Erasmus and the Seamless Coat of Jesus

ERASMUS
AND THE SEAMLESS COAT
OF JESUS

De Sarcienda Ecclesiae Concordia
(On Restoring the Unity of the Church)

With Selections from the Letters
and Ecclesiastes

Translations with Introduction and Notes
by
Raymond Himelick

Purdue University Studies
Lafayette, Indiana
1971

© 1971 by Purdue Research Foundation
Library of Congress Card Catalog Number 70-151515
International Standard Book Number 0-911198-29-6
Printed in the United States of America

. . . *The peasants raise dangerous riots and are not swayed from their purpose, despite so many massacres. The commons are bent on anarchy; the Church is shaken to its very foundations by menacing factions; on every side the seamless coat of Jesus is torn to shreds. The vineyard of the Lord is now laid waste not by a single boar but at one and the same time the authority of priests (together with their tithes), the dignity of theologians, the splendor of monks is imperiled; confession totters; vows reel; pontifical ordinances crumble away; the Eucharist is called in question; Antichrist is awaited; the whole earth is pregnant with I know not what calamity. (Erasmus, in* Puerpera, *Craig Thompson translation)*

. . . *We all hold there is a number of Elect and many to be saved, yet take our opinions together, and from the confusion thereof there will be no such thing as salvation, nor shall any one be saved; for first the Church of Rome condemneth us, wee likewise them, the Sub-reformists and Sectaries sentence the Doctrine of our Church as damnable, the Atomist, or Familist reprobates all these, and all these them againe. Thus whilst the mercies of God doth promise us heaven, our conceits and opinions exclude us from that place. There must be therefore more than one Saint Peter, particular Churches and Sects usurpe the gates of heaven and turne the key against each other, and thus we goe to heaven against each others wills, conceits and opinions, and with as much uncharity as ignorance, doe erre I feare in points not onely of our own, but on anothers salvation. (Sir Thomas Browne, in* Religio Medici)

. . . Men are now-a-days, and indeed always have been since
the expiration of the first blessed ages of christianity, so
in love with their own fancies and opinions as to think faith
and all christendom is concerned in their support and main-
tenance; and whoever is not so fond and does not dandle them
like themselves, it grows up to a quarrel which . . . is made
a quarrel in religion, and God is entitled to it; and then
if you are once thought an enemy to God, it is our duty to
persecute you even to death, we do God good service in it. . . .
All these mischiefs proceed not from this, that all men are
not of one mind, for that is neither necessary nor possible,
but that every opinion is made an article of faith, every art-
icle is a ground of a quarrel, every quarrel makes a faction,
every faction is zealous, and all zeal pretends for God,
and whatsoever is for God cannot be too much: we by this
time are come to that pass, we think we love not God
except we hate our brother, and we have not the virtue of
religion unless we persecute all religions but our own. . . .
(Jeremy Taylor, in The Liberty of Prophesying*)*

. . . To certain zelants all speech of pacification is odious.
. . . Peace is not the matter, but following and party.
(Sir Francis Bacon, in "Of Unity in Religion")

PREFACE

THE LAST TWO decades of Erasmus' life were attended by a persistent irony, one which his own ironic mind must have wryly appreciated: he was a religious reformer who was appalled by the Reformation. The present selection from his writings shows an Erasmus by no means willing to disclaim his past and exasperated in about equal measure with the shrill voices on both left and right who could not, or would not, understand what his past had been all about. Huizinga has called attention to the "tragic defect" which prevented Erasmus from drawing "ultimate conclusions," and everyone knows the celebrated quip suggesting the same inferential flaw: "Here I stand. But also here, and here, and here!" But no one, I think, can read his words in these selections without sensing the real "ultimate conclusion" that left him to pursue a lonely evasive action in a polemical no-man's land. That conclusion has an inescapable relevance for our own day.

With one exception the translations which follow are my own and, with a few more exceptions, to the best of my knowledge many of them are not available elsewhere in modern dress. There is such a translation of the *De sarcienda Ecclesiae concordia,* but it is not annotated or provided with much other editorial help. At least four of the letters included here can be found elsewhere and have been so noted in the text. The letter to Abbot Volz appears here in its early Tudor translation, presumably by William Tyndale, with spelling and punctuation modernized for the convenience of the general reader. It, like the *Enchiridion* which it prefaced and the *Paraclesis* of Erasmus' New Testament, provides a significant view of Erasmus as reformer and the insistence upon a need for a renewal of the "Philosophy of Christ." It was such statements as the Volz letter, of course, which necessitated much of what we see in the later correspondence. It seemed fitting to print it here as most sixteenth-century Englishmen would have known it, in the vigorous, sometimes pugnacious, English of the greatest of Tudor biblical translators, a Protestant martyr—and the chief polemical adversary of Erasmus' great friend, Sir Thomas More.

The letter to Volz appears *in toto*. In most of the others, however, I have excerpted only those parts that bear more or less directly upon the developing rent in the fabric of Christendom and the forces that were producing it. Such passages—significantly long as a rule—serve to reinforce and illuminate what had led Erasmus to choose Psalm 83 (Vulgate numbering) for commentary in the *Concordia*. They also get us closer to the man himself in their mingling of occasionally unguarded candor with sophistical tight-rope walking, of urbane reasonableness with a kind of querulous asperity and self-pity. And they are repetitive; but if we are sometimes tempted to wonder if Erasmus had only one string to his bow, we can hardly escape the basic consistency of the Erasmian message which virtually nobody wanted to hear.

My thanks are due to Professors Harold Watts and Walter F. Staton, Jr., for their comments and suggestions, to the librarians of the Folger Shakespeare Library for their courtesy and helpfulness during the time, all too short, I spent there, and to Mr. and Mrs. James Redmond for their help in preparing and checking the typescript.

The Latin text used for the *Concordia* and the excerpt from the *Ecclesiastes* was that in *Erasmi Opera Omnia*, ed. Jean LeClerc, Leyden: 1703-1706 (Hildesheim: Georg Olms Verlagsbuchhandlung, 1961-62), 9 volumes. It is cited in the notes as *LB*, followed by volume and column number. For the letters I must record my debt to the definitive edition of P. S. and H. M. Allen and H. W. Garrod, the *Opus Epistolarum Erasmi*, published by the Clarendon Press (Oxford, 1938-58). In the designation of the epistles translated I use the abbreviation *EE*, followed by volume and letter number. In the footnotes appended (for a great many of which I am again indebted to this edition) Allen, when cited, is followed by *page* number of the volume being used.

CONTENTS

1   Introduction

29   De Sarcienda Ecclesiae Concordia

110 Selections from the Letters

        Paul Volz   110

        Albert of Brandenburg   133

        John Slechta   141

        Lorenzo Campeggio   150

        Louis Marlian   161

        Jodocus Jonas   165

        Duke George of Saxony   174

        Simon Pistorius   176

        Willibald Pirckheimer   179

        Martin Bucer   180 and 205

        John Longlond   183

        Justus Decius   188

        John Botzheim   189

        Hermann Von Weid   192

        Cuthbert Tunstall   194

        Balthasar Mercklin   198

        Jacopo Sadoleto   201

        Unknown   210

213 Ecclesiastes

220 Selected Bibliography

INTRODUCTION

THE GLOOMY OBSERVATION of the first epigraph found its way into a dialogue mainly taken up with Renaissance pediatrics, feminism, and Aristotelian psychology. It first appeared in 1526, nine years after Luther had posted his *Theses* and six years after the papal bull of condemnation. If, as Craig Thompson has reminded us, the passage is an effective comment on the progress of Lutheranism in those years,[1] those which follow it point up the fact that Erasmus' premonitions were well-grounded. His speaker was not quite sure what calamity the earth was pregnant with, but the century of Browne, Taylor, and Bacon was to see the progeny first hand in—to pass over Civil War in England and a thirty-years conflict on the Continent—the enthusiastic sub-division of Protestantism into Brownists and Familists and Anabaptists and Socinians and Sabbatarians and Quakers and many, many more. As a modern critic has observed, "The harsh sectarianism of Puritan England was in effect the inevitable first fruits of the Reformation, of the appeal which Protestantism had made from the authority of the Church to the conscience of every believer. This was the entering wedge of an individualism that eventually was to go far beyond the intentions of the Protestant Reformers. . . ."[2]

The very recent Peasants' Revolt alluded to by the speaker of Erasmus' *Colloquy* was, of course, no less reprehensible to Luther. What Erasmus seems to have understood more clearly than Luther and the other Evangelical leaders was that to substitute an appeal to scripture itself for an officially-ratified Catholic interpretation of scripture, and at the same time insist that there could be only one meaning, not only in broad outlines but in the most wire-drawn details, was to invite the wholesale proliferation of sects. From every-man-his-own-priest to every-man-his-own-church—this seemed to be the built-in logic of a movement whose power lay in its appeal to untutored and uncritical masses. As P. S. Allen has reminded us,[3] in the 1520's Oecolampadius, Zwingli, and others were

1

already sounding their own variations on the main theme of that movement, and almost every town in southern Germany had its own version of Reform. The one thing all versions shared, of course, was a violent hatred for whatever smacked of Rome. In Switzerland and elsewhere images were being pulled down in the churches and burned; inmates of monasteries and convents were turned out or— if their own sympathies lay in that direction—pouring out of their own accord.

The *Liber de sarcienda Ecclesiae concordia* was not to appear in print until seven years after Erasmus' speaker had sketched in the reason for it. Even a year before that dialogue, however, a letter written from Basel had mentioned "something in hand" which, if not the present book, had the same intent, that of checking the increasingly bitter dissension of Christians. But Basel was violently Protestant and it would not be safe to publish the treatise *nisi loco commutato;* first it had been his health and pressing tasks that stood in the way, but now it was the "bloody tumult of affairs." [4]

Nevertheless, when Erasmus' effort to quiet the hurricane did appear in 1533, it was at Basel, with Froben of course as printer. During the same year it was reprinted at Antwerp, Leipzig, and Paris; and within a year it had two German translations, one Flemish, and one Danish.[5] In the light of events of the century following, of course, one is not surprised to find that, after this initial flurry, the number of editions suggests no great demand. The sixteenth century saw nine more, in Latin, German, and Flemish; the seventeenth even fewer.[6] His *Enchiridion Militis Christiani,* first published a generation earlier, went through more than a hundred in an equivalent length of time.

Interesting, too—and perhaps somewhat puzzling—is the fact that such editions and translations as there were remain limited to areas most closely identified with evangelical reform; there were no editions in France for more than a century, none in Spain, none in Italy, and none in England. And, needless to say, no translations seem to have been published in the vernacular of any of those countries.[7] The ecclesiastical right wing was apparently adamant. A few months after the appearance of the *Concordia,* John Choler was informing Erasmus that "certain cardinals" at Rome were displeased by the little book, and Erasmus could only marvel at the wrong-headedness of some men who seem determined to apply only stupid remedies to this general evil of the world. He was hoping that lesser points of disagreement could be straightened out by the authority of a synod, and to this end "meus libellus videbatur satis appositus."

Apparently, though, it had only reminded the conservatives of a book of Luther, also published in 1533, attacking the Mass. Erasmus disclaimed any knowledge of Luther's treatise, but he was at a loss to see how anyone could object to the way *his* handled the subject, "quum ille nullum articulum tractet aut diligentius aut reverentius quam de Missa." Such malicious charges were only too familiar. With some bitterness he recalled a recent book by a Franciscan—a book without learning or talent, but loaded with venom—in which Erasmus, along with Luther, Zwingli, and Oecolampadius, had been accused of being a soldier of Pilate and of drawing people away from the Church, presumably to form his own sect.[8]

The tone of weary disenchantment and resignation one finds in his reply to Choler can hardly have been much of a change from the mood in which he had written his little book. He had chosen as his subject a psalm dealing with the loveliness of peace and concord within the Church. As his prefatory letter suggests, however, the very theme was an anachronism. There would be no peace until men loved peace more than they loved their own way of shredding the seamless robe of Jesus. If Christ deigned to put this love in their hearts, his book would be unnecessary; if He did not, it would be useless.

To turn from the *Enchiridion,* coming at the beginning of Erasmus' career, to *De sarcienda Ecclesiae concordia,* coming near the end of it, is to sense something of what, in the thirty-odd years intervening, had happened to Erasmus and the force he preeminently stood for, Christian humanism. The cheerfully prescriptive method of the earlier work suggests both his conviction that to *know* the *philosophia Christi* was essential to following it and his confidence that man was educable, via the humanistic fusion of classical wisdom with Christian dogma, in that philosophy which for Erasmus was simply a quintessential "seamlessness." The older man who wrote the *Concordia* seems less sure, if not of the importance of the advancement of sacred learning, at least of man's enthusiasm for light rather than heat. The joyful harmony of the Church Triumphant which he sees in his psalm had little in common with the cacophony of wrangling voices all around him. He had seen the *Enchiridion* itself, that "little dagger" designed to help the soldier of Christ defend himself against the world, the flesh, and the devil, being used, in effect, by some Christians to dismember the Body of Christ; and, of course, by others he had long been accused of assisting in that surgery. A critic writes to tell him that he himself shudders even to mention the abominable heresies Erasmus has either condoned or been responsible for—and then forces himself to name at least five. He could list "six hundred more" if he had time.[9] A monk preaching before Francis I is sure that Erasmus is one of the four precursors of the Antichrist.[10]

Although the fiercely combative temper of the times was not conducive to the success of the *Concordia,* it is also unlikely that even a sympathetic reader would have found it comparable in literary merit to some of the earlier pieces, such as *The Praise of Folly,* certain of the *Colloquies,* or extended *Adages* like *The Complaint of Peace.* It lacks most of their wit and elusive irony and sense of drama. No one would think of tagging it as another example of humanistic *jeu d'esprit.* His subject here is intensely serious, of course; but so, for that matter, was the subject of *The Praise* and "The Shipwreck." Perhaps its most evident quality is a strong sense of urgency, particularly in the latter portion; this urgency, it seems, pushes him into hammering out his theme *sans* playful grace notes or subtly ambiguous nuances.

Not that by modern standards the *Concordia* is a model of straightforwardness and tight construction. To use P. S. Allen's description, it is "as torrential as the most fluent orator's tongue, whirling along in eddies and backrushes which sometimes return almost to their starting-point."[11] On this point, of course, the twentieth-century reader must remind himself that leanness and economy were not literary virtues for the Renaissance. The age preferred fullness and amplitude. When Erasmus launches into an extended bestiary passage on the significance of the nesting instinct, they would have seen this as a demonstration of one of the methods of supplying *copia* which he had long ago set down for the instruction of school boys. And when he pulls up suddenly to say he has been rather prolix and is now going to hurry on, they would not necessarily have taken the first part of his statement as an admission of fault or the second part as his precise intention. The "eddies and backrushes" are part and parcel, it seems, of an exegetical method intent upon establishing a continuum of relevance for the scripture it deals with. Almost every verse finds its meaning exemplified in early Hebrew history, in events of the early Church, and ultimately—Erasmus' real concern—in the present. The scriptural commentary, with its eddies and backrushes, takes up roughly two-thirds of the treatise; the rest of it is concerned with the Erasmian position in that unhappy present.

For the general reader this final section will no doubt have the greatest interest. He will find there the Erasmus he expected to find. The exegete of the psalm, however, may not be so familiar a figure. To some he will seem to oscillate between the quite "modern" or "advanced" on the one hand and the very medieval on the other. The oddly incompatible—for us—mixture will be found to exist both in his assumptions about the nature of Christian piety and in his critical techniques. But if the discovery startles us, it is no less important for that reason to our understanding of the man and of his times.

To say that he "oscillates" is of course misleading. The old and the new co-exist and even blend here (an observation true in varying degrees of most Renaissance figures) in a way that causes us more discomfort than it would have Erasmus. When he engages in linguistic analysis, or compares a reading of Jerome with that of Augustine or the Septuagint writers, we are struck by this anticipation of a much later textual criticism. We note as well the cool detachment which, as Renaudet has remarked, obviously declines to consider the Vulgate as a divinely inspired book, but sees it, like any other text, as vulnerable to linguistic deficiencies and error.[12] At the same time, though, we need to remind ourselves that the purpose of such textual criticism, of all scholarship and learning, for Erasmus was a truer knowledge of God. This meant the restoration, as nearly as possible, of the true text of scripture and of the early Fathers, the original *fontes* of that knowledge. Men had to go forward by a backward motion; he did not intend to emanicipate men from the old Christian pieties, but to return to them.

In comfortable co-existence with the scrupulous minutiae of textual criticism, the reader comes across quite different methods of exegesis. A good many years ago Seebohm observed that Colet might not have approved of the *Enchiridion's* "tendency to interpret the text of Scripture *allegorically*, rather than to seek out its *literal* meaning," but that Erasmus himself corrected that tendency "in after years." [13] The last part of Seebohm's remark is not altogether borne out by a reading of the *Concordia*. Not that Erasmus disregards the literal or historical reading Colet had favored, but it would be hard to show that he preferred that meaning to the exclusion of an "allegorical" or "mystical" interpretation. On one occasion he candidly confesses that, granting the possibility of reading a certain passage literally, he himself prefers the "hidden" or recondite sense.[14]

Renaudet, noting Erasmus' fundamental preference for the New Testament, relates it to his insistence upon an allegorical reading which could make the Old Testament a repository of truth for Christians, prefiguring the story of Christ: "Toute l'action du Christ se trouve ébauchée, de façon obscure et symbolique, dans les livres de la loi; les prophetes l'annoncent expressément. Il n'est rien dans la doctrine du Christ qui ne corresponde à un passage de l'Ancien Testament." [15] Thus the psalmist's "My soul fainted" leads Erasmus directly to Pauline commentary upon flesh and spirit, and Isaac becomes a representation of spiritual joy which could not be born until "flesh" in Sara and Abraham had lost their hold upon them.

It may be argued, of course, that this is merely a "figural" mode of reading scripture and that, as Erich Auerbach insists, a distinction must be made between this kind of interpretation and the genuinely allegorical, that the figural method is allegorical only in the widest sense, differing from most of the allegorical forms known to us "by the historicity both of the sign and what it signifies." [16] Erasmus, however, was prone to use the terms *allegorical* and *mystical* in a pretty wide and inclusive sense. In his *Ecclesiastes* he advises the student preacher that there are two ways in which only the historical sense is admissible, 1) when an event is told as having happened, or 2) when it is told as going to happen and is to be understood *simpliciter*, with no hidden meaning suggested. In all other instances the explicator must look for "vel Typos vel Allegorias"; although he makes a distinction (allegory is more specifically related to the doctrinal and preceptive), typological and allegorical readings apparently have more in common with each other than either has with the literal or historical.[17]

To return to the matter of the "modern" versus the "medieval" in Erasmus, the distinction here may have in a large measure been blurred out. Reading scripture according to its "manifold senses"

was, of course, a practice already venerable in 1533. Certain twentieth-century approaches to poetry, however, will have gone far
to inoculate the reader against shock. As Helen Gardner has
pointed out, "mystical interpretation" can hardly any longer be
said to be alien and repellent to the modern mind.[18] The passage
linking the eighth and eightieth psalms with his subject, eighty-
three, is a case in point. All three commemorate victory. Number
eight, however, the number of the day on which Christ rose from
the dead, is really about man created after the image of God, intended to be a little lower than the angels. The second of the
triad, as indicated by the number eight multiplied by ten (i.e., the
decalogue), refers to man restored to justification through the Law.
Eighty-three, one hardly needs to explain, adds to original excellence and justification through the Law the ultimate Christian
mystery of the Trinity and signifies the grace of the Gospels by
which man can have faith in and hope for an abode in heaven.

Such a passage does indeed, as one of my colleagues has put it,
show an Erasmus happily in the bosom of his times, but even from
this numerological symbolism one can move to some recent criticism of Spenser and Milton without a very perceptible jar.

However much this section seems to be a tessellation of old and
new, the imposition of one kind of context and experience upon
another, we cannot escape certain inferences from it which help
define what we mean when we say "Erasmianism" or, in a more
inclusive sense, "Christian humanism." Whether these inferences
serve to illuminate or merely to qualify, with some sense of loss,
will depend upon the assumptions and predilections the reader
himself brings to the work. Certainly he will find no hint here of
the casuistical old man ("senem versipellem aut bilinguem"), the
irreverent mocker of things holy whom Etienne Dolet was describ-
ing two years later: "Ridet, eludit, delicias facit, lacessit, increpit,
laedit, cachinnum etiam in Christum tollit" ("He laughs, he jeers, he
cracks jokes, assails, censures, rails, provokes loud laughter even at
the expense of Christ Himself").[19] However wrong Dolet was, even
in terms of the author of *The Praise of Folly* or *Ciceronianus*, the
notion of a fundamentally sceptical and secular Erasmus has had
considerable currency from his own day to this. For this notion
the first half of the *Concordia* ought, if nothing else, to serve as
corrective.

We see here, that is, a man who not only has been steeped in the traditional piety of past centuries, but who has no thought of discounting the full, suprarational Christian mysteries. If this book in any way defines the philosophy of Christ, it does not suggest a merely secular morality or social gospel drained of any genuine religious content. The Christ one finds here, as Harold Watts has remarked, is a far cry from a warrant for liberal agitation. Man's relation to Him is an individual relation, with Church as mediator; it is not man, however, who stands at the center of this perspective, but Christ. And, although Christ is supremely relevant to all sorts of purely human experience, that experience has to be understood in relation to Christian Gospel. The "good life" in this world is not so much one that uses Christ as one that is used by Him.[20]

Nevertheless, for Erasmus, and the other Christian humanists as well, the real evidence of the philosophy of Christ was its translation into the everyday conduct of human life; it did not lie in the verbalizing of Christian dogma or in a mindlessly meticulous obedience of ecclesiastical rules, and certainly not in the observance of ritual and ceremony. In this sense he was a secularist. He insisted that piety must also be moral, that in terms of this world religion must also be an ethic, and his preoccupation with outlining the grammar and syntax of this translation of Christ into day-by-day living led his critics to suspect an insufficient awareness, if not an abandonment, of more revelational truths. To Luther he was, among a good many other things, a Pelagian and an Arian.[21] To a more sympathetic modern critic Erasmus effected a "singularly organic fusion," which, parenthetically, would not have made him less reprehensible to Luther. Possessing a "diversity of allegiance," on the one hand to a secular ethic and on the other to a supranatural religious inheritance, he had managed to synthesize the two elements in his life and thought. If in the process there occurred a "vitiation of the supranatural in Christianity," that vitiation was not premeditated or sought, "or even recognized on those terms." The good life, for Erasmus, always implied the world, but it also implied an archetype in the life of Christ. The "finest achievement of secularism is the living of an ideal rather than its contemplation, a hope in the present rather than an expectation for the future." There are inherent contradictions between "a revealed religion whose principal aim is salvation and whose metaphysic is essentially supranatural" and on the other hand an ethic which is essentially worldly. The Erasmian synthesis, however, was able to key down these contradictions and keep them from becoming explicit.[22]

The first half or more of the *Concordia* makes plain enough, I think, that the supranatural element still had meaning for him and that the common-sense pleas for accommodation, the softening of hardline dogmatism, do not stem from any deep-seated religious scepticism. He was a sceptic, but not about matters of faith. If his Christianity has struck some as being drained of its mysticism, it is not because its mysteries did not count for him but because he never supposed they were intended as a kind of spiritual hallucinogen. He writes of the New Jerusalem with utter confidence, but this is a joy that must wait. In the meantime there is a difficult and complicated present which seems to have lost sight of any temporal relation to that Church Triumphant. Red Cross, one recalls, had to leave his lofty eminence in the House of Holiness and go down to fight the dragon.

If there was a divided loyalty or "diversity of allegiance" here which we are more aware of than was Erasmus, his synthesis is of a piece with the "shelving process," to use Margaret Mann Phillips' phrase, whereby he managed to subscribe to two opposing views at once concerning man's place and destiny, accepting the orthodox Christian doctrine of the Fall, and the resultant infection of human will, but retaining the humanistic emphasis upon the potentialities for good that also exist in the nature of man.[23]

By the same kind of process, apparently, he could comfortably domesticate his abundant learning and a devout belief in the moral efficacy of "good letters" with a fundamental anti-intellectualism. His scepticism was of the classic pyrrhonic brand which Montaigne was later to demonstrate in *Sebond*. Mistrusting metaphysical speculation and the presumptuousness it seemed to him to derive from, Erasmus was led to a position, at odds with both the radical Reformers and the conservative Schoolmen, that salvation cannot depend on knowing an inaccessible absolute Truth. He saw, as Preserved Smith has pointed out, that to seek and find this absolute brands the seeker as either a child or a dogmatist. The all-important matter in religion had to be the life, not the dogma. Beliefs were interesting, even rather important, but they were subordinate to the moral issue.[24]

If the latter portion of the *Concordia*, then, shows us the more familiar Erasmus who stands for compromise and reconciliation, we may suppose that tolerance here means, not the rejection of or indifference to the Christian truths at stake, but a suspicion that revelation had not been so lavishly distributed as most men liked to think. The schismatics were invoking scripture with the passionate conviction of men singularly chosen for the confidences of a burning bush, but already the voices they listened to were becoming competitive. Those who could agree in denying the Real Presence in the Eucharist could agree on little else about the sacrament. Indeed, they scarcely agreed with themselves from one day to the next. Every new dogma, however silly, could find some people to take it up. The thorny question of the will could be left to those who fancied themselves as theologians; it made an interesting subject of debate, as Smith has said,[25] but (the implication is clear) not much more.

It is in this context, surely, that we must consider some of Erasmus' suggestions and recommendations that strike us as disappointingly lame and inconclusive. When he supports traditional and orthodox dogma against the new and heretical, he is not implying that the consensus of time and of numbers or the ruling of an official council ensures infallibility, only that it takes a good deal of intellectual arrogance to suppose that Providence has waited centuries to vouchsafe its fullest light now at last to a comparative handful. It is his Pyrrhonism more than his Catholicism which rejects the heresy.[26] If the Church has been vague at times in spelling out definitions of recondite points of doctrine—as he concedes that she has been in the matter, for example, of the Real Presence—that very vagueness, for Erasmus, has the virtue of allowing some flexibility within a framework of ecclesiastical unity. On the whole, men should define as little as possible. In definition lies division, a fierce contention over words when the crying need of Christendom was agreement upon essentials.[27]

If this more familiar Erasmus sounds like the voice of sweet reasonableness and tolerance, then we do well to remind ourselves that the reasonableness stems in part from his anti-rationalism, and that his spirit of accommodation was no more hospitable to heresy than to belligerent orthodoxy. Wallace Ferguson is right in saying that Erasmus voiced no doctrine of unqualified toleration, that he had basically little sympathy with heresy, which seemed to him "unnecessary and perverse." [28] By both temperament and conviction, however, he was not only irenical but pragmatic. Coercion from either side accomplished nothing in changing minds or rooting out erroneous doctrines. More often its result was precisely the opposite of that intended:

> There are some who while they are feebly bleating
> "Heresy! Heresy! To the fire! To the fire!" and making
> the most sinister interpretation of any equivocal remark, or
> distorting by misrepresentation what was said with piety, have
> won a large measure of sympathy for the very ones they
> were marking for extermination. Again, those who under the
> praiseworthy label of the Gospel set in motion such things as
> are diametrically opposed to the Gospels, are vastly helpful to
> the sects of those very people whom they wanted to suppress.[29]

On pragmatic grounds persecution is a failure; on Christian grounds it is an anomaly, a contradiction in terms.

Unmistakable here, also, is Erasmus' readiness to distinguish between the heresy and the heretic. People could err in all innocence; an erroneous doctrine should be condemned only when it was accompanied by intractable stubbornness ("cum indocili pervicacia coniuncta est") or seemed maliciously bent on disrupting the peace of the Church with its perverse teachings. And for that matter there were heresies and *heresies*. Just as some poisons were more deadly than others, some heterodox teachings were relatively innocuous. In any case, the belief a man held mattered less than his conduct.[30] Ten years before the *Concordia* he was telling Botzheim that he had never broken off a friendship with anyone on the basis of that person's Lutheranism.

"My disposition is such," he confessed, "that I can love a Jew if only he is an agreeable dinner companion and friend, and doesn't blaspheme against Christ in my presence. Moreover, I consider this civilized behavior pretty effective in minimizing friction."[31]

Such a remark, of course, suggests an urbanity and tolerance not very typical of the age. That it was not completely unique, however, is suggested by a passage in *Utopia*. More's convert to Christianity there, waxing so hot in his zeal that he could not rest at ease in his own opinion but "must utterly despise and condempne all other, calling them prophane, and the folowers of them wicked and develish and the children of everlastinge dampnation," makes such a public nuisance of himself that he is finally exiled as a "sedicious person and a raiser up of dissention amonge the people." Generously latitudinarian as far as beliefs were concerned, a reasonable society could draw the line at bad manners, a self-righteous incivility that insisted upon stirring up trouble. Even a disbeliever in the immortality of the soul could keep his views with impunity so long as he did not "dispute in his opinion" among the common people.[32]

Whether this sweet reasonableness disappeared in an older and grimmer More is, of course, a moot question. Nevertheless, even the Catholic polemicist of years later could suggest that if Tyndale, Frith, and Barnes would at least be "reasonable heretykes and honeste, and wryte reason & leue raylinge" there might be some possibility of compromise.[33] He did not suppose they would ever do so, but the remark sounds a note of regret that the Christian church could no longer be what Seebohm thinks the Utopian church indicated, the position of the Oxford Reformers that "the Church was intended to be broad and tolerant, not to define doctrine and enforce dogmas, but to afford a practical bond of union whereby Christians might be kept united in one Christian brotherhood, in spite of their differences in minor matters of creed." [34] As Lacey Baldwin Smith has pointed out, there was comparatively little alarm over heresy *per se* in the early sixteenth century. What hardened the resistance of the Church and state was awareness of a political and social complication, the fact that the new doctrines, when preached publicly before the butchers of Cambridge, could lead to sedition, tumult, and riots.[35]

The treatment of heresies in the *Concordia*, as we might expect, shows Erasmus' concern with such very palpable effects as the causing of Christians to mount hostile barricades in the very house of the Lord. Beginning with Moses' trouble with Dathan and Abiron he moves forward in time—but only up to a certain point. Not the least interesting, and suggestive, aspect of the treatise in this respect is what he chooses not to drag into the open. We hear of Cainites and Ophites, of Nicolaitans and Adamites, of Circumcellions and Sabellians and Donatists and Eunomians and, of course, Arians and Manichaeans. (That he omits the Pelagians would not have surprised Luther.) Rarely, however, does he name an important dissident sect much less than twelve centuries anterior to Erasmus' own troubled present. The word *Lutheran* occurs only once, and then only in an anecdote illustrating a common error of the anti-Lutherans. He mentions the wretched Anabaptists, persecuted with equal zeal by both the Protestant and Catholic parties, but only as an example of delusion rather than wilful malice. His one reference to the Sabbatarians, we must suppose, would have been equally peripheral in terms of the real threat being posed to Christian unity.

Heresies long dead, obviously, had the virtue of being no longer inflammatory. They served to illustrate a principle without probing any particular tendernesses of bias the reader might be cherishing. Other considerations may have entered in as well. Some of the sects, such as the Cainites, Adamites, and Nicolaitans, exemplified aberrant extremes of doctrinal perverseness. Any serious Lutheran or Oecolampadian or Zwinglian could hardly have found them less distasteful than did Erasmus. And many of them were Gnostic groups, including of course the Manichaeans, who had posed a serious threat to early Christianity and whose doctrine, it is interesting to note, Erasmus refers to in the present tense, in contrast to his handling of the Priscillians immediately after. How much of a current menace he considered Gnosticism as a cult is open to question. The characteristics attributed to it by a modern Jesuit critic, however, suggest clearly enough what would have been repugnant to the Christian humanist; it "displays itself in a love for an unattached mysticism, for fantastic theogonies . . . it is sure to despise the body and what is most human, but usually it has to permit some of the least savoury expressions of carnal desire; it is esoteric and appeals to a strange craving in human nature for hidden symbols and double meanings." [36]

Explicitly the *Concordia* decries the Manichaeans for rejecting the entire Old Testament as "something handed down not by God but by the Prince of Darkness" and falsifying the New according to their own fancy. Like all heretics, they pervert Scripture by accommodating it to merely human modes of thinking, rather than to "Christ, who is Truth." Implicit here, one may suspect, is Erasmus' classically rational distaste for systems of wholesale occultism, the vaporizing of religion into frivolous speculations about "essence" and a romantically apotheosized Evil, a mysticism too unattached to establish guidelines for Christian conduct, too esoteric to have any relevance for the broad base of Christian laity. Granting that the *Concordia* shows no inclination to discount the ineffable mysteries in religious faith, nevertheless Erasmus—*mutatis mutandis*—is not unlike Frost's climber of birches: he mounts *toward* the heaven of a mystical realization of divine love, but only so far as the branches can bear a human weight. Unlike Frost, of course, he knows perfectly well where such love is bound to go better. Until such time, though, earth *is* the right place for it; this is the heart of the Gospel and of any viable Christian doctrine as well.

And this is the cardinal point, clearly, of the Erasmian compromise with which the concluding pages of the *Concordia* are concerned. Given the fallibility of human reason confronted with the arcane secrets of Divine Providence and the multi-colored biases of response to such inviting bones of contention as saint worship, fasting, feast days, visual arts and music, confession, and the Mass, what could possibly restore unity to Christendom but the charitable readiness of every Christian to bethink himself that in the bowels of Christ he might himself be a little mistaken, and in any event to love his brother more than his own opinion?

Implicit in the Erasmian insistence upon the importance of accommodation here is the humanistic distinction between matters crucial and essential to salvation and those which are merely adiaphorous, neutral in themselves though capable of being used either for good or ill. In general, the *Concordia* voices the reasonable man's plaintive wonder that new brooms cannot rest until they have expelled not only the dust and clutter of empty ceremonialism and superstition, but every stick of traditional furniture as well. The voice, of course, is the voice of conservatism, but its tone makes it a reproach to the shrill and intransigent types of both right and left.

In the matter of church music, indeed, the mean of Erasmus seems if anything relatively closer to the extreme of the Reformers. His readiness to exclude the use of any instruments and to curtail the role even of *a cappella* singing will make many readers wince a little. It suggests a regrettable underdevelopment of this aspect of his sensitivity in favor of the scholar and moral philosopher. We are ready to suspect that he really was impervious enough to alpine scenery to sketch out *The Praise of Folly* in the midst of it. We may think of Doctor Johnson, who on being reminded that he was listening to a violin piece of extraordinary difficulty could only regret that it had not been made impossible.

There is some ground for the suspicion that, as far as Erasmus was concerned, unheard melodies were indeed sweeter, particularly if they had to be heard to the accompaniment of winds and percussion. Without knowing the quality of the performances and instruments, we can hardly make categorical judgments as to what his strictures reveal about himself. Typical enough, however, is the wry complaint to a correspondent some years before the *Concordia*: Christians were now using drums as the Corybants once did, as if madness were a requirement not only in warfare, but for weddings and holy days and church services too. If there were any drums in hell, feast days there must be celebrated there on no other instrument. If Plato thought that there was a correlation between the greatness of a state and the kind of music it employed, what would he have thought if he had heard this horrendous din raised by Christians and listened to by pious virgins during the performance of the holy office? [37]

None of this suggests that Erasmus would have been moved to rapture by a baroque mass. It does suggest, however, a kind of austere purism which deplores anything it sees as violating the decorum of simple piety:

> There was a time when the Church admitted nothing but
> the words of the reader and preacher. Then singing was
> gradually introduced, but of a plain sort very closely following
> speech rhythms, not blurring out the text but impressing it more
> deeply upon the consciousness of the listeners. Now things have
> come to such a pass that churches reverberate with cornets,
> with reeds, with trumpets, and even with drums; scarcely
> anything can be heard above the mingled din of voices and
> a kind of music more gaudy and voluptuous than anything
> the theaters of pagans ever had.[38]

It is not, he insists, that he would ban music in religious rites; he would merely require a musical setting in keeping with the sacred text. The current practice of introducing wantonly frivolous popular tunes—and sometimes without even deleting the brazenly lewd lyrics—into a church service, this was as absurd as outfitting Cato in the trappings of a Thais.[39]

It may be true, as Father Surtz has suggested, that More and Erasmus held differing opinions on the general question of the "need of aids for the senses in religion." [40] However, what More had written years earlier about music to the monk John Batmanson, strikes the same note. Batmanson had attacked *The Praise of Folly;* More answered that the book contained more true piety

> than do certain hymns which some of your friends
> think place all the Saints under their obligation. These songs
> in honor of the Saints are such silly ditties, no clown could

> ridicule them with sillier ones, try as he would; yet, in our
> day some of this trash has crept into the churches and is
> gradually assuming such a prominent position, particularly
> because of the accompanying music, that we have become much
> less inclined to listen to the serious and solemn prayers
> arranged long ago by the holy Fathers. As a matter of great
> concern to Christianity, the Popes should ban all that sort of
> nonsense. . . .[41]

Shortly after the publication of the *Concordia* English humanists
in the service of a government no longer deferring to pontifical
policies may have helped define the Erasmian influence upon a
nonpapal Catholicism. The first Royal Injunction, 1536, mentions
"the abrogation of certain superfluous holy days" effected by the
Ten Articles by Convocation and enjoins the clergy not to

> set forth or extol any images, relics, or miracles for any
> superstition or lucre, nor allure the people by any enticements
> to the pilgrimage of any saint, otherwise than is permitted
> in the articles . . . but they shall exhort as well their parishioners
> as other pilgrims, that they do rather apply themselves to the
> keeping of God's commandments and fulfilling of His works
> of charity, persuading them that they shall please God more
> by the true exercising of their bodily labour, travail, or
> occupation, and providing for the families, than if they
> went about to the said pilgrimages; and that it shall profit more
> their souls' health, if they do bestow that on the poor and
> needy, which they would have bestowed upon the said
> images or relics.

A second injunction two years later limits the use of images and
the number of candles or tapers to be burned "afore an image or
picture" and urges the clergy to remind their flocks that "images
serve for none other purpose but as to be books of unlearned men
that cannot know letters, whereby they might be otherwise admonished of the lives and conversation of them that the said images
do represent. . . ."[42]

However More might have felt about such accommodation to
Protestant austerity, Erasmus most certainly would have counted
all such loss a gain. About these external adjuncts of worship he
had stated his position again and again: at best they were nearly
irrelevant to the essentials of Christian piety; at worst they became
a hazardous surrogate for it. God is best seen with closed eyes and
lifted heart; how could merely human hands, which fail even to
capture the real *man* in a statue, presume to have represented

deity in that way? The very attempt was evidence of an astonishing thick-wittedness in Christians who were unable even to conceive of God except in the crasser terms of wood or stone.[43]

In that even more sensitive area of transubstantiation and the eucharistic sacrifice, however, we cannot be so sure where Erasmus really stood. What he has to say in the *Concordia*, as well as in his letters, suggests a rather roomy zone with boundaries carefully left vague and elastic enough to provide all Christians with a common meeting ground. Although he will abide by the doctrinal rulings of the Church in such matters, his emphasis is upon the symbolic and ritualistic commemoration. He makes no attempt to defend transubstantiation against its Lutheran critics[44]; the questions raised about the dogma of the Real Presence by a crudely literal naturalism [45] can be settled by a synod. For Erasmus they are both irreverent and irrelevant.

He shows little disposition, however, to make a point of heretical deviations from the Church's position, possibly because he saw that position as one determined not so much by revelational dispensations from on high as by exigencies of time and circumstance. Early Christians had had ecclesiastical sanction for beliefs at variance with current teachings simply because the Church had not yet considered it necessary to define the official dogma sharply.[46] And on the matter of the Eucharist not only was her definition vague but biblical authority was slight. Four years before the publication of the *Concordia*, Erasmus was pointing out to Justus Decius that Scripture offered no firm evidence of Apostolic consecration of the bread and wine. Were it not for the "very substantial agreement of the Church" he himself would be able to adopt the sacramentarian view of Oecolampadius.[47] In a letter to Tunstall the next year he was even more unguarded; the Church had never clearly explained the Real Presence; furthermore, the importance of the sacrament lay in the faith of the partaker. Nor did he consider it irreligious to call the Real Body a type or symbol, since it was the invisible Body that symbolized the unity of Christ and His Church.[48]

Two years later he was declaring his "utter astonishment" that Martin Bucer should have found him in essential agreement with the Evangelicals. We may be astonished that he was astonished. We may even see in some of his denials of heterodoxy a little of the verbal virtuosity with which, long before, he had dodged the imputation of authorship of *Julius Exclusus*. Still, however supple in doctrine Erasmus may seem at times, his fundamental temper *was* as far from that of the Protestant reformers as from that of an intransigent Catholic conservatism. If, in his hands, Catholic dogma would have dwindled into nothing, Protestant dogma would have fared no better.[49] His great mission in life, the brotherhood of men in humane Christian values, was not to be served by arid caviling on the ninth part of a doctrinal hair. As Renaudet has put it, ". . . l'exégèse érasmienne, sans attaquer de front dogmes et pratiques, s'efforce de les réduire insensiblement a des symboles, pour en dégager peu a peu, sans revolution et sans violence, les quelques affirmations essentielles où se résume pour lui l'essence du christianisme."[50]

If, as Renaudet goes on to say, Erasmus "ne dissimule pas la pensee de pacification qui inspirera son oeuvre," that *pensee,* he knew, was not widely shared. When Reginald Pole, for example, addressed his own *pro ecclesiasticae unitatis defensione* to his royal cousin three years later, his bristling tone and argument were calculated not so much to restore peace and concord as to assign blame for their absence. Like Erasmus he cites the sacrilegious revolt of Dathan and Abiron, but unlike Erasmus he makes a point of specifically equating that revolt with the action of Henry and the English church: however heinous the behavior of those Mosaic schismatics, compared to their sixteenth-century counterparts, their offense was modest. Heresy for Pole is not misguided enthusiasm or a well-intentioned mistake. With sly cunning Richard Sampson and his kind had twisted scripture to their own satanic purposes and obfuscated a very plain truth. Just as the serpent of old, inflamed by malice and hatred for man, had deceived our first parents with the specious charm of his persuasion, so the English heretics were seducing men with a fraudulent show of piety when their whole aim was to subvert genuine godliness.

Especially vulnerable to such wiliness, Pole argued, were the untutored, the "homines . . . literarum ignaros." Just how vulnerable can be inferred from the massive array of exegesis and disputation he considered necessary to dispose of heretical arguments. Much of Book II, for example, is given over to his demonstration of the primacy of the Bishop of Rome. He buttresses his case for Peter as the Rock with copious citations of patristic and scriptural authority, analyzes the sense in which the Apostle was the Rock, the sense in which after the Passion he became a surrogate for Christ, and why it must follow that his successors—even the bad ones—representing as they did the *persona Christi*, contained in their persons the unity of the Church. Henry, therefore, had effected a "duplex" church; Christ's Church was still the pope's, and Henry's, clearly, belonged to Satan.[51]

True, he was addressing a king who fancied himself as a theologian and who would perhaps have considered less ponderous and sophisticated weapons unworthy of his mettle. True also that Pole had been affected by the Anglican schism in a way more directly personal than the Reform had ever touched Erasmus. Even More and Fisher were still alive at the time of the *Concordia*. Such facts may account, at least in part, for the contrast between the *Defensio* and the *Concordia;* but they do not diminish it. The doctrinal hard line, the *ad hominem* acerbity of Pole's treatment of schismatics— all this suggests as well a difference in cast of mind and temper between two men who were, after all, on the same side. Pole, too, had hoped for a renovation of the Church within the existing framework of that Church. He could even be counted among the number of Erasmian humanists—as, for that matter, could Sampson and Starkey and Lupset and Tunstall, and the other scholars who had put themselves at Henry's disposal. It is interesting to note that Pole accused Sampson of distorting and misquoting Erasmus; he doubted that his adversary could have read all the work of that "virum in literis exercitatissimum," for he was sure much of it was too learned and too difficult for Sampson to understand.

But perhaps there was something in Erasmus that Pole, too, did not understand, or at least could not accept. The attribute which ultimately put off most of Erasmus' contemporaries and left him standing pretty much alone and disregarded was clearly enough not his erudition but his incomprehensible (to them) refusal to put that learning to work in the promotion of one or another doctrinaire version of the New Jerusalem. His difficulty for moderns—ecumenicity notwithstanding—is probably much the same. However much belated stitching we attempt in the fabric of institutional Christendom, the proclivity for robe-rending seems to be endemic in human nature and the voice of Erasmus too low-keyed and tentative to make very appealing other less exciting adjustments of the world's ills, whatever the terms being currently applied to the malaise. He will have no attraction for the messianic or for anyone with a recipe for instant millennium. He will offer little comfort to any self-constituted elect, or the fierce innocence of a cocksure and self-righteous zealotry. If he thought a simple Christian faith was what men needed, a fervid simple-mindedness he certainly did not. Knowing that the best in us could often be turned to the worst effects and that this was perhaps the most cunning pitfall Old Nick had left us, he saw the aggressive ideologue of the Reform as differing in no important way from the repressive bigot of the Catholic Establishment. Whichever side had its violent way, one tyranny would merely be substituted for another; the real casualty would be the philosophy of Christ. The only sure betterment in religion, or in culture, or in society, was that which came about by gradual enlightenment, not by force; and only in an atmosphere of peace and mutual forbearance could such an evolutionary process take place. This was the steady conviction of his whole life. Whether any such conviction can carry the field over the heady thrill of apocalyptic certainties is a question still in doubt.

NOTES

1. *The Colloquies of Erasmus* (Chicago, 1965), p. 268.

2. Wm. P. Dunn, *Sir Thomas Browne: A Study in Religious Philosophy* (Minneapolis, 1950), pp. 45-46.

3. *Lectures and Wayfaring Sketches* (Oxford, 1934), p. 86.

4. See *EE*, VI, 1608.

5. *Ibid.*, X, headnote to 2852.

6. Cf. *Biblioteca Erasmiana*, F. Van Der Haghen, ed. (reprint of 1893 edition), pp. 116-117.

7. Anthony à Wood (*Athenae Oxonienses*, I, 423) mentions a translation "done by" Richard Taverner in 1545 but does not include it among works published by Taverner. No such translation is listed in the *STC*.

8. *EE*, X, 2906.

9. *Ibid.*, IX, 2513.

10. See A. Renaudet, *Études Erasmiennes (1521-1529)* (Paris, 1939), p. 116.

11. *Lectures and Wayfaring Sketches*, p. 82.

12. *Études*, p. 153.

13. *The Oxford Reformers* (London, 1869), pp. 173-174.

14. In his *Ecclesiastae Sive De Ratione Concionandi (LB,* V, 1061C-1062D) Erasmus refers to the four ways of interpreting Scripture as the historical, the aetiological (or etymological), the analogical, and

the allegorical. His aetiological method, he admits, tends to merge with the allegorical; the analogical is that reading which seeks to find perfect agreement between the Old and New Testaments, and, with a touch of irony, he comments upon the pious men who have sweated earnestly over this task of showing that "nihil praecipi in Novo Testamento, quod in Veteri non praecipiatur, neque quidquam esse gestum, quod non sit vel a Prophetis praedictum, vel typis adumbratum" (1062C). He is not immune to such typological efforts himself, however.

Erasmus' classification differs somewhat in terminology from that of the medieval explanation:

> Littera gesta docet,
> Quid credas allegoria,
> Moralis quid agas,
> Quo tendas anagogia.

A literal sense, that is, deals with historical fact, an allegorical with belief, a moral with right action, and an anagogical with man's ultimate destination. In his well-known letter to Can Grande, Dante applies these methods to Psalm 114:1-2: "When Israel went out of Egypt, the house of Jacob from a people of strange language; Judah was his sanctuary, and Israel his dominion." Allegorically, says Dante, the verse refers to "our redemption wrought by Christ." In the moral sense it means "the conversion of the soul from grief and misery of sin to the state of grace." In the anagogical it refers to "the departure of the holy soul from the slavery of this corruption to the liberty of eternal glory" (in *The Latin Works of Dante Alighieri*, London, 1904, pp. 347-348). But Dante goes on to call all three "mystic," even though they have their special denominations, so "they may all in general be called allegorical."

15. *Études,* pp. 136-137. In the Old Testament, Renaudet observes, Erasmus liked and referred most to those books best in accord with the New Testament spirit, e.g., Isaiah, Ezekiel, Jeremiah, the Psalms, Proverbs, and the Book of Wisdom (the latter books appealing to the compiler of adages). He knew the historical books but read them, like those setting forth Judaic law, for his own purposes: "mais il ne les allègue que pour en tirer des symboles religieux ou des allégories morales."

16. See "Figura," in *Scenes From the Drama of European Literature* (New York, 1954), p. 54.

17. Cf. *LB,* V, 1043B-C:
> Inter Allegoriam autem & Typum hoc interest. Quae
> facta narrantur ut aliud significent, typos ac figuras appellamus:
> ut serpens aeneus in stipite pendens, typus fuit Christi sublati
> in crucem in salutem omnium credentium; Allegoria magis sita
> est in doctrina ac praeceptis, cujus generis fere sunt, quae
> lex Mosis praecepit de aedificando Templo, de vestitu
> Sacerdotum, de ritibus Sacrificiorum, de Circumcisione, deque
> cibis mundis & immundis. Caeterum quod ad tractationem
> attinet, eadem est ratio Typorum & Allegoriarum.

18. See *The Limits of Literary Criticism* (London, 1957), pp. 29-30.

19. A product of the well-known controversy over literary style: *Dialogus. De Imitatione Ciceroniana, adversus Desiderium Erasmum Roterodamum pro Christophoro Longolio* (Lyons, 1535), p. 44.

20. I am indebted here to comments of Professor Watts on reading the manuscript of my translation.

21. A letter from John Choler in 1534 (*EE*, X, 2936) urges Erasmus to defend himself against Luther's attacks, lest the world take his silence as a sign of fear or uneasy conscience. Luther's talents for invective were generous: is it not enough, Choler asks, "quod te bilinguem impostorem, artificem satanicum, regem amphibolum, confusissimam Babilonem, ethnicum et Epicurum vocet, Anabaptistam, Sacramentarium, Arrianum, Donatistam, hereticum ter maximum et versutum Christi irrisorem clara voce appellat . . . ?"

22. Eugene F. Rice, "Erasmus and the Religious Tradition," *Journal of the History of Ideas* 11 (1950):387-411.

23. *Erasmus and the Northern Renaissance* (London, 1949), p. 82. Mrs. Phillips points out that Erasmus saw man always as thirsting for his pristine state of goodness. In his *Enarratio Primi Psalmi* (*LB*, V, 174D-E) he describes this universal yearning of all men for beatitude and praises the efforts of pagan philosophers to understand it (while he deplores the contrasting behavior of many Christians). With a note of regret, however, he concludes that the pagans could not have arrived at that beatitude "quia defuit unicus ille verae sapientiae Doctor, Christi Spiritus."

24. *Erasmus* (New York and London, 1923), p. 336. On Erasmus' Pyrrhonism see also Renaudet, *Études*, pp. 125, 129-130, and 146. The French critic observes that the humanist's scepticism would not permit him to believe that philosophy or theology could arrive at an understanding of first causes or "les realites supremes." For this reason he never debated or argued about the supernatural character of the Christian revelation.

Thomas Lupset took the same position in his "Exhortacion to Young Men." In the study of the New Testament, he advises, "meeke downe your wittes. Presume not, in no case to thynke, that there you vunderstand ought; leue deuisinge thereupon: submit your selfe to the expositions of holy doctours and euer conforme your consent to agre with Christes church." (*In Life and Works of Thomas Lupset*, J. A. Gee, ed. (New Haven, 1928), p. 244.

25. *Erasmus*, p. 351.

26. Renaudet, *Études*, p. 171. That is, Erasmus censures heresy more as a moralist with no liking for intellectual arrogance than as a theologian armed to do battle for the one and only Church. His distrust of metaphysics, though it assuredly did not make him the Arian or the antitrinitarian he was sometimes accused of being, led him to present an

image of Jesus which seemed too human for some, a christology which, without being rationalistic, skirted all the questions raised by the School-men, a Holy Spirit which remained more metaphor than divine person.

27.   Cf. Allen, *Wayfaring Sketches*, p. 98, and Philip Hughes, *A History of the Church* (New York, 1947), III, 472. As a result of Erasmus' lack of "doctrinal precision," in Hughes' words, "Catholic dogma thins out until it vanishes to nothing. . . ."

28.   See "The Attitude of Erasmus Toward Toleration," in *Persecution and Liberty: Essays in Honor of George Lincoln Burr* (New York, 1931), pp. 171-176.

29.   *Concordia*, p. 84.

30.   For Erasmus' views on heresy, see for example his letter to Nicholas of Hertogenbosch in 1521 (*EE*, IV, 1232); one to Jacob Hochstrat in 1519 (*EE*, IV, 1006); his *Ecclesiastes* (*LB*, V, 1981B). His comment in the last-named work is characteristic:

> Haeresim autem appello, non quemvis errorem, sed pervicacem malitiam, alicujus commodi gratia perversis dogmatibus turbantem Ecclesiae tranquillitatem. In genere vero omne crimen cum impietate conjunctum est. Quisquis enim admittit scelus, aliquem rem creatam Creatori praefert, & a Deo ad Satanam deficit, unde & Paulus avaritiam idolotariam appellat.

The position of Jeremy Taylor more than a century later was essentially Erasmian:

> . . . if a man mingles not a vice with his opinion, if he be innocent in his life though deceived in his doctrine, his error is his misery, not his crime; it makes him an argument of weakness and an object of pity, but not a person sealed up to ruin and reprobation. . . . For it cannot stand with the goodness of God to condemn those who err, where the error hath nothing of the will in it; who therefore cannot repent of their error, because they believe it is true. . . . ("Liberty of Prophesying," in *Works* [London, 1847-1854], V, 383-4.)

31.   *EE*, I, p. 17 (in the *Catalogus omnium Erasmi Lucubrationum*).

32.   *Utopia* (Everyman ed., 1946), pp. 101-103.

33.   *The apologye of syr Thomas More*, 1533, p. 74.

34.   *Oxford Reformers*, p. 491. As Bacon put it, "Christ's coat indeed had no seam, but the church's vesture was of divers colours."

35.   See *Tudor Prelates and Politics* (Princeton, 1953), pp. 33-37.

36.   M. C. D'Arcy, S. J., *The Mind and Heart of Love; Lion and Unicorn, A Study in Eros and Agape* (New York, 1947), pp. 47-48.

37.   *EE*, VI, 1756. The allusion to Keats' ode is not facetious. In his commentary on Psalm 38 (*LB*, V, 427C) he draws an analogy between bad music and bad living. Good *living* is the music that really pleases God: "Ne Christianorum quidem musica grata est, nisi totus homo sibi

consonet, atque externus cum internus congruat." *In Psalmum 4* (*LB,* V, 243B-C) develops the same theme:

> Nos intelligamus Deo gratissimam esse musicam, quum nulla in parte vita nostra dissonat a praeceptis ipsius, quum oratio nostra cum vita concordat, cum suavissimum fraternae concordiae concentum, nulla dissidiorum aut opinionum turbat dissonantia, quum lyra querula deplorat admissum, quum cymbalis bene sonantibus gratias agimus, quum tuba libere personat sermonem Evangelicum.

38.   From *Ecclesiastes* (*LB,* V, 942A-B). Cf. *In Psalmum 85* (*LB,* V, 523F): "Corporis vocem oportet esse modestam. At hodie quidam in templis mira vocis ostentatione tonant verius, quam canunt, quum interim animus sit otiosus. Habent & pietatis officia vocem efficacem."

39.   See *Christiani Matrimonii Institutio* (*LB,* V, 718B-C).

40.   Edward L. Surtz, *The Praise of Wisdom* (Chicago, 1957), p. 195.

41.   The translation is from the Elizabeth F. Rogers edition of *St. Thomas More: Selected Letters* (New Haven and London, 1951), p. 120.

42.   See *Documents Illustrative of English Church History,* ed. Henry Gee and William J. Hardy (London, 1921), pp. 271-278.

43.   *In Psalmum 85* (*LB,* V, 533E-534A).

44.   Cf. Renaudet, *Études,* pp. 171-172: "La seule tradition de l'Église l'oblige à reconnaître, dans l'Eucharistie, plus qu'une commémoration symbolique de la dernier Cene de Jésus."

45.   The kind of questions denounced in England in a "Proclamation concerning the irreverent talkers of the sacrament" issued at the beginning of Edward VI's reign. Fines and imprisonment were decreed for those who search and strive irreverently

> whether the body and bloud aforesaid is there really or figuratly, locally or circumscriptly, and having quantity and greatness, or but substantially and by substance only, or else but in figure and manner of speaking; whether his blessed body be there, head, leggs, armes, toes and nails, or any other ways, shape and manner, naked or clothed; whether he is broken and chewed, or he is always whole; whether the bread there remaineth as we see, or how it departeth . . . with other such irreverent, superfluous and curious questions. . . . (Quoted in C. W. Dugmore, *The Mass and the English Reformers* [London, 1958], p. 116). Cf. the letter to Balthasar Mercklin, pp. 122-124 below.

46.   See his Annotations on I Corinthians (*LB,* VI, 696C):

> . . . diu satis erat credere, sive sub pane consecrato, sive quocumque modo adesse verum corpus Christi. Ubi rem proprius contemplata est, ubi exactius expendit, certius praescripsit. Non erant Haeretici qui olim credidissent Spiritum sanctum a

Patre duntaxat procedere, & haud scio, an maxima pars
Christianorum primitus ita crediderit. Expensa re, definit
Ecclesia quod hodie sequimur.

Heresy has thus long been simply a matter of differing from what ecclesiastical authority has decided must be defined. Dugmore (*ibid.,*
pp. 8-9) points out that Augustine apparently had no thought of the
eucharistic sacrament as a repetition of Christ's sacrifice, considering
it merely a "sacramentum memoriae." The Reformers tended to use
Augustine in this regard; the consecration, effected by the celebrant's
imitating the acts and words of Christ, was not what perfected the
Eucharist, but rather, the use of the faithful.

47.   *EE,* VIII, 2175; see also p. 188 below.

48.   *EE,* VIII, 2263, and p. 195 below.

49.   Cf. Philip Hughes, *A History of the Church* (New York, 1947),
III: 472.

50.   *Erasme: Sa Pensee Religieuse et son action d'apres sa correspondance (1518-1521)* (Paris, 1926), p. 55.

51.   On this point, at least, Starkey had misread his man. Much too
hopefully, he has Pole saying, "I think the authority given to Saint Peter
was nothing of the sort which nowadays the Popes usurp, but it was
only to declare penitent hearts, contrite for their sin, to be absolved
from the faut thereof, and that it should be no more imputed to them."
The "dispensation of laws," having been ordained by man and given
to the See of Rome by man, could of course be taken away by man
(*A Dialogue Between Reginald Pole and Thomas Lupset,* ed. Kathleen
M. Burton, [London, 1948], p. 118).

*A letter to Julius Pflug, written as a preface
to the first edition of* Liber de sarcienda
Ecclesiae concordia, *published by Froben
at Basel. (EE, X, 2852)*

H OW DEEPLY YOU are grieved by this constantly worsening
discord and with what heartfelt longing you, and all devout
men, sigh for that desirable peace in the Church, most admirable
Julius, has been the theme of a great many of your letters to me,
where you are always sounding the same old tune and, with great
urgency, pressing me to show how to quiet this tempest. Although
what you are insisting on is not a whit more realistic than if you
were to order a pygmy to hold up the sky in place of Atlantis,
nevertheless you will accept no excuse from me.

You are quite wrong, my dear Julius, about my unawareness.
But the greater your error, the more it reveals your extraordinary
devotion to the house of God, in which you occupy no inconsiderable place, and occupy it most deservedly because of your outstanding virtues; these virtues become you all the more because
you do not preen yourself at all on their account but acknowledge
the bounty of the Lord. If Christendom had many such men, either
these tumults would never have arisen or they would long since
have been lulled into quiet. But just because I have been caught,
as they say, between the devil and the deep blue sea so that I can
neither refuse what you urge nor effectually perform it, I have
found a kind of middle course with which I may in the future
conciliate you to some extent. I have discussed Psalm 83, in which
the spirit of God powerfully recommends to us the concord of the
Church. It is no insignificant help and encouragement in this kind
of undertaking, where a good part of the success, clearly, lies in a
well-disposed will, which never lacks the assistance of a beneficent
Divine Will. Therefore if Christ deigns to grant that the love of
peace in the Church which you are so poignantly eager for should
seize the hearts of all men, it will soon come to pass that neither
you in your solicitations nor I in my reluctance to comply will be
making a futile effort, but we will each be congratulating the other.
But I will keep you away from the psalm no longer.

Written at Freiburg on July 31, 1533.

PSALM LXXXIII
Vulgate Version

In finem,
Pro torcularibus filiis Core, Psalmus

Quam dilecta tabernacula tua Domine virtutum! Concupiscit, & deficit anima mea in atria Domini.

Cor meum, & caro mea exultaverunt in Deum vivum.

Etenim passer invenit sibi domum:& turtur nidum sibi, ubi ponat pullos suos.

Altaria tua Domine virtutum: rex meus & Deus meus.

Beati, qui habitant in domo tua Domine: in saecula saeculorum laudabunt te.

Beatus vir, cujus est auxilium abs te: ascensiones in corde suo disposuit, in valle lacrymarum in loco, quem posuit.

Etenim benedictionem dabit legislator, ibunt de virtute in virtutem: videbitur Deus deorum in Sion.

Domine Deus virtutum exaudi orationem meam: auribus percipe Deus Iacob.

Protector noster aspice Deus: & respice in faciem Christi tui.

Quia melior est dies una atriis tuis super millia.

Elegi abjectus esse in domo Dei mei: magis quam habitare in tabernaculis peccatorum.

Quia misericordiam, & veritatem diliget Deus: gratiam, & gloriam dabit Dominus.

Non privabit bonis eos, qui ambulant in innocentia: Domine virtutum, beatus homo, qui sperat in te.

PSALM LXXXIV
King James Version

To the chief Musician upon Gittith, A Psalm for the sons of Korah

How amiable are thy tabernacles, O LORD of Hosts!

My soul longeth, yea, even fainteth for the courts of the Lord: my heart and my flesh crieth out for the living God.

Yea, the sparrow hath found a house, and the swallow a nest for herself, where she may lay her young, even thine altars, O LORD of hosts, my King and my God.

Blessed are they that dwell in the house: they will be still praising thee. Selah.

Blessed is the man whose strength is in thee; in whose heart are the ways of them. Who passing through the valley of Baca make it a well; the rain also filleth the pools. They go from strength to strength, every one of them in Zion appeareth before God.

O LORD God of Hosts, hear my prayer: give ear, O God of Jacob. Selah. Behold, O God our shield, and look upon the face of thine anointed.

For a day in thy courts is better than a thousand. I had rather be a doorkeeper in the house of my God, than to dwell in the tents of wickedness.

For the LORD God is a sun and shield: the Lord will give grace and glory: no good thing will he withhold from them that walk uprightly.

O LORD of Hosts, blessed is the man that trusteth in thee.

DE SARCIENDA ECCLESIAE CONCORDIA

WE HAVE CHOSEN the eighty-third[1] psalm for comment because in it the Holy Spirit, arguing with the utmost plainness and cogency, urges upon us that blessed and lovely peace of the Church, a subject useful and beneficial at any time, but in this age of proliferating sects more essential than any other. Therefore, whoever loves the kind of peace which, according to the blessed Paul, surpasses all understanding,[2] and which alone protects and shelters from all evil our hearts and bodies in our Peace-Maker Christ Jesus the Lord, let him pay close attention to what I have to say. The heading of this psalm offers some difficulties, but having disposed of these as briefly as possible we will move more briskly to the contemplation of a prospect at once very beautiful and very pleasant. This superscription varies somewhat in the manuscripts, whether by intention of the scribes or because the uncertain meaning of the Hebrew has resulted in inconsistency. The Septuagint translators have "For the conclusion, a psalm of the sons of Korah for the wine presses." Jerome has it this way: "For Him who conquers, a psalm of the sons of Korah for the wine presses."

When you hear *in finem*, or "for the conclusion," you should understand that the psalm is talking about Christ, who is the "end" or "ultimate," this is to say, the fulfillment of the law to all believers. There is no true and perfect righteousness except through genuine trust in Him who alone purifies, by faith, the hearts of men.[3] When you hear *Vincenti*, "the conqueror," or *pro Victoria*, "for victory," you are reminded at once of Paul's remark that no one achieves that glorious wreath which never withers except him who has competed in the right way.[4] A student of the Hebrew has suggested that in place of *Vincenti* it could have read *Effundenti sanguinem*, "to one who sheds his blood," not a slight, harmless

29

skirmish but a fierce battle, or as the Greeks say, *aspondon pole-mon*. When those who fight wars for this world expose their bodies so often to the weapons of the enemy and stake their lives on the dice of unpredictable Mars for the sake of a public celebration, for the sake of applause, or maybe a triumphal ceremony—and this, looked at more realistically, is something absurd and trivial rather than impressive, something no serious man could contemplate without laughter since its whole glory is bounded by a single day—why will not the soldiers of Christ work to achieve that everlasting triumph in heaven? How great is the glory of the martyrs, who by shedding their blood conquered kingdoms through faith, dedicated themselves to righteousness and realized the most abundant promises! Their praises resound throughout the whole earth and they celebrate, to the applause of angels, an everlasting victory with Christ as their general in the heavenly Jerusalem. But these, heeding the words of Paul,[5] mortify in the love of Christ their own earthly qualities, lust, greed, wrath, and other passions habitually hostile to the spirit, and thus conquer Satan in no easy warfare.[6] Now there is also in this very psalm a reference to tents, part of the language of warfare.

Going on a little further, the fact that "for the wine presses" is included has somewhat disturbed Saint Augustine because nothing is said of wine presses in the psalm itself. He therefore resorted to allegory.[7]

One can, indeed, sometimes consider the psalm headings as referring to facts of history, as in Psalm 33: "The Psalm of David, when he changed his behavior in the presence of Abimelech, who sent him away, and he departed." Sometimes it deals with the holy day when it was customarily sung, as in Psalm 91, which has the heading "A Psalm for the Sabbath day," or 92: "The song of praise of David on the day before the Sabbath," or in 94, "A Psalm of David on the fourth day of the Sabbath." We need not reject the historical sense to make place for the allegorical, for one may become the foundation and support of the other, and that which is known makes it possible to bring in more effectively the mystical and recondite meaning. Therefore, when the prophetic heading includes the words "for the wine presses," it is referring to the seventh month, which for us is September. In olden times, since the sun enters the Ram in March, they made that month the beginning of the year; and in counting from this—since the fifth month, later called July, was then called Quintilis and the one following, now August, was called Sextilis, and so on clear up to December—they chose a name in accordance with the number. Moreover, seeing that the seventh month is the time of the grape harvest, it was more meaningful and in keeping with a divine significance to say "for the wine presses" than "in the seventh month." Thus Horace, to indicate early spring, spoke metaphorically, with some charm, of "Zephyrus and the first swallow." [8]

At the same time also, holy days are indicated, on which the prophets engaged in singing contests. Hence the superscriptions of several psalms refer to lilies or roses, indicating spring time and the celebrations held at that time of the year. Among the Jews there were three of special importance: the Passover, commemorating the miraculous crossing of the sea; Pentecost, the law given and received on Mount Sinai; and the Tabernacles, about which we shall speak shortly. The first fell at the beginning of spring; the second, in summer; the third, in autumn. For on the fifteenth day of the seventh month there was the Feast of Tabernacles, so named from the tabernacles to be erected; they were commanded to dwell in tents for seven days in memory of their past history, the flight from Egypt, and their living for forty years in tents as they journeyed through the harsh and boundless wastes, to commemorate God's showing them the way by means of a fiery pillar at night and a pillar of cloud by day,[9] His loving kindness which kept them from being deprived of food and drink. Neither their clothing nor their shoes were worn out.

At this time the temple itself was a tabernacle, or tent, and remained so until Solomon built that magnificent Temple of Jerusalem held in awe even by the heathen. In order that they might not forget the merciful providence of God and that they might not fail to hand down awareness of such a miracle to their posterity, they were commanded to observe annually an eight-day Festival of Tabernacles about the time of the grape harvest, and this was on the seventh month. Thus in a certain sense it is the Sabbath of the months. Just as in days it was the seventh day, and in years also it was the seventh year that provided its rest to the earth, on this Sabbath of years there was a jubilee covering hebdomads of seven years. Of these eight days of the seventh month, therefore, the first was the Sabbath, being the beginning of the third week, just as the eighth was the beginning of the fourth. Both were spent in rest and fasting. The intervening days were given over to sacrifices, hymns, and to solemn rejoicing and thanksgiving. But the eighth was, so to speak, the start of a new feast day, namely a coming together or collecting, because then, besides the cost of the sacrifices and gifts, something could be collected from everyone for the expenses of the tabernacle. Leviticus 13 and Numbers 29 treat of these matters.

Accordingly, although there is no explicit mention of tabernacles in the heading, it is nevertheless implicit that on the month appointed for the celebration of the Feast of Tabernacles the fruits of the earth had already been harvested. Moreover, virtually the whole month was taken up in feasting and sacrifices so that, at one time, the priests might be provided for and the people might understand that they had a duty to bring as the gift of Divine Providence whatever the land produced. And, having been reminded by the tabernacles themselves that when they had journeyed through the arid, barren desert the Lord permitted them to lack nothing, but had rained manna from heaven and sent water gushing from the rock,[10] they were not to misuse such fruits of the earth in a selfish way when the crops were unusually abundant, nor were they to be down-hearted if some year turned out to be a hard one. For who could suppose that He who clothed the lilies of the field, who provided for the little sparrows,[11] would cease to provide what His servants needed, especially when the prudence of righteous men could be satisfied with very little?

How much more shameful that some Christians today, showered with overflowing abundance by divine benevolence, are moved, not to give thanks, not to be generous with the Church or with the poor, but to lewd pleasure, easy living and self-gratification. On the other hand, if they do not prosper very well, then forgetting earlier bounties and distrustful of the future, they raise prices, reduce their contributions to charity, cut down on what they give the Church, and avoid paying their bills. How much more appropriate for those who glory in the title *Christian* to increase their gifts to the needy when the year's harvest is rather meager! God did not give rich crops so that the grain could mould in your barns but so that the overflow could be used to relieve the poor. See to it that you don't appear unworthy of previous prosperity, that in years to come you may deserve greater favors from the Lord.

Furthermore, as the prophet Zachariah makes plain in chapter 14, that Feast of the Tabernacles which was observed by the Jews, was a *typichos* which pointed to the festal celebration of the Catholic Church. "There will be a plague in which the Lord will crush all the Gentiles who have not come up to observe the Feast of the Tabernacles." In this same chapter occurs mention of wine presses, so one can see that the subject of the psalm was drawn from this passage of the Prophet, or vice versa.

Jerome has meticulously noted that three psalms have headings which refer to a winepress: the eighth, which is entitled "David"; the eightieth, entitled "Asaph," and this eighty-third, entitled "to the sons of Korah." What they all have in common is that they all recall a victory. Number eight, moreover, is devoted to the glory of the resurrection; for this is the day the Lord made when He arose from the dead, the day on which we are commanded to rejoice and be glad with holy dancing. Where there is resurrection there is life, and life is righteousness, just as sin is death.

The first day, then, which Psalm 8 deals with, was an appropriate subject for the praise of man created in the image of God, and showing man thus created as to be nearest to angels. The second one of the three deals with man recalled to innocence through the law, a fact which is pointed up by eight multiplied by ten, symbolizing the Decalogue. The third reveals man elevated by the grace of the Gospel to the point of perfection where he could live corporeally here on earth while, through faith and hope, having communion with heaven. To these ten eights is joined a three because by the light of the Gospel the whole world has clearly recognized the mystery of the Holy Trinity. The Jews had known the Father; but afterwards the Son, who had taken on human nature, was seen on earth and dwelled with men; finally He was received into heaven, with the Spirit imparted from above restoring the minds and tongues of all. Then at last the world clearly acknowledged one God in three Persons, three Persons in the same divine nature: the Father, the Son, and the Holy Spirit.

Moreover, since the Gentiles were in the habit of celebrating harvest time with profane and shameless rites in honor of a sportive Bacchus, wantoning with frenzied games, lewd dances, and smutty language—several vestiges of which secularity we grieve to see holding over to the present day—Moses converted this public merry-making to the reverent offering of thanks, changing bawdy posturing to the ceremonial dancing of prophets (for we read that David danced before the ark in honor of God), and suggestive songs and indecent lyrics to mystic psalms. Thus he converted the impious worship other nations were giving to devils into the worship of the true God.

The Gentiles had their own contests on these holidays, in which men something less than sober and with filth-smeared faces scattered ribald verses from carts among those they met on the street. As a prize the winner received a goat, a lid worthy of the pot, as the saying goes.[12] *Here*, on the other hand, there was a contest between prophets, full of piety and reverence. It is from this practice that many of the psalms have *pro victoria*, "for victory," in their titles. A contest of this kind existed also in the assemblies of Christians at the time of the Apostles. One man spoke with tongues; many engaged in the act of prophecy. Nor did unbecoming contention seethe here: if revelation had come to someone else, the first speaker fell silent. The person outdone was not displeased with himself but gave thanks to the Spirit who was willing to teach through another that which had escaped him. And the winner was not proud in heart, knowing that all this was the vigor of the Holy Spirit, who distributed to each one His gifts just as He willed.

Such was the competition of singing and dancing among these prophets. We learn by this example that whether we are distressed and disheartened by adversity or generously blessed with prosperity, we should do everything to the glory of God. Nowadays many Christians call upon God only in sickness or in war or in other perils; thus they compartmentalize their situations, reserving bad times for God and giving the pleasant ones over to Satan. At the burial of loved ones you may see some appearance of piety; at weddings, celebrations, and dinner parties not a trace of Christian character. People think they have amply paid off God if they live a little more strictly during Lent, but how loose is their liberty up to that time! Again, after the restrictions of the Easter period how eagerly they return to the pleasures they have left off! But it behooves us to have Christian joys no less than hardships. As long as we are committed to these tabernacles here, the vicissitudes of our affairs will differ. There is a time for birth and a time for dying, a time for being wed and a time for refraining from marriage, a time for rejoicing over the birth of children and a time to mourn their death [13]: but the Christian should have no time devoid of faithfulness. Let the fast be observed on the approach of a feast day, but let it be a devout one; the feast day is a time for rejoicing, but a spiritual rejoicing. In that place some are sad, but in accordance with the will of God; here some of us are glad, but in the sight of the Lord. As Isaiah says, speaking in chapter 9 of the Evangelic joys: "They will rejoice before you, as those who rejoice in the harvest." Those are rightly glad who are glad in the sight of God, who with a just understanding give thanks to Him for their sorrows as well as their happiness. Those people who give over their times of rejoicing to gaming, drunkenness, obscene talk, and whoring may be happy as the world sees such things; but in the eyes of God, they are mad. Perhaps we dwell too long on these matters. Would to God we had no reason to do so!

Let us therefore clear up the mystery of the heading. Psalm 8 is ascribed to David, a word which in Hebrew means "strong of hand"; Psalm 80, to Asaph, which means "the gatherer"; this Psalm, 83, to the "sons of Korah," which is to say, "Calvary." In this rather recondite sense all three names signify "Christ." He was the creator of man unfallen; the Father, through the Son, made the universe and whatever is in heaven or earth. This no one but the all-powerful could do; hence, Paul writing to the Hebrews calls the Son "the word of His Father's might." [14] At the same time man fallen and debased to such a degree that he now had to be compared with brutish beasts and had become like them, or even worse, him He restored by means of law and, until the fullness of time came, enclosed him so to speak within the bars of justice. Whence the term *synagogue*, and the Psalm of Asaph resoundingly challenges us to observe the law: "Israel," it says, "if you will hear me, there will be no strange God for you." Finally the Lord himself openly acknowledges the role of the Unifier in the Gospel: "Jerusalem, Jerusalem, you who kill the prophets and stone those who have been sent to you, how often have I wanted to gather you together as a hen gathers her chicks under her wings, and you would not!" [15] At length, when the time was ripe, the "son of Korah" was also made, who, having suffered on the hill of Calvary, gathered the whole world unto himself, and when He rose again triumphed over Satan in His very overthrow.

At this point, perhaps, some question perturbs the reader as to how Christ, the son of God, can be called "the son of Korah," who, since he was an important Levite, sought the office of high priest and, aligning himself with Dathan and Abiron, stirred up practically the whole populace against Moses and Aaron, as we are told in the sixteenth chapter of Numbers. Of the many who stubbornly supported him, some were swallowed up alive when the earth parted and others were consumed by fire sent down from heaven.

The allegory is not pointless, though. In terms of the flesh Christ drew His origin from the Jewish people, who were obstinately rebellious against God and about whom He complains through the Prophet Isaiah: "I have stretched out my hands all day to a people not believing, and speaking against me."[16] Again, in the psalm: "For forty years I have been devoted to this generation, and I have always said they err in their hearts."[17] In the Acts of the Apostles Stephen censures this stiff-necked rebelliousness in them: "You have always resisted the Holy Spirit."[18]

Many of the psalms, moreover, have "son of Korah" in their headings, although the specific name of no one is mentioned; it is as if "son of Korah" was enough to be said in their praise, although in the general opinion of men it might seem a shameful thing for those condemned by the loathesome example of a criminal father to be pointed out by name. Who could bear to be called the son or grandson of Judas? Nevertheless, Scripture graces with praise the posterity of Korah, with the name of the forebear whose impiety made more lustrous the piety of the sons; although they had been bound by the strictest obligations of nature to this author of rebellion, nevertheless the love of religion in them took precedence over natural sentiment, inasmuch as they either—as seems likely— came to their senses and, loyal to Moses, separated themselves from their father; or they remained with him in such a way as to indicate no complicity in his wicked design, and when he and his followers were swallowed up the sons were spared, as you read in Numbers, the twenty-sixth chapter. Nor were they removed from service in the tabernacle because of their father's crime, but performed the honorable function of door-keepers, as recorded in the twenty-sixth chapter of First Paralipomenon.[19] They excelled, moreover, in the spirit of prophecy.

Therefore, since God does not charge sons with what their parents have done unless they themselves copy their actions, the common run of men behave unjustly when they blame children for the misdeeds and punishment of their ancestors as if they themselves had committed the crimes.

"How dare you open your mouth," they say, "when your father was convicted of embezzlement and put to death for it? How dare you show your face in public?"

But it is a finer thing to see the descendants of evil men achieve outstanding virtue than a good man born of good parents. Still, those people act even more unfairly who hold against the children, not the sins of their parents but their good fortune or their losses.

"I have found out," they say, "that his father was a slave," or "I have seen him when he was a beggar."

The very people who say such things are making excuses for themselves because, abandoned to vice, they are subject to the vilest bondage to Satan, or because they are getting rich by squeezing the poor. It is no crime to have had a slave for a father, but it is the worst of sins to be yourself a slave to lust and greed and the other offenses. There is no disgrace in begging your bread if you have to, but refusing to share the bare essentials of life with the needy and living by plunder, that is an opprobrius fault. Those who condone real transgressions in themselves, criticize their neighbors for circumstances not of their own making.

How much more gracious is God toward us! He does not make us responsible for transgressions which grieved Him over and over again. What sin was more deplorable than Korah's? What punishment more miserable? Not, indeed, by the judgment of man which is often deceived, but of God. And yet the word of His prophet chose to describe Korah's sons with their father's name rather than their own, as if it were a mark of honor.

It is a similar kind of inhumanity that leads us to apply the word *Maronite* as a term of abuse to those of Jewish descent who have been converted from the false religion of their parents to the true one, when it ought to be all the more honor to them for this reason. In view of our own provenance is it reasonable to thrust the faults of ancestors upon their descendants? Are not those who do this descended from people who, to the reproach of the true God, worshipped sticks and stones, or shed the blood of martyrs? But back to the matter at hand.

Korah, Dathan, Abiron, and On tried to divide the tabernacle, just as heretics and schismatics have always tried to split apart the Church; and just as the prompt wrath of God fell upon those who, even though warned, refused to give up the madness of their impious deeds and turbulent endeavors, so doubtless the flames of hell await these others. Regarded in this light, we must all be sons of

Korah in the sense that a son must not, in spite of religious faith, cleave to father, or brother to brother, or wife to husband, or son-in-law to father-in-law; but we must all withdraw from the tents of the wicked, if not bodily, surely in the matter of this discord of minds. If any error steals upon us through our thoughtlessness, let us listen to Moses and, once advised, follow the better ways so that after the tasks of this life have been endured we shall drink the wine of everlasting joy on the mountain of the Lord and, living harmoniously in the tabernacle of God which is the Church, shall be received into that heavenly Tabernacle of the Church Triumphant.

I see that in explaining the superscription I have been rather more tedious than I had intended. We will therefore hurry on to the psalm.

"How delightful are your tabernacles, Lord of Hosts, etc."

The abrupt opening of this psalm reveals an uncontrollable yearning of the heart, like that of Psalm 72: "How good is God, O Israel, to those who are pure of heart." Augustine's reading is more felicitous: "How lovely (amabilia)," or in the Greek, *agapeta*. Nothing is more agreeable, nothing more lovely, nothing more secure or stable than the concord of good men in good deeds; conversely, nothing is more vile, nothing more deplorable, nothing more debilitating than the conniving of evil men in evil deeds. The wicked, to be sure, have their own tents, a fact which this psalm, as well as the one immediately preceding it, notes. "Since they have consulted together with one consent, they also have drawn up a covenant against you: the tabernacles of the Edomites and Ishmaelites and Moab and the Hagarenes; Gebal and Ammon and Amalek, the Philistines with the inhabitants of Tyre." [20] And the second psalm says: "The Princes have banded together against the Lord and His Christ." [21]

Now, there is only one Church, although Paul speaks in this way of his teaching thus "in all churches," [22] because he knew that there are many churches in terms of differences in place and people even if there is only one in the profession of faith and the sharing of the sacraments. In the same manner of speaking, we read of many tabernacles of God even though there is one true tabernacle embracing all the elect, since all are the same in Christ.

On the other hand, there is no common tabernacle for the wicked since they are all at odds with one another in worship and the tenets of faith; but the ungodly differ with the ungodly in such a way that however they disagree on various styles of terminology they are all nevertheless equally at odds with the tabernacle of God. At one time the Greeks and Romans scoffed at the Egyptians who worshipped Serapis the bull and long-tailed apes and even onions, but at the same time they themselves were worshipping, as the true God, pieces of stone or wood, or spirits concealed in these objects. So it was that the Spartans had tabernacles different from those of Asia. Gaul had Druids as priests of their own kind of religion, but they were hostile to the true worship.

Dathan, Abiron, and On typify these priests. Each one was standing in his own tent ready for a fight. They were divided among themselves, agreed only on this point that they should attack Moses, just as various religions of diverse Gentiles, at odds with one another, nevertheless persecuted the Jews with marvelous harmony and accord—and, then, Christians, with even greater unanimity. Korah, moreover, who did not depart bodily from God's tabernacle but was far away from it in his heart, is a type of the divisiveness of heretics who, indeed, strive to seem to be proponents of the true faith. Just as Korah was trying to remove Aaron from the sanctuary, so they are trying to persuade adherents of Catholic doctrine that the latter are despotic foes of the Church. And just as every heresiarch shouts, "Christ is here, not there!" so Korah's band was saying "The entire crowd is holy, and the Lord is in them."

Before the coming of the Saviour to the Jews, the Sadducees and the Herodians [23] had their own tabernacles, but they were not lovely, not beautiful. Indeed, with the light of the Gospel already pouring itself over the earth, how many execrable tabernacles of heretics have stood in opposition to the tabernacle of the Lord! Who does not shudder even to read about the parade of obscenities in the tents of the Ophites,[24] who worshipped a serpent instead of Christ; of the Cainites,[25] who had Cain the fratricide and Judas the betrayer as their especial saints; of the Nicolaitans,[26] who shared their wives; of the Adamites,[27] who male and female came naked to worship—on the pretext, naturally, that they typified for us Adam and Eve, still innocent though out of paradise. However, they shunned matrimony.

What absurdities of dogma, what monstrosities of vileness in the tabernacles of Basilides,[28] of Colarbasus,[29] of Priscillian [30] and Marcion.[31] Who could read about or study the detestable cult of

the Manichaeans [32] without nausea? Who would not abominate
the blasphemies against Christ—or rather against the unified Trinity—on the part of the Sabellians,[33] the Arians,[34] the Eunomians? [35]
By what deceptions and tricks, with what savagery they have tried
to obscure the truth of Catholicism!

It will be worth the effort to review one or two of the stratagems
from which one may infer what malice those tabernacles conceal.
Since with Scripture and logic they were not strong enough to overcome Athanasius,[36] the invincible defender of Catholic truth, they
set out to crush him with invented slanders. They so provoked
Constantine, the Emperor, with their spiteful innuendos against
this holiest of men that he ordered a commission convened at Tyre
to examine him, and selected one of his associates to preside over
the hearing.

Two charges in particular were pressed: one, that he had raped
a woman and, two, that he had used the severed forearm of a
corpse for purposes of black magic. Hiring a worthless woman to
play a role in this spectacle was no problem, but to prove the
charge of magic they had sent for one Arsenius, once a reader for
Athanasius, who, fearing the reproaches of the bishop he had ma-
ligned, had fled from him. For several days the Arians had kept
him hidden so they might plausibly pretend he was dead. As he
knew, however, what they were trying to do to Athanasius, whether
because he was revolted by the enormity of the crime or because
he wanted to seize the occasion to get back into the good graces of
his bishop, he secretly stole out of hiding one night and came by
boat to Tyre and Athanasius, where he laid open the whole business to him.

Here was a man as notably devout as extraordinarily shrewd,
in accordance with God's injunction combining the openness of a
dove with the guile of a serpent. He orders Arsenius to hide there
until he is called to testify.

The woman appears before the assembled council, a coffin is
brought in for the shuddering spectators, and the amputated human arm which had been placed in the casket is exhibited. Horror
seizes the hearts of the respectable men! Who would suppose that
priests would perpetrate such things? The woman tells what she
had been taught to tell: that she had once welcomed Athanasius
hospitably and that night, though she thought she had nothing to
fear from him, he had violently ravished her.

Athanasius was brought in to reply to these charges. Relying now on his craftiness, he instructed Timothy, his elder, to answer the woman while he kept silent, for he knew she did not know him, even by sight.

When she had concluded her harangue, Timothy said, "Woman, do you say that I forcibly violated you?"

Then feminine stubbornness answered. "You!" she said. "You, I say, robbed me of my virtue in that very place, at that very time, and by force."

They blushed, of course, at a calumny so easily exposed. Still, Athanasius was not set free, nor was the woman punished for her perjury, since the accusers were also the judges. So they passed on to the second charge.

"See," they say, "the thing speaks for itself. This is the arm of Arsenius. Explain to us, Athanasius, your reasons for cutting it off."

With the same cunning this clever man asks them whether they were well acquainted with Arsenius, whose arm this was. Some of them replied that they knew Arsenius by sight quite well. Athanasius asks that he be permitted to bring in someone on his own behalf when he needed him for the case. Permission was granted. Arsenius was then brought in, his face uncovered.

"Look," he says. "Here is Arsenius alive. See here! a right arm. And here! a left arm, both whole. Explain to him where you cut off that arm you have there."

Now what do you think? That Athanasius was cleared of this charge? On the contrary, he would have been torn to bits at the hands of his enemies had not Archelaus, the Emperor's legate who was presiding over the commission, rescued the holy man from their clutches and sent him away by a secret passage. What objections could they raise after being so patently exposed? They clamored that the fellow was a magician who had deceived men's eyes by sleight of hand, that such a trickster should by no means be allowed to live. Far from being acquitted, Athanasius is sentenced by the council just as if he had been legally convicted. Throughout the whole world the disgraceful report is spread, and by the edict of imperial judges a man worthy of heaven is hunted in every nook and cranny on land and sea. Rewards were offered to anyone who turned him in alive or, failing in this, brought in his head.

Isn't this like what the Jews did to Christ? Who, indeed, ever heard even by gossip of a more heinous crime among pagans? I have illustrated the nature of the tabernacles of schismatics and heretics. What should I say about the savage cruelty of Circumcellions, of the cunning of the Donatists,[37] their trickery and violence? Those who have read Augustine's commentaries [38] on these matters are familiar with them.

But all this belongs to the past. More reprehensible is the fact that even within our own memory we know of meetings where, after much glorifying of God in song, that night when the lights are out men tumble about with women in promiscuous praise of Venus. Consider it a trifle, if you wish, that mothers have voluntarily handed over their own babies to be slaughtered because they had been convinced that, butchered in this fashion, they were to be considered among the special saints. This madness seems to have derived from the sect called *Kataphrygas* who made a practice of preparing the Eucharist of meal mixed with the blood of an infant. They covered him with tiny prick wounds; if the child happened to die he was worshipped as a martyr.

You see, then, what fantastic extravagances men fall into once they abandon the tabernacle of God and transfer themselves to the tents of the unholy. Now, if you compare an exceptionally pretty girl with a homely old maid, the one seems even more lovely, the other all the more unattractive. Thus it is with the prophetic and spiritual eye as it compares the synagogues of Satan with the tabernacle of God, where heavenly truth reigns, where peace that surpasses understanding abounds, where a love glows that is incapable of dissimulation and invincible faith is triumphant, where with one voice and one mind are sung the praises of God. Seeing this, one cries all the more strongly, "How lovely are your dwelling places, Lord of hosts!"

The concord of righteous men gives us an image of that celestial Church in which there are no warring opinions, for then men see the glory of the Lord, not in shadowy outline, but face to face.[39] Perfect harmony of souls and perfect love hymn God's praises with voice and heart. Add to this the fact that the eye of the spirit, sharpened by the light of faith, discerns more than the physical eye. What more does it see? It sees Christ abiding in the midst of His own and blessing His throng; as He himself proclaimed in the Gospel: "Wherever two or three have gathered together in my name, there I am in their midst." [40] It sees the angels employed in infinite numbers and deepest reverence as attendants and protectors of the holy gathering.

In the tents of the ungodly, where Satan resides, everything is diametrically opposed; never more deadly than when he is posing as an Angel of Light, the wicked spirits are present, inciting to every evil. No need to mention the contrasting results! What happened to Korah and his conspirators everybody knows. It was a terrible sight for the earth to gape wide and swallow up their living bodies, for so many thousands of men to be wiped out by fire rained down from on high, or by bolts of lightning; the next day when the rebellion of the people broke out afresh, fourteen thousand perished by burning. But more terrible still is it for both soul and body to be cast into hell.

What some people say, that the Church is invisible, is not altogether false. Only God looks into human hearts and truly knows who are His own. Nevertheless, there are many kinds of evidence for surmising where the Church of God is, and where the synagogue of Satan. The manifest sins of many provide a means of judgment. But this visible Church itself, consisting of an admixture of the bad with the good, contains the utmost joy and grandeur as often as it unites for the achievement of piety. Wherever a man gifted with the power of prophecy talks from the heart and shares the word of God, the people listen to what he says with devout reverence and attention, not as to the words of man but of God. Whenever the person teaching is so inspired that you can see Christ's spirit speaking through human lips, one sees at the same time the power of that Spirit operating in the listeners. Some are sighing, others are bursting into tears, still others have smiling faces; in brief, you may say that all are transfigured. Again, when in the established worship each one makes use of his own talent, one gives the scriptural reading, another sings praises to God, a third offers prayer in the name of the whole congregation and discusses the divine mysteries, others assist the one performing these things, and the people meanwhile do homage to the whole in reverent silence. Who, watching these things, does not confess that they are "the lovely tabernacles of God"? In like manner, when a solemn occasion of the Church takes place with the ceremonies fittingly performed, even those who are observing only for the sake of observing are stirred by a kind of reverential delight.

Finally, every lawful gathering of men for an honorable purpose

has a certain worthiness, even pleasure, of which sort is that of
students of a profession or that of men of contrary views in regard
to a public debate. Alcibiades, when about to make his first speech
before the Athenian people, felt nervous. Socrates quieted his ap-
prehensions this way:

> "Is it possible," he asks, "to disregard a mere tanner?"
> "Yes," replies Alcibiades.
> "Or a potter?"
> "Easily," he answers.
> "Or a carpenter? Or a stone-cutter?"

When Alcibiades had replied that he could talk with composure
to any of these people he was asked about, Socrates said, "But that
populace you are afraid of is composed of these people."

So you see that if the mere fact of nonentities assembled in a
body produces weight and respect in itself, how much more worthy
of respect is a throng of devout men come together to worship the
living God! Such power, indeed, has a multitude single-mindedly
praising God that it inspires awe even in worldly men, as Paul
gives witness when he says that the ignorant or the disbeliever who
has entered the Church of the godly falls down on his face and
worships God, acknowledging that God was truly in their midst.
Balaam, of course, was a prophet, even though an evil one. Nevertheless, having viewed the tents of the Israelites from the mountain
he was moved to cry out, "How beautiful are your tabernacles,
Jacob, and your tents, Israel." [41]

He saw also the victorious death of those who continued steadfast in the fortress of the Church. "Let my soul die the death of the
righteous," he says, "and my last end be like these." [42]

The holy prophet discerns the beauty of these tabernacles when
he exclaims in the Song of Degrees, "Lo, how good and joyous to
dwell together as brothers." [43]

And Peter saw, but as if in a dream, when he had beheld the
glory of the Lord on the mountain and had listened to Moses and
Elias conversing about the glory of death in the Lord: "Lord," he
says, "it is good to be here. Let us build three tabernacles in this
place." [44]

In that matter, certainly, there is true harmony, when the Law
and the Prophets, agreeing as one that Christ is the Minister of
the New Testament, make it known not by the letter but by the

spirit. This does not happen in the synagogues of the Jews, who twist the law, not towards Christ but toward some Messiah or other whom these unhappy people still look for in vain after countless ages. Nor does it happen in the tabernacles of the Manichaeans, who reject the entire Old Testament as something handed down not by God but by the Prince of Darkness. The New they accept or discount, I should say, after it has been falsified in many instances according to their own fancy. In fine, nowhere in the tents of the heretics is scripture accommodated to Christ, who is Truth, but rather it is perverted according to human modes of thinking.

This has always been characteristic of heretics. True, the Priscillians rejected the authority of no book of either the Old or the New Testament, but since they considered any part that did not jibe with their own doctrines as totally inconsequential, they twisted them into an outlandish meaning with their perverse interpretations.

But to return to the course of the psalm. If you understand by "the tabernacles of God" that Church still waging war on earth, think of these things as being said by a new convert, either a converted pagan or Jew, or a sinner returning to his senses, whether heretic or schismatic. But if you think it refers to that part of the Church which already rejoices with Christ, then think of the speaker as any godly man, longing like Paul to be released [45] and to be with Christ, saying "How lovely are your tabernacles, O Lord of hosts." The sudden opening of the discourse evinces intense desire arising from deep contemplation. It is no idle word choice when, addressing the Lord, he says *your*. Whatever excellence or strength or felicity is in the Church is from the Lord, not from men. By His own grace He redeemed the Church for Himself; He rules it, He guards it against all onslaughts. And whoever opposes the Church rebels not against men, but God.

Zachariah plainly says this in his second chapter: "Whoever has touched you touches the apple of my eye." [46] And Paul hears the words "Saul, Saul, why do you persecute me?" [47] Again, just as in the Gospel He acknowledges that any kindness done to the humblest user of the name of Christ has been done to Him, [48] so any evil done against the Catholic Church He considers an offense against Himself.

Since the Church has such a defender and advocate, all conspiracies of godless men against her are fruitless. That is why the psalm adds, "Lord of Hosts." The word here is *virtutes,* not *aretai,* the opposite of vices, but *dynameis,* which means *potentia,* or power. The sacred letters not infrequently refer to God by this name, as in Psalm 23: "The Lord of Hosts is Himself the king of glory, *dynameon."* For He had excelled, "A Lord strong and mighty in battle."

In the Old Testament books He is often called the "Lord of Sabbath," which in Hebrew means *powers* or *armies,* a word which this psalm has in the Hebrew. *Dynameis* in mystical writing sometimes signifies a special class of angels whose help God uses for guarding his elect. Elisha saw this host when he told the boy who had been terrified by the sight of the armies of the Syrians: "Do not be afraid. There are more on our side than on theirs." And at the prayers of the Prophet the eyes of his servant were unveiled and he then saw for himself the mountain covered with horsemen and chariots of fire.[49]

"No one," says Christ, "can take from my hand those the Father has given me."[50]

The Song of Degrees is in accord with these: "Unless the Lord builds the house, they labor in vain who do build it."[51]

In Paul's time the Church was fortified, not by wealth, not by men, not by any resources of this world; yet he speaks with utter confidence: "If God be for us, who can be against us?"[52] And soon his faith is exalted to such an extent that when the Church was harassed on all sides by countless evils, he was not afraid to say, "I am convinced that neither death, nor life, nor angels, nor principalities, nor things present, nor things to come, nor height, nor depth, nor anything in creation has the power to separate us from God's love, which is in Christ Jesus our Lord."[53]

Where did you get such faith, Paul, in the midst of so much dying, so many perils threatening from within and without? What was the source of that strength in men few in number, untutored, isolated, weak, and oppressed? Of ourselves, he says, we can do nothing, but our Lord is the Lord of Hosts.

So, whether you think of *virtutes* as angels, the protectors of the Church, or as miracles, either sense indicates that the Lord of the Church is absolutely invincible. Since He is all-powerful, all the legions of angels are ready at His nod, and He who alone performs great wonders has done anything He willed in heaven and earth alike. The early Church grew strong by miraculous rather than human aids, and since anyone who lives devoutly in Christ Jesus suffers the harassment of the irreligious, being, in worldly terms, unimportant and few in comparison to the ones who oppress them, "Lord of Hosts" was a phrase used to comfort an insignificant flock.

In the Gospel it is He who says: "Fear not, little flock, for yours is the kingdom of heaven." [54] And again, "Have faith, for I have overcome the world." [55] He alone was able to bind the strong man and take away his goods.[56] "We have been considered," He says, "only as sheep for the slaughter." [57]

What creature is more weak and helpless than the sheep? But why does Paul presently say that the wolf became a sheep? "The weapons of our warfare are not of the flesh but the power in God to destroy fortresses, to overcome stratagems and every lofty eminence that exalts itself against the wisdom of God," [58] etc. In the same passage he chides the Corinthians because when they were as yet carnal men they saw only those things which were apparent, and judging the Apostles by outward shows, because by worldly standards they were not only weak and insignificant but even wretched, they made light of them even though these men were rich in spiritual gifts, fortified by spiritual armor. Thus the power of this world filled their eyes when they evaluated the Church by outward show and not only disregarded it but even shrank from it in aversion.

Such were those who customarily were inclined to put off baptism until their dying day and never entered the house of God unless in tears and calamity. But he who inwardly perceives, with eyes of the spirit, the glory of the King's Daughter [59] says with the prophet, "My soul faints and longs for the house of the Lord."

Ordinary goods are sought with moderate passion, but those things which eye has not seen, nor ear heard, nor have reached the heart of men,[60] things which God has made ready for those who love Him, ought to be desired with consuming eagerness. This greatness of desire the Prophet expresses when he speaks of "growing faint for the house of the Lord." *Epithymein* refers to the ordinary or commonplace, but *ecleipein* is nothing less than a yearning of more than human intensity. The Greeks use *leipothymian* when a man, through some powerful and sudden emotional disturbance, loses consciousness and is not himself for a time. Violent terror or awe sometimes produces this state in one; whence we say he is stunned or stupefied. Sometimes it is great grief or joy surpassing our hopes, or hopeless love. So it is that in secular tragedy Phaedra sinks to earth like one dead when she sees Hippolyte,[61] and history tells of a woman dying at the unexpected appearance of her son, whom she had believed slain in war. Psalm 108 has used the word in the same sense: "My soul has grown faint for your salvation. My eyes fail for your word." [62]

What the bride says in the Song of Solomon is relevant here: "Support me with flowers, comfort me with apples, for I am faint with love." [63] That which she asks support for she puts to the test lest it waste away. For what is true physically is also true spiritually. Between force and object a temperate relationship is required; otherwise, when something strikes a sense with too much intensity, that faculty is overwhelmed. The unclouded sun, for instance, blinds you if you fasten your eyes on it, and a clap of thunder brings on deafness. Authorities have told us that at the town of Stadisis where the Nile plunges over falls with thunderous noise, natives are born deaf.[64] Again and again we see people losing their sanity because they so passionately devote themselves to an immoderate enthusiasm for subtleties. It has been written of Aristotle (how truthfully I am not concerned with now) that after he had racked his mind long and hard but without success in his zeal for tracking down causes as to why the Sea of Euboia, unlike other seas, flowed in and receded seven times a day, he threw himself into that same sea, crying "Since I don't get you, you may get me!" [65]

It is small wonder that those people who, not content to believe what Scripture teaches us about the Holy Trinity, minutely scrutinize questions vastly exceeding the capacity of the human mind, fall to raving, so that wishing to be more than humanly wise they lose ordinary common sense. Solomon has a prediction about them: "He who pries into majesty is overcome by its glory." [66] Isaiah also has something to say about such people "who search into secrets as if they were not secrets." [67]

But you have been wanting this long time to hear what those extraordinary benefits may be which surpass human understanding, and which one who is filled with longing to enter the house of the Lord has so meditated on that for very wonder his soul is overwhelmed. Can anyone, however, adequately comprehend the greatness of the distinction, the bliss that sinful man, caught in the snares of Satan, is without his deserving chosen for through faith and baptism, transferred from the devil's slavery to the number of God's children, ingrafted on the body of Christ,[68] made one with Him, and changed from heir of hell to heir of the kingdom of heaven, elected to that glorious fellowship of all the saints from the beginning of the world to the end of time, whether in heaven or earth? Such is the honor and glory the new Christian is assured even in the *atrium* or antechamber of the Lord's house, before his admission to the inner sanctum. *Atrium,* properly, is the word given the entrance of the houses of nobles; thus we have the term *servi atrienses* for those servants who had as their charge the waiting-rooms. Why should it be strange, then, that anyone who contemplates, with eyes of the spirit, the majesty of God's dwelling-place should be emotionally over-wrought and, ravished by helpless longing, be possessed by desire for things divine and surpassing human nature?

Horace, an articulate man, has little to say when summoned by Maecenas and this, as he himself remarks,[69] hesitatingly. And it not infrequently happens that men in other respects notable and learned have an attack of nerves when they are about to address a distinguished assemblage of prelates and princes and suddenly become so flustered that they are unable to come out with what they have been working on for months. But what is the augustness of a gathering of that sort compared to the glory of the Church?

The eyes of faith, moreover, see more truly than the eyes of the body. Accordingly, those who come to baptism without real feeling and as if by coercion do not yet perceive what felicity they are being given, and to that extent they are not worthy of receiving what they are being summoned to. You see, if a messenger should come to some fellow rotting in a stinking jail and say, "Cheer up! Today you will enter the palace a free man; you will mingle with noblemen of the Royal Court and be an intimate of the King," wouldn't there be some danger that he might faint away through sudden joy? And having been given access to the light and pomp of the palace after the gloom of prison, would he leave? But what jail, what pit is so foul as that in which those persons are imprisoned whom Satan has tied to him with the chains of their own vices? Or where was there ever a palace, even if you rolled into one the magnificence of every one of them, which can be compared with the majesty of the Church?

Accordingly, if people dilatory and lackadaisical about accepting the one kind of favor would deserve some censure, how much more justly ought we to rebuke those who live nasty, disordered lives in the inner chambers of this palace? I think some hidden meaning lies concealed in the very words of the Prophet: he does not say, "I have fainted," but "My *soul* fainted." He does not say, "I have rejoiced," but "my *heart* and my *flesh* have rejoiced."

The voice of the soul in sacred writings sometimes strikes a rather uncertain and human note, as when Paul speaks to the Corinthians: *psychikos* that is, "Natural man does not receive those things which are of God." [70] Thus James calls "sensual" the wisdom of this world which spurns faith and looks at the divine with merely human understanding.[71] So it is that the "flesh" of man refers to something rather gross which is continually at war with the spirit of God. The word "heart" really means the spirit or the mind of man. The source of the vital spirits, according to physicians, is in the heart. It is the flesh, then, which in Paul's words "cannot possess the kingdom of God." [72] And it is flesh, whose fellowship the Spirit of God does not endure.[73]

So think of this as the basest part of man. Thus it is that the soul repels the Spirit of God, as Saint Jude says, leveling his finger, so to speak at those who, pursuing those things which are of this world, withdraw in sects and factions from the fellowship of the Church. "These," he says, "are the ones who cut themselves off, sensual creatures, lacking the spirit." [74] And it is man's heart that is not entered by those things which God has prepared for those who love Him.[75]

Therefore, since the whole man, joining together all his own faculties, is not capable of receiving heavenly gifts, what remains but that this whole should faint and give way in itself, so that recreated and lifted up by God's spirit it may understand through faith how enormous are those blessings which divine benevolence freely bestows on us through the Son, if we enter His tabernacle in the right spirit. To faint or fail in this sense is to succeed, to be deprived of life is to come alive, to lose oneself is to gain oneself, to fall is to be raised up, to be robbed of one's own powers is to become powerful in Christ, to die is to be transfigured in God. Unless the physical part is put side, the spiritual part does not come to life, just as in the process of nature the dry, shapeless seed is buried so the green tree may grow. The ugly caterpillar gives way to the brightly embroidered butterfly. The old cicada withers away to produce the vigorous new singer from its dry husk. Therefore, after the whole man has given up, and yielded to the tabernacles of God, his flesh and soul and heart then rejoice together in the living God; for the Spirit of God makes everything new through faith and the whole man becomes a "new creature in Christ Jesus." [76]

It is the flesh which sees the saving quality of God and, according to Paul, is the spiritual body; [77] and it is a clean heart which God creates in us and an upright spirit which He restores in our inmost parts. There, surely, is the source of that spiritual joy, not the riches or honors or pleasures of this world, not beauty or strength of body, not human wisdom, but the loving God who gives life to the dead. As the blessed Paul counsels us, only he "who glories in the Lord" glories with assurance.[78]

The Scriptures repeatedly refer to God with this word *living*, not only to distinguish Him from lifeless images but also to proclaim His omnipotence. He is said to be "living" who is *effectual*. It is no great matter for us to believe that God is *alive*, since brute beasts are alive, but He alone is *living* in the sense that He is real Life itself, the source from which life flows like a fountain to all men. "I am the way," God declares, "the truth and the life." [79]

When the "old man," [80] therefore, has been mortified and buried in baptism, the new man, who is assuredly dead to self but holding the living Christ unto himself, is wholly exultant, giving thanks to Him by whose undeserved grace he has been thus transformed. Sarah did not give birth to Isaac—"joy of the spirit," that is—until after her womanhood had failed her. Besides, by whom did she become pregnant? By Abraham, flesh which had withered but was vital and flourishing in the sap of faith.[81]

As for the rest, the Prophet preferred to tell us by means of allegory the reason for his joy: "For truly the sparrow finds a home for herself and the turtle-dove a nest where she can place her young." What a magnificent idea the prophetic spirit expressed in a homely figure. Just what is it that you so rejoice in that it causes you to leap triumphantly for joy when a little while before, you had fainted away? Because, he says, "the swallow finds her home and the turtle-dove a nest where she can place her young."

Instinctively all kinds of living creatures prepare some place for themselves where they can rest securely after their exertions, and in this they demonstrate marvelous diversity of ingenuity. Many, like the stag, retreat to some distant, out-of-the-way place where hunters have a hard time finding them. Wild boars hide themselves in thickets, lions and dragons in the remote passages of caves. The hare fools his pursuer by backward leaps so that he won't find his hole. The snake is safe in his caverns and rabbits protect themselves in underground burrows. Ants lie hidden throughout the winter in hills they have constructed. Bees make their hives in hollow trees and cover them over on the outside with a tough, bitter crust for protection against damage. Fish have their own places of concealment. Most birds betake themselves to remote wooded areas or marshy places. The eagle builds its nest on steep crags, the plover on the ground. Kingfishers hang theirs on the water, woven with such cunning they cannot be destroyed even by a sword, and no one has yet found out just how they build their little floating homes. Many others make their nests of twigs and straws artfully entwined in the chimneys of houses or suspended in a tree. Swallows and sparrows also have shown us how to build walls out of moist clay mixed with chaff. To make a long story short, every creature finds a place where it can safely rest, bring up its young, find its own contentment—and there is nothing it desires more earnestly. It has the natural instincts to protect itself and reproduce its kind.

But someone will wonder why, of all the kinds of living creatures, only birds should be mentioned, and of those only the sparrow and the turtle-dove. Of all the kinds of animal life birds are the most paltry. The earth has elephants, the sea whales, both huge. Among the birds, moreover, it is the tiny sparrow with its disregard and life free from worry which is recommended to us by the word of God. The Holy Spirit does not love minds swollen with arrogance and burdened by concern with creature comforts and, for this reason, earth-bound. He loves those who are lowly in His eyes, despicable in terms of the world. He loves all those who cling to the providence of God. Now, if God thus clothes and feeds little two-for-a-penny sparrows,[82] why should you go frantically about piling up money, by hook or crook, for the old age you may never reach or for children, grandchildren, great-grandchildren—money which may go to people you least would want it to. And if not one sparrow falls to earth—for this occasionally happens, some say, from excessive sexual union [83]—why should you, who have been elected to the flock of those about whom the Saviour has said that not even a hair from their head will be lost without our Father's foreknowledge,[84] rush to fortune-tellers and astrologers because you are afraid of dying before your time?

The turtle-dove has this in common with the dove, that its song is a sigh and it is innocent of promiscuity, even of taking a second mate; it has been reported that when its partner dies it never takes another. For this reason its voice pleases the bride in the mystical Song of Solomon: "The voice of the turtle," she says, "is heard in our land." [85] In other respects larks and nightingales sing far more sweetly in spring, but the sighs of the turtle-doves please the bride.

All those who scorn this world in the hope of life in heaven, as long as they are busied in this dwelling-place of the mortal body, sigh heavily, as the Apostle says, not because they want to be divested but invested, so that what is mortal may be swallowed up by life.[86] Add to this the fact that in the Old Testament the turtle-dove was the offering of the poor, so that the insignificance of this bird is comparable to that of the sparrow. Who was more sublime than Paul? Yet he talks like a paltry sparrow when he speaks of himself as being prematurely born, the least of the Apostles and utterly undeserving of the name, finally as the dross and offscouring of this world.[87] But this worthlessness is the only thing that makes us precious in the eyes of God. This lowliness makes us great and noble in the presence of a just judge.

Would you like to hear about the importance of this sparrowlet? "I can do all things," he says, "in Him who strengthens me." [88] Wouldn't you say that out of this sparrow or turtle-dove He has made a lion?

The values of God and those of this world are diametrically opposed to each other. Therefore, as the world loves and glories in those things which are of this world, so it despises and rejects what is not of the world.

"They have gone about," he says, "in the pelts of sheep and she-goats, needy, impoverished, oppressed, wandering in the solitudes in mountains, and caves and grottoes of the earth."

What could be more contemptible? But hear of their honor. "Of these," he says, "the world was not worthy." [89]

Who was of meaner estate than Paul, as the world sees it? He calls himself dross, the refuse, that is, which is cast away. But how great was that same man, so despised by the world, to Christ, who calls him the vessel chosen by Himself.

But why talk about other holy men when the Lord of Glory himself speaks through the lips of David: "I am a worm, not a man, the reproach of mankind and the cast-off of the commons."[90] And that very One so despised by the world is He in whose name every knee bends, in heaven, earth, or hell,[91] He who is of one communion in glory with God the Father.

No one living righteously, then, is displeasing to Him, even if he is an object of scorn and hatred to those imbued with the spirit of this world. Indeed, we must struggle with all our might lest we offer some little offense to Him, but nevertheless it is strong evidence that we are acceptable to Christ if, without any sin of our own, we are anathema to the world.

Now when I say "the world" I am not referring to a profession, to clothes, to food, to rank, but to a heart that is empty of Christ's spirit. The common run of men, like many others, misuse the word, calling "worldly" those who have not been admitted to the sacraments or who do not lead a monastic life. The professional religious, by the same token, people describe as "out of the world," or "dead to the world." But just as any robe, however drab or *hieroprepes*, may conceal a worldly spirit, so under whatever secular dress you wish, even a military, there can lie a spirit alien to this world, even if an ostrich feather flutters in his slitted cap.

Perhaps someone is wondering now just how we slipped so suddenly from the subject of the tremendous exaltation of the whole person to talk about his sighs—from the sublime, as they say, to the ridiculous.[92] These two conditions may seem incompatible; nevertheless, they are related in such a way that as long as we inhabit this mortal tabernacle and carry a heavenly treasure in earthen vessels,[93] one thing cannot be separated from the other. What is more, one condition may give rise to the other. Every joy of those of us who walk by faith is in hope of goods to come. The more clearly we discern these goods with the eyes of faith, the more confidently we hope for them, the more deeply we sigh, as if every delay is irksome to our impassioned longing. Also, the more we sigh for that life, the more the heart and flesh rejoice in the living God. While we have sadness in the world we have comfort in Christ.

Here nothing is perfect, nothing secure. We know in part and we prophesy in part;[94] he who stands must be on guard lest he fall. We walk in the midst of snares and it is very hard, not to say impossible, to dodge them all. These trials which this life comes equipped with, even if they are not strong enough to deprive us of that love which is in Christ Jesus, still often distract us from that spiritual exaltation of mind and make us groan in desire for that day when what is perfect will come. Who in such an exile would not sigh for such a homeland?

Do you wish to hear the turtle-dove sighing? Read Psalm 119: "Alas, for me! Because my sojourning has been prolonged: I have lived with the inhabitants of Kedar; my soul has long been in exile. Lord, free my soul from iniquitous lips and a deceitful tongue."

For righteous men a large part of their distress is suffering patiently the behavior and the talk of evil men. What Ecclesiastes says is apposite here: He who increases his knowledge increases his sorrow; in much understanding is much vexation.[95] The sun's light is shared by everyone, but not the light of faith. *Kedar* in Hebrew means "darkness." Moreover, whatever those having the spirit of this world strive for is nothing but vapor; they hate the illumination of truth and prefer the shadows. And, although there is perhaps even more contrast between a man enlightened and made spiritual by faith and one carnally devoid of it, in this sojourn abroad the faithful have to live side by side, in the same cities and in the same houses, with people otherwise disposed. So it was that while alive Lot was agonized by the spirit of Sodom and prayed to be rescued from his daily life with wicked men.[96]

But you have heard only the heavy sighs of this turtle-dove: "Alas for me, because my sojourning has been prolonged." Now listen to him rejoicing in the hope of promised bliss: "I exult," he says, "in these things which have been told me. We will go into the house of the Lord." And listen to another remarkable turtle-dove groaning in longing for his heavenly homeland: "I am a wretched man; who will free me from the body of this death?"[97] Now hear him rejoicing: "I am overflowing with comfort, with abundant joy in all our affliction."[98]

We see that these laments have always been most poignant in men who are panting for supernal happiness. Hence the withdrawal of the prophets into secluded spots. Hence, at one time after the Passion of Christ such flocks of men taking refuge in the Theban desert because they were unwilling to endure the wickedness and barbarism of idolatrous worship. Hence the beginning of monastic life: they were more content to associate with lions and panthers than with wicked men. Some, including the blessed Jerome, with-

drew into the wastes of Syria. Some concealed themselves on secluded islands, while others—like Saint Benedict—took possession
of almost inaccessible mountain peaks. Many, such as Bernard and
Patrick, hunted out rough marshlands scarcely habitable for any
living creature and still others sought cliffs and places fearful even
to look at. Of this number was Bruno, or whoever was the founder
of the Carthusian order. The weariness of this exile here won these
devout men over to such retreats; they were eager to separate themselves from the inhabitants of Kedar.

But wherever you turn here, wherever you go into hiding, you
are in exile. Note, then, that however much you may long for
some secluded retreat, as a man you are rushing off to humankind
and that even as you try to avoid all association with men you are
lugging man with you, carrying around a mortal body whose burden the Apostle was lamenting.

Saint Basil, we read, called back to social concourse the monks
who were spending their time in seclusion, far from human society,
because, a shrewd man, he knew that many of those secluding
themselves were not really devout but arrogant, puffed up with an
unfounded assumption of sanctity, peevish, spiteful, captious, devoid of commonsense, and unfitted for every human task. Chrysostom also acknowledges that experience had taught him the same
lesson whenever these people were summoned from those fasts of
theirs, or their vigils, or their beds on the bare ground to do the
work of the bishop.

They were looking outside of themselves for what should have
been sought within. They were building nests, but hardly in the
house of the Lord, since that kingdom of God is within us.

Here the very course of our commentary suggests that we come
back to the word *nests*. A nest is where man's longing finds peace,
where he tranquilly supports his offspring, that is to say, his work
and his consuming interests. That man is called happy who, when
he has understanding, desires nothing more. This understanding
is accessible to no other creature in this life: Nature has set limits
to the felicity of other animals which, once they have arrived at
that state for which they were created, have fully realized their
own kind of contentment. But the human soul, being divine and immortal, finds nothing in this life which really satisfies it unless it
has realized that condition for which it was created. And what is it

that man was made for? That he may have understanding of both mind and body, that he may love and glorify God his Creator and Redeemer and his Lord.

"This," says the Master, "is life eternal, that they may know You, the one true God, and Jesus Christ whom You have sent." [99]

To understand is to see, and to see is to enjoy; to enjoy is the ultimate goal of bliss. This bliss will not fully exist except in the resurrection of the righteous. There is, however, a kind of nest in the anteroom of the Church though it is one fixed to and dependent on the hope of things to come. Apart from the Church there is no hope of real felicity. So expansive, so measureless is the human mind that God alone can fill it, even if you add to it innumerable worlds [100] exclusive of God.

Why is it that even in inanimate things you may see that each and every one is drawn to its own peculiar abode? As soon as a rock dropped from a height hits the earth, it comes to rest. How eagerly a flame is attracted to its own place! What is this which sometimes rocks the earth so hard it dislodges mountains and stones except the north wind struggling to break through to the place where it was born? Thus it is that a bladder full of air, when forcibly pressed down into water, springs back up.

Now, the human spirit is a flammable thing which, though hindered by this absurd little body of clay, still does not rest until it mounts up to the seat of its beginning. By nature, indeed, all men hunt for repose; they seek something in which the spirit can rest, but because they fashion a nest in things meaningless or transient, the more they seek for tranquillity the more caught up they are in hurly-burly. What else do the many books of the ancients look for, books on the *summum bonum*, on the characteristics of the good man, on peace of mind, which the Greeks call *euthymia?* One man builds his nest in knowledge, another in freedom from pain, another in pleasure. Some place it in the condition of virtue which they call wisdom, many in the habitual practice of virtue.

But all of these people, according to Paul, "became vapid in their own imaginations," [101] and while their tongues boastfully promised *euthymia* to others, they themselves were restless of heart. Why? Because they did not rejoice in the living God.

And if the princes of wisdom have babbled so foolishly, what can be said of the simple-minded ones who measure happiness by

affluence? After they have got what they set out to get, they see
the utter truth of the words of Horace: "Care attends the swelling
bank roll" [102] and

> However great your pile becomes
> It's smaller than your itch for it.[103]

Others, though they scorn wealth, covet power and authority. What
else did Alexander the Great work for with such great chaos of
states? But how much of the world could he bring under his control? And even if he had subjugated all of it, when he learned from
Democritus that there were countless other worlds, he groaned
because he had worked so long for a piece of only one. What did
Julius Caesar not do and endure to hold first place in the Roman
world? He held it, but his heart found no peace in it. Quite the
contrary, oppressed by cares and the consciousness of his crimes,
he was disheartened to the point that he preferred death to the
weariness of life, albeit the unexpected death. Where the mind is
guiltily aware there is no true repose.

Human desires know no limit. This man assures himself that he
will be happy if he can find as his wife some handsome girl with
a handsome dowry, but instead of eliminating his problems he dis-
covers a whole army of them. That man promises himself a blissful existence if he can win some ecclesiastical preferment, but when
he has it the passion of pursuit has grown fiercer. One benefice is
appetizer for another: he has fought his way to the abbot's office
and now he seeks the bishop's mitre—and one mitre gives way to
another more sumptuous. Now his heart pants for a cardinal's rank,
and when he gets this he courts the Triple Crown.[104]

But does ambition rest even here? Let Julius II [105] answer us,
whose old age was tormented by insupportable turbulence of affairs. As for the rest of it, let others judge.

It is no trivial explanation Saint Augustine makes of the word
offspring as our good works [106] which, unless you place them in the
nest of the Catholic Church, come to no fruition. Phocion and
Aristides, Trajan and Antoninus and many more acted courage-
ously, justly, and conscientiously in regard to their native land. We
can praise the temperance of Zeno, the probity of Xenocrates, the
humility of Socrates, but because they acted without Christ they
did not attain to true felicity. The Emperor Julian devoted huge
sums of money to relief of the poor, but he opposed Christ.

In like manner, some remarkable, almost incredible, virtues are displayed in many heretics. The Ebionites [107] had great contempt for material wealth; the Euchites,[108] prodigious persistence in prayer; the Manichees, great restraint and asceticism of life. But they did all these things in vain because they did not place their progeny in the nest of the Church. Instead, each one nested in his own tabernacle and thus illustrates the old proverb "the bad crow lays the bad egg," and "if you look for young ones from the turtle-dove, you must keep out the vipers." [109]

Therefore, if we are looking for true peace of mind, we must persevere in the tabernacle of the Lord of hosts and remain in the unity of the Catholic Church, which is Jerusalem and is built as a state in which citizenship leads to that very condition. This is that blissful peace which another psalm speaks of: "I shall rest and sleep in peace unto the thing itself, because you, O Lord, have made me steadfast in hope." [110] Zion, too, is a mountain in Jerusalem, on which were the tabernacle and the palace.

In Hebrew, moreover, Zion means "a high place." So let us climb toward this peak. How? In the despising of things worldly and in eagerness for celestial life. There, worn out after the long meanderings of error, after the barren worries of human concerns, we shall come upon a rest where we shall be warmed into life again and find rest, as Psalm 14 says: "Lord, who will dwell in your tabernacle? Or who will find rest on your holy mountain?"

Let us proceed without the blemish of heresy and going forward in faith which is active through love, let us do justice, not of the Judaic kind but the evangelical, all of which we are seen to do rightly when we yield ourselves to God. Moreover, in order for us to soar up to the top of this mountain, let us be sparrows in our humility of mind, the meanest and least important in our own eyes, not anxious about tomorrow but casting all our uneasiness on Him who has our love. Let us be turtle-doves in blamelessness and purity, and knowing that we have here no lasting home, sigh unceasingly for the heavenly Jerusalem. Let us listen to the voice of God as He offers true peace of mind: "Come to me, all you who labor and are heavily burdened, and I will refresh you. Put my yoke upon yourselves and learn from me how gentle I am and humble of heart, and you will find rest for your souls." [111]

In terms of human understanding of course, such words are foolish. What peace is there for the lowly and the meek who are

kicked about and driven out of their own homes? Or what rest for
those wearing the yoke? A yoke means slavery, and according to
the Greek proverb "there is no rest for slaves." [112]

But those who are meek after the example of Christ possess the
earth, and those who, as the world looks at things, are of no account, in Christ are exalted even unto heaven, and those who submit their necks to the easy yoke of Christ are in reality free. And
those who submit without quibbling trust His promises. Let us follow the prophetic guide to mysteries who shows us forthwith how
amiable, how beautiful, how admirable are the dwelling places of
the Lord and what soft peace is in them.

Next, moving from the anteroom, he reveals to us the altar of
the Lord, a holier and lovelier part of the temple, "your altar, Lord
of Hosts, my King and my God." Among the Jews, reverence for
the temple, its outfitting, and richly ornamented altar was great.
Hence those words, "Temple of the Lord, Temple of the Lord,"
and it was their most sacred oath to swear by the temple and its
altar. Nor was God speaking lightly when He said, "Destroy this
Temple." [113]

But such things as those were nothing more than symbols of
spiritual truth. While the Prophet is saying this, his mind is filled
with another tabernacle not made by human hands, he contemplates another altar which so strikes him with wonder that, stunned,
words fail him.

Some readers suppose that this passage about "your altar, Lord"
refers to the earlier one, "How lovely are your tabernacles, how
lovely your altar." Augustine, however, relates it to the words following: "The swallow finds a home for itself, the turtle-dove a nest"
so that it appropriately follows "your altars" and we understand
altar itself to mean nests in which we find our peace.[114] It seems
more plausible to me that the words should be broken off, to better
convey the feeling of wonder. Thus when we see the house of a
prince standing in grandeur, we say in amazement, "the Palace of
Kings." And just as here the emphasis is on the word *kings*, so in
the passage of the Prophet the strong stress is on the pronoun *your*.
You are the one Lord of Hosts, and this is *your* altar, worthy of
you, pleasing to you.

Again, in place of *hosts* (virtutum) the Greek has *dynameon*,
which we talked about earlier, the Hebrew *Sabaoth*, that is *armies*.
The repetition has the function of letting us know that the Church,

though weak and despised in the eyes of the world, is nevertheless invincible with the Lord of Hosts as its defender, invulnerable even to the very gates of hell.

This is not an altar stained with the blood of bull calves, he-goats and rams. The Lord long ago disdained this kind of sacrifice. Why? God is Spirit and delights in sacrifices of the spirit. He takes no pleasure in the slaughter of herds but in the mortification of those desires antagonistic to spirit.[115] If in the love of Christ you have overthrown the greed for money in yourself, and that property which you once worshipped in place of God you now devote to Christ's members, you have offered the most pleasing sacrificial victim to God. If you have slain your debauchery and lechery, made the glutton temperate and the incontinent pure, you have presented an acceptable offering to God. If when you have been injured by your neighbor you repress your boiling anger in the grace of Christ and forego evening the score with him, you have sacrificed to God in the most appropriate way. If strong in faith and zealous in love you surrender yourself and all you have to God's will, prepared to endure both death and torture to see Him, you have placed a pleasing burnt offering before the God of Hosts.

This is the understanding, the spiritual worship to which the Apostle warmly urges us in the twelfth chapter of Romans—living, holy sacrifices pleasing to God. God takes no delight in the smoke of incense or myrrh or the gum of the storax tree,[116] but He loves the perfume of the spirit; it is in the pledges and prayers of devout minds, the deeds of grace, the sacrifice of praise where God likes to be worshipped. Through such offerings as these lies the road to seeing God's salvation, which is the burden of Psalm 49: "The Lord of Lords will be seen in Sion." Those prayers are acceptable which are made with faith and in the name of Christ. The deed of grace is the rite performed not just in good times but in bad. The sacrifice of praise will be pleasing if, in accordance with Paul's admonition, whatever we do, whether in word or deed, we do it not to our own glory but to the glory of God.[117] The offering really attractive, because it is spiritual, is made perennially throughout the world on the altars of the Church.

In this nest we rest in safety for the moment, for the altars are not those of men but of the hosts of the Lord, whose will no one can withstand, who wishes to be worshipped in simplicity and humility and to bestow on the down-trodden the gifts of the heavenly kingdom. On this account He himself gives thanks to the Father in the Gospel: "You have hidden those things from the knowing ones and the clever, and made them known to babes; so it was, Father, because it was your will to do so." [118]

You have nothing to fear of the world or of Satan if the Lord of Hosts receives you into His tabernacles. He watches over that which He has ordained, He rules as He walks in the midst of His creatures, He perfects that which He has made. The Lord of Hosts watches, the King rules, the Deity elevates to the kingdom of heaven. "My King and my God." Psalm 43 speaks in the same way: "You are my King and my God."

The words of the second Psalm can fittingly be applied to Christ, the Head of the Church: "By Him have I been made King over His holy mountain of Sion." All things are under the dominion of God. Demons recognize His omnipotence and they tremble, but the language of faith is its own: "My King and my God." No one can say "Lord Jesus" except in the Holy Spirit; yet far and wide we hear the voices of those who call Him Lord Jesus. No one can say "my King and my God" except someone who yields himself with utter trust to the will of God and awaits from Him alone the prize of everlasting happiness.

Another psalm [119] calls blessed that people to whom the Lord is God. Similarly, as in a number of other places in Scripture, in the twenty-sixth chapter of Leviticus the Lord speaks as follows: "I shall place my tabernacle in your midst and my spirit will not abandon you. I will walk among you and be your God and you will be my people." The one who is called King here is afterward called Law-maker. If we acknowledge Him as King, therefore, we must comply with His laws. If we acknowledge Him as God, we should love nothing more than Him; more accurately, we should prize nothing at all unless we do it for His sake. The name *King* reminds us that we have been redeemed by the blood of Christ from the despotic rule of the devil and that in place of a most execrable and cruel master we have entered into the justice of a most gentle Ruler.

Up to this point our expounder of mysteries has shown us the lovely tabernacle of God, led us into the vestibule, pointed out the altar and the spiritual sacrifices. Now he indicates those priests who are worthy of God as they perform the sacred rites in the temple of the Lord. "Blessed are those who dwell in your house,

O Lord," he says. "They will praise you for generation after generation."

Those strong in faith, rooted in charity, already dwell not in the anteroom but in the house of the Lord. *Dwell* is the word for steadfastness. And why are they blessed? Because they are dripping with money? Because they dazzle us with medals? Because they swim in voluptuousness? Hardly! Why then? "Because," he says, "they will praise you for generation after generation." There is the peaceful haven which the sparrow finds, there the quiet nest of the turtle-dove. This is the ultimate purpose of man's creation, that he may recognize, love, and sing the praises of his Creator, his Redeemer, his Ruler, and Rewarder.

By human standards it seems more blessed to receive praise than to give it. In worship the opposite is true. The felicity of God, to be sure, is not heightened by anyone's praise, but anyone who does praise Him is blessed by the very fact that he does so. But not everyone who sings "glory to thee, O Lord" is praising Him—only those in whose hearts love is alive, the bond of perfection, and in whom the peace of Christ to which they have been called abounds, who mutually encourage one another in psalms, hymns, and spiritual songs of gratitude, who in their hearts are singing the praises of God. Even if God is to be lauded vocally, "Let us accompany in spirit, let us psalmodize in mind." In the mouth of the sinner praise has no beauty; choral harmony is not pleasing to God when the heart is sourly dissonant with the vocal concord, when, in fine, outside of God's house, or the Church, there is no hymn acceptable to God. If we wish to be full of joy we must so praise the Lord with one heart and mind as the angels do, among whom there is no rancor.

All creation praises God, each part in its own fashion. It is not only the heavens that declare the glory of God, but every kind of life, the elements themselves and whatever is produced from them. As long as by their very appearance they tell of their Creator's omnipotence, His wisdom and goodness to us, they shout the praises of God. Here in the Psalms, as well as in the Canticle of the Three Children,[120] not only the sun and moon but herds and fish and mountains and hills and seas and rivers are summoned to the praise of the name of the Lord. Only evil spirits and wicked men are not invited to join this symphony, because by them, or rather through what is in them, the Lord's name is used in blasphemy.

What He wishes for Himself is what the Prophet goes on to say: "They will praise you for generation after generation," and under this passage is placed "Selah," which Jerome translates as "always." However, there are those who do not think this word has the sense of "eternally" because it is found nowhere in Scripture except in the Psalms and sometimes in passages where there is no suggestion of "everlastingness." They think instead that "Selah" had something to do with pauses in the music, that it marked a changing of the melody. The Psalms were, of course, performed by voices and musical instruments.

Today, too, certain musical signs indicate a way to alter the singing. Not every melody is appropriate to every sentiment. Thus, in the dialogue of comedies flutes sounded certain modes, or perhaps they played before the performance so that the audience understood what kind of subject—whether grave or otherwise—they were dealing with.

In this psalm, actually, this closing implies the beginning of another subject. But however one takes this, certainly the words "for generation after generation" describe eternity and therefore cannot apply to the temple at Jerusalem, which did not last much more than two hundred years. Although the Jewish populace had persuaded themselves that the law and worship of that temple would last as long as the world did—just as the Romans convinced themselves that there would always be a capitol—today there is no trace of that capitol to be seen at Rome, nor any part of the temple of the Jews at Jerusalem. The eye of the Prophet, then, was looking at a different temple, where the name of the Lord would be praised forever. This, indisputably, is the Catholic Church.

But what praise can be everlasting when they who do the praising are only mortal men? This Church, the glorifier of God, awaits its apotheosis; it knows no end. Just as the devout are never deprived of love, so the lauding of the deity rehearsed here is fully realized in heaven. Once the spirit has soared up from this earthy housing it is already caroling clearly its praises to God with the angels and spirits of the blessed, until in a renewed body which is no longer animal but spiritual the whole man sounds praises of his Creator without end or interruption.

The Church Militant here on earth and the Church Triumphant on high are one and the same, except that the latter manifestation of it is more pure. It is analogous to that air next to the earth we

trod, an atmosphere which according to some philosophers extends
to the orb of the moon, but here is heavier because of the infection
of the earth while there it is more rare.[121] But there is nothing to
prevent each and every one of us, even conceding the weight of
this corporeal body, from praising God without ceasing. Who can,
you ask? Anyone can. If whatever we plan, whatever we talk about,
whatever we do, we do it to the glory of God, if even when we are
eating and drinking, even when we sleep, or refresh this poor little
body of ours with sports, we praise our God.

"Glorify the Lord," says the Apostle, "and carry Him in your
body." [122] Not all members of our body speak, but they all glorify
God if they work for righteousness, even if the tongue is silent.

After the Prophet, caught up, as it were, in ecstasy, has come
to that heavenly Jerusalem where there is no harm to assail us,
no cacophony of minds to mar the melody, no exigency to disturb
the hymns of God—for as the blessed Paul says, "Whether we are
beside ourselves, it is for God, or whether we are sober, it is for
you" [123]—as if returning to consciousness, he reminds himself that
he is a man and points out to those sharing in this exile the way
to arrive at that blissful tranquillity.

"Happy are they who dwell in your house, O Lord" (referring to
the angels and those devout souls who live with the angels). Here
he speaks with the suggestion of a change in the harmony: "beatus
vir," or as Jerome translates from the Hebrew, "beatus homo." The
word *vir* does not exclude women: "In Christ there is no man or
woman, no slave or free man, but a new creature." The term *homo*
reminds us of our weakness, which unless God's mercy extends its
hand to us, cannot even enter the anteroom of the Church, let
alone soar up to that supernal seat of the blessed.

The means of access to the Church is faith, without which baptism means nothing; but no one bestows faith on himself. It is the
gift of God, by which God goes before and draws to Christ His
elect. Man, to the extent that he is man, is carnal and smacks of
nothing but the world. Perceiving this, the Prophet now sings in
more gentle harmonies: "Blessed is the man whose help is from
you," or as Saint Augustine puts it, "whose adoption." [124] The Greek
is *antilepsis,* a word appropriate to someone who extends a hand
to someone trying to climb higher. The City of the Church is built
on a high place, just as the Temple of Jerusalem was on Mount
Sion. Jerome uses the word *strength* (*fortitudo*) instead of *help*

(*auxilium*). The terms differ but the idea is the same. It takes strength to triumph over difficulties, but man can do nothing in himself. Faith assuredly gives man personal power so that he fears neither the world nor Satan. Those who place their whole trust in God, then, are precisely the ones made hardy enough in the Spirit to ascend the mountain of the Lord.

There were fifteen steps leading up to that famous Temple of the Jews which Solomon built.[125] On the first step the Prophet laments the deceptiveness of tongues and the weariness of exile. On the second he is renewed by the gift of faith, saying, "I have lifted my eyes to the hills, from which help will come. My help is from the Lord, who made heaven and earth." Faith is what makes our steps resolute and unhesitating. This is what Paul says to the Corinthians: "By faith you stand." [126] And to the Romans: "But you stand by the faith." [127] Saint Peter, too, urges us to be strong in faith and resist the devil.[128]

Ultimately, indeed, the indomitable soul is one who, helpless in himself, gets his courage from God. Isaiah is referring to this when he says it will come to pass "that this song will be sung in the land of Judah." The song is of the evangelic promise, for in Hebrew "Judah" means "acknowledging." What, specifically, is the song? "A city of strength is our Sion." Sion is the Church, but what is the source of this strength for the weak? "A deliverer will be appointed for her as a wall and an outwork." [129] You are hearing about an invulnerable fortification. He also says, "Your strength will be in silence and in hope." [130] If one has no doubt as to His promises, he waits in silence; and hope of such felicity as one can never be made to regret, because it never deceives, buoys the spirit even when it is confronted by affliction and death. In this life, of course, there is no perfect happiness; yet there is a certain real measure of happiness when we consider how brief is the whole span of this life and how our afflictions mean nothing compared to the glory to come which will be revealed in us.[131]

In connection with this, think how good and infallibly trustworthy He is who has pledged this; as we deny Him He remains faithful and He is unable to refuse Himself as long as we remain constant in faith and charity, enclosing ourselves within the protective house of God where, when we have grown all the way to the fullness of Christ, we may mount the fifteen mystical steps to the everlasting Tabernacle and, passing through the forty-two months,[132] come joyously to that land of peace which in the Gospel the Lord has promised the meek.

We press upward in a steep ascent since we are aiming at a towering eminence. No one is suddenly transported from the depths to the heights. We need someone to show us the way, as God led the Israelites, who represent us typologically, through impenetrable deserts. We need One to extend a hand from on high and draw the struggling man upward. None of this can we do for ourselves: "It is the Lord who works in us, both as to the will and the achievement." [133] Through faith He opens our eyes so we can see where we are, so we may abhor what we are and sigh to be what as yet we are not.

The first help from God, then—which is to say, the first step toward bliss—is to lift our eyes to the hills. From on high comes our grace to love things heavenly and despise things earthly. Anyone who looks complacently at his own wisdom, his own strength, his own merits; anyone who is preoccupied only with ceremonialism, with the indulgences and dispensations of popes, has never arrived at that kind of joy. What does he do, that candidate for bliss to whom the Lord has granted through faith that by scorning the base concerns of the world he may lift his eyes to hills of eternity? The *anabaseis*, the steps of ascent, he constructs in his own heart. What is here called *anabaseis*, in the Songs of Degrees is called *anabathmous*, which is a stair but only for those going up, since in Latin one is said to climb and descend by the same steps. Besides, in this matter of devotion one ought not ever to turn back, but forgetful of what is behind move always toward those things to be accomplished. When Eurydice looked behind she sank back into the Underworld; when Lot's wife looked back she was turned into a pillar of salt.[134]

Piety, you see, has its own stages, just as has the life of man. New-born Christians, just recently baptized, are nursed on milk like babies; those who are mature are proffered the solid food of deeper mysteries. Paul "speaks wisdom among the perfected," but among the uninitiated he professes to know nothing "but Jesus Christ and Him crucified." [135]

Therefore, he who lifts his eyes unto the hills is setting up the steps to climb by. Where? "In his heart." No wonder, since one climbs that hill not by foot but in his passions. There are *outward* steps which, though they need not be censured, are nevertheless irrelevant unless those other steps are fashioned inwardly. From the layman is made the cleric; from the cleric, the sub-deacon; from sub-deacon, the deacon; from deacon, the arch-deacon; from him, the elder; from the elder, the bishop. Similarly, from layman comes the monk; from regular canon, the Dominican; from Dominican, the Franciscan; from Franciscan, the Benedictine; from Benedictine, the Carthusian.

Now, there has been much argument about these ranks among the very ones who set them up and arranged them in accordance with matters external. Some think the Franciscans stand on a more exalted rung because they stalk about in bare feet and do not touch money. On the other hand, there are those who esteem the Dominicans more than these because they eat no meat at home. Some prefer Benedictines to both of these orders because they chant long hours in churches and never go out of their house. Nowadays those rate number one with everybody who rub their skins raw in iron corselets instead of undershirts.

These steps, no doubt, are a contribution to piety if with God's help the true steps are being raised in the heart. If you have stopped living like a thug, that is no inconsiderable step to devoutness. If you not only return what you got by fraud but in the love of Christ, lavish your own wealth on those in need, you have mounted a still higher step. If you have become gentle instead of fierce and violent, you have ascended another rung in your heart; if you are intent on doing good to everyone, you have betaken yourself to a still higher one. Finally, if you not only give no thought to evening the score with those who have deeply offended you, but in the grace of Christ are happy to wish them well and do them good—then you have achieved a truly lofty step.

I have brought up these things as examples; each person must examine himself as to other matters also. These are the steps ordained in the human heart, the innermost recesses of the mind. The happy man orders in his own heart those steps by which we move toward perfection, not pluming himself in front of man but proving himself to the Inspector of hearts and asking for help nowhere but from the Lord. And he meditates on these things in the vale of tears, for what else is this whole world but a dark valley, a place of being born, of giving birth, of dying, of sickening, of being in want, of making voyages, of waging wars—full of a thousand other occasions for weeping to which not even the powerful, the rich, the royal, are immune. This is that valley of Achor, "place of tumult and perturbation," that is, into which Achan was hurled, as the seventh chapter of Joshua has it. The Lord put us in this place after we forfeited Paradise through disobedience, so that, spending some time in exile, we might through the obedience of faith and observance of God's precepts struggle to return to our native land.

It is not that aspect of this valley which should grieve us. The Son of God himself deigned to descend into it that we might have "the way, the truth, and the life." However long we live in this mortal body, then, we are involved in the valley of tears. Someone will say, "Well, if we have to stay in this vale of tears, there is no point in man's ordering the steps of ascent within his heart." But according to Isaiah, chapter sixty-five, the valley of Achor is turned into pasture land for cattle. In the second chapter of Hosea, Jerusalem is presented as the expression of hope. Besides this, one ought to keep in mind the fact that man climbs up to the ark of Sion by the affections, not by foot; in the heart, not by staircase. The body holds fast to the valley; the mind struggles upward on the mountain. So it seemed to our King that by means of the passing trials of this world we might attain an immortal crown.

Nor should this seem a harsh law of this warfare. Our King, who established the law for us, has Himself taken it upon Himself. It is no reason for despondency; He who calls us to the struggle will Himself give us a blessing, helping us in perils, strengthening us in afflictions so that we can endure them. Our Director of Games summons us to a contest and has offered tremendous prizes to those who compete according to the law. He presides not only as overseer and judge but also as helper. He gives us strength and keeps up our spirits.

As the Apostle says, this "blessing" does not mean praise but bountifulness: "He that sows sparingly will reap sparingly; he that sows bountifully will out of his bounty reap life eternal."[136] The inexorable law is that "he who does not despise father and mother in comparison to his own soul, is not worthy of me," [137] and so on. I would call it a hard law and one to be appalled at unless abundance of grace is added which, in order that He might show that it was both free and by no means niggardly, He preferred to call *eulogia* rather than by another name.

Under Mosaic law grace was distributed rather more meagerly, but as soon as the kindliness and good will of our God shone forth,

He gave us salvation not according to the requirements of justice, for what we had done, but according to His mercy; and through the font of rebirth and renewal He poured out His spirit abundantly upon all flesh.

Now, with men saying well is often one thing, doing well another; in fact, the "blessing" of man is frequently a mischief, a *maleficium*, not a *beneficium*. But for God, to speak good is to do good. People act with a show of piety when they fall on their faces to receive the bishop's blessing, but how much more godly it is for us to be prostrate before God to obtain *His* blessing! Notice, too, how much more God's benediction accomplishes: "They will go," He says, "from power unto power and the Lord of Lords will be seen on Sion."

Here someone will be puzzled by the sudden shift in number of the verb. He merely said *"He* is blessed whose help is from you and *he* disposes in his heart." Here it is *"They* will go from virtue unto virtue." How is it that all at once one becomes many?

In mystical literature the blessing of God produces fruitfulness, just as His curse causes barrenness. "The earth is cursed because of your deed; when you work her she will produce thorns and thistles for you." [138] On the other hand, when God had created man from damp clay and a wife out of a single rib from the left side, He blessed them, saying, "Increase and multiply, and fill the earth." [139] Similarly in Psalm 106: "He blessed them and they multiplied exceedingly."

Such things, obviously, are symbolic of spiritual conditions. After we have been freed through the grace of the Gospel from the curse of the Law and through the Holy Spirit a benediction has been shed upon the Apostles, how quickly the worship of the true God, which before was penned in, so to speak, in one corner of the earth, spread itself abroad through all the nations of the world! What throngs of virgins, of martyrs, of testifiers to faith sprang up! Whence this marvelous proliferation? Whence, except from God's blessing?

"Your sons," He says, "will come from afar, and your daughters will rise up at your side." [140]

Thus that forsaken and bereaved woman marvels at her unlooked-for-fertility when she says, "Where did those sons come from?" [141] They came from every nation under the sky—from India, from Cadiz, from Thrace, from the Goths, from the Scots and the

Irish. Having multiplied by God's blessing, therefore, and being bold in faith and of high hope, they will go "from virtue unto virtue." Even here it is not *arete* (goodness), but *ek dynameos eis dynamin* (from power to power) which Jerome translates from the Hebrew as "from strength unto strength" (*de fortitudine in forti tudinem*). It requires no inconsiderable strength to give up, for Christ, the pleasures, the affluence, the plaudits of this world; but it takes even more to repress the feeling of devotion to parents, wife, and children, and by far the greatest fortitude of all to be indifferent to death and pains worse than death because of a love for life celestial.[142]

When people ascend a staircase, the higher they climb the more exhausted they become, but for those who mount these steps, their eagerness and strength increase with the ascent. How in the world could this be except by a divine blessing rather than by merely human powers? From where else could come such resolute endurance, such ardor on the part of Apostles and youths and young girls in filthy jails, in beatings and torture, even in death itself, which makes the human mind quail just to think of? This could never have happened without the Law-giver and Overseer's increasing His bounty to match the intensity of the trials. Men marvel at them because they consider only the outward affliction, not the inward blessing.

A certain man celebrated for his piety has spoken to the point about the ascetic life of monasteries: "Many see our crosses, but not our ointments. They see the body racked by vigils and fasting and toil; they see the solitude and the self-denial of all carnal pleasures, but they do not see how exquisitely the spirit panting for heaven is refreshed in this wretched, worthless body." [143]

But what, finally, is the prize sought in such strenuous exertions? "The God of Gods," the psalm says, "will be seen in Sion," or as Jerome has it, "They will appear before the God of Gods in Sion." This is the prize of all contests, the answer to all prayers, the height of felicity. "Lord," he says, "show us your face and we shall be saved." [144] And Philip says 'Show us the Father and He will be sufficient for us." [145]

Of course, no one ever "saw God." He is invisible to the physical sight but visible to the pure heart. So it is that in the Gospel the Lord calls those blessed who are "pure in heart, for they will see God." [146] But you should understand, too, that "heart" here is not that organ of the body which is the source of blood and vital spirits. Rather, it is the mind of man illuminated by the radiance of faith. Therefore, God is sometimes seen in this life by the pure in mind, but only as reflected in a mirror and as a shadowy figure, not as on Sion. Outside of the Church no one sees God, for no one has this purity of mind. And if there are those who imagine that they see Him, they hallucinate; they are really looking at an illusion rather than God.

To appear in the presence of the "God of gods" is no every-day kind of happiness. What does it mean to do this? It means to come in the fullness of trust into the presence of Him who knows every dark corner of the human heart. One dare not do this except with an absolutely cleansed and sound conscience.

God will be seen by the wicked, true, but in another sense; His aspect will be frightening, whereas to the just it will be loving. He is not a different deity, but the eyes viewing Him are different. To sick eyes a light is painful which to the healthy is delightful. "We must all present ourselves before the tribunal of the supreme Judge" [147] from whom there is no appeal. The soldier who has done his duty faithfully and energetically in war, the servant who has zealously employed the talents of his Lord sets out cheerfully to meet his Commander and his Master, and is going to hear, "Receive the crown of life eternal, and enter in to the joy of your Lord." [148]

The happy man is he who is not afraid to open up his conscience to his Lord, saying with King Hezekiah, "I beseech you, Lord, remember, I pray, how I have walked openly before you in truth and with upright heart, and the good I have done in your eyes." [149] With like confidence that stoutest of all Christ's soldiers presents himself before his General: "See," he says, "we speak openly before God in Christ." [150] And speaking of himself to these same Corinthians: "Not walking in cunning, nor falsifying the word of God, but in the palpable evidence of truth commending ourselves to the whole conscience of men, in the presence of God." [151] And in still another place: "I have fought the good fight, I have finished the course, I have kept faith. As for the rest, a crown of righteousness has been kept for me." [152]

Is it not a great joy to be thus able to appear "in the presence of the God of gods in Sion," to the mirrors of the perfection of the Gospel. "God of gods," he has said, meaning the Judge of all judges. Now, whether you interpret "judges" as peoples, or as devout men for whom God's word was made, or as angels who themselves are called *Elohim,* or Gods, or as demons, or as men in the service of demons who allow themselves to be worshipped as gods, He alone is "God of gods," Judge of the universe, as Psalm 81 witnesses: "God stood in the Synagogue of the gods and in their midst He decided between them," but He himself can be judged by no one.

It is not the sight of angels or of prophets or of any of the saints that brings man true joyfulness; only the God of gods offers this. And in order for us to achieve it, the Lord bestows His blessing, but only upon those who pray for it. He wishes to be prayed to earnestly, not for the purpose of reminding Him, but to make ourselves worthy by our praying, so that He may bestow His blessing the more bountifully. In this respect we appear before God both whenever we call upon Him in pure prayer and when we give Him thanks for the benefits we have received.

"Lord God of Hosts, listen to my prayer. God of Jacob, hear me." He is the God of the angels and here He is called God of Hosts. He is also the God of men who imitate the Patriarch Jacob. By wrestling with an angel he won a blessing, and he also said, "I have seen the Lord face to face, and my soul has been made whole." [153]

This follows: "Look upon us as our Protector, Lord, and be mindful of the countenance of your Christ." Now, one who requires a protector has not yet achieved complete freedom from danger. He still fears the fiery darts of evil spirits assailing us from above, and he prays to the God of Hosts to be a shield against them. "Shield" is Jerome's translation of what the Septuagint writers called "hyperaspistes," or great shield. Great is the power of demons, but the sole Lord of Hosts is more powerful than all of them. If He deigns to be our shield we need fear no darts. The one who says, "Lord, defender of my life, why should I be afraid?" is safely sheltered under this shield.[154] In another passage he says again, "Lord, you have girded us as with a shield of your good will." [155]

There is no shield made by man which renders the whole body of a man invulnerable; in fact, the very shield sometimes betrays a man. The person protected by the shield of God, however, cannot be wounded in any part. To be watched over by God is to be shielded; He watches over one He loves and wishes well. For this reason the psalm I just now referred to calls it the *"scutum benevolentiae,"* the "shield of goodwill," in Greek, *eudokia.* Jerome translates it as *"placabilitas,"* the "conciliatory disposition."

Those who armor themselves in their own merits and rely on them as a shield will find out for themselves whether they are safe. Those who put their confidence in ritual, in the veneration of saints, or in a vestment, as if these would preserve them from the onslaught of Satan, are not using a sufficiently reliable shield. One safely trusts the grace of God and His promises. To look upon God is bliss, but we cannot look upon Him unless He has first looked upon us. When we were fumbling blindly in a more than Cimmerian darkness, He deigned to watch over us. He opened our eyes, and when we were hostile to His love, He made us ready to love Him in turn.

"Look upon the face of your Christ." I don't think we ought to worry about the question whether this refers to the person of David or of someone else who can be reconciled with commonsense. In Greek *Christ* means "the anointed one," like *Messiah* in Hebrew. All are Christ's who have been reborn in Christ. From the countenance of these persons God never averts His eyes, but guards them like the apple of His eye,[156] provided only that they do not turn their face from Him. "Anointing," moreover, is the prerogative of kings and priests. Both have their own quality; those whom the Blessed Peter addresses are in accord with their own name: "You are a chosen race, a royal priesthood, a holy nation," [157] etc. But there is One who is Prince of all Christs, the one who is called "Prince of Peace," [158] and "Priest for ever after the order of Melchizedek," [159] whom God particularly "anointed with the oil of gladness before His comrades." [160] On His face, because it was free from every blemish, God the Father rejoiced to look—on Him whom He acknowledged as His dearly beloved Son, in whom He was pleased.[161]

What is it that the Prophet wants, then, in saying, "behold, and consider the countenance of your Christ"? Whatever God bestows on us is bestowed through and on account of the Son, not on account of the good works we have performed. "We all offend in many things." [162] He alone is the Lamb innocent of every stain. Therefore, God our Defender, if our countenance—our conscience, that is—offends you, look instead upon the countenance of your Son whom you love unexceptionably, and through His merits grant us what we ourselves do not deserve.

Since the Jews had not learned the mystery of the incarnation, disavowing in their prayers their own merits, they appealed to God in the memory of the Patriarchs, Abraham, Isaac, and Jacob, whose goodness had been acceptable to God. But Christians ask nothing from the Father except through Jesus Christ, whom we have as an effective pleader in heaven and who has made His own faith a guarantee for us so that whatever we ask of the Father in His name we may receive. The one who wrote this psalm had not seen Christ in the flesh; but with the eyes of faith, which look far ahead, he saw that He was going to come, just as Abraham many, many ages before the advent of Christ had seen that day and rejoiced. Whenever we seek something from God, even though we ask it with confidence we should not base that confidence on a sense of our own benefactions but on the gratuitous promises of God. Let us not say, "behold my fasts or my contributions to charity, my vigils, my sleeping on the hard ground," but "consider the countenance of your Christ."

Paul teaches this to the Ephesians in chapter 3: "In Christ Jesus our Lord let us have our trust, and approach in the assurance of His faith." Why through His faith? Because He must be trusted wholeheartedly who does not go back on His promises even if He should promise what seems to us impossible. Who would have thought it possible that human and divine nature could be thus made one so that they could be assimilated in one person? But He made the promise and kept it. Who believed it possible that a man would actually sit at the right hand of God the Father? He made the promise and He kept it. Then what can you not hope for from God if only He considers the countenance of His Christ?

So that you may understand, moreover, that this interpretation is not merely some dreamy sentiment of my own, but that the Prophet, recognizing his own worth, had run for succor to the countenance of Christ, listen to what follows: "One day in your dwelling is better than thousands." Of course, there is no reason why this cannot be read, at a more literal level, as a reference to the Israelite captives in Babylon. They were gripped by a passionate longing for their native land; they [163] were weary of heathen superstitions and sighed for the ancient rites and that splendid temple of theirs which Solomon had built. It seemed to them that they had been paganized by too-long association with unbelievers.

But we prefer to follow a rather subtle interpretation. The psalmist did not append the number *thousands* just so that you might think of a striking contrast. He does not say "in your home" or "in your sanctuary" but "in your *atria*," the antechambers of the temple, as it were, into which even the common people were admitted. For this reason, Paul, in writing to the Hebrews, calls it "the worldly sanctuary" [164] or *kosmikon* because it stands open to the whole world. Nor, in the Hebrew is it "one day," but merely "day," for there is no day where the sun of justice does not shine and where truth is defiled. Day does not exist, then, except in the Church. Those who are outside Her are in night, as Zechariah, speaking in his last chapter of unbelievers, has prophesied: "On that day there will be no light, but freezing cold." Shortly after that he speaks this way about the faith of the Church: "And there will be one day which is known to the Lord, not day or night." [165]

The rising of the sun produces the ordinary day; its falling, night. Then what is this day that is not a day? Isaiah explains in chapter 60: "You will have no sun in daylight, neither will the rising moon shine on you at night. But the Lord will be your everlasting light."

Both prophets have presented the situation described in Revelation: "And the state will have no need of the light of the sun, because the Lord omnipotent will be its light." [166] Further on in the same chapter I have just quoted from, Isaiah declares that there is no light except in the Church, referring to these people who have not accepted the faith of the Gospel: "For see how darkness will cover the earth and a thick mist its people. But the Lord will arise above you and His glory will be seen upon you." Then he comments on those people who, having abandoned ancestral superstition, have believed in the Gospel: "Gentiles will walk in your light and kings in the radiance of your rising." [167] When he says *hyper chiliadas* (over a thousand) he does not specify items, and thereby encompasses universal goods brought together as one, something impossible to man outside the Church. For what felicity is possible for a man if he walks in darkness? As long as we serve in this tabernacle we look upon the Sun by means of faith, but in that celestial temple there is only day, because there is no flux, no darkness of mutability, no mists of error or ignorance to obscure the light. Eternity knows no rising and setting of the sun.

In the meantime, though, to walk in the light of faith and to follow in simplicity of spirit Him who said "He who follows me does not walk in darkness" [168]—this is a greater joy than all material goods, a greater one than power, than renown, than the pleasures of this world. To those people whose eyes Christ has not yet opened, this seems a stupid thing to say, but if you were to question those in whose hearts Christ has begun to shine whether they would reap the benefit of the whole world by sacrificing their devoutness, they would scorn, they would shun and abhor your words. They have come to know how great is that Good which they already possess as earnest money, so to speak, and how incalculable is that to which they are eventually to be brought.

Now consider the point with me: how passionately is the speaker holding fast to the house of God who says these words, "I have chosen to be a nobody in the house of my God rather than to live in the tents of sinners." What is it to be a "nobody?" To lie on the threshold or in the waiting-room and to be despised, the lot of beggars. But so great is the majesty and bliss of the Church that what is most abject in it far surpasses all the attractions of the world. Just as in the heavenly Jerusalem are many mansions [169] of which the meanest is better than all the palaces of kings, so in the Church, as in a great house, are vessels of various kinds, some more splendid than others, but the cheapest of them more precious than the whole world. In the natural body of a man one member has more dignity than another, and they of course perform diverse roles, but they are all animated by the same vitality. That is the way with the mystical body of Christ, the Church: there are different ranks of men, different gifts and functions of the Spirit, but all are members of Christ and they look forward to the same inheritance. That which is most base is more sublime than any eminence of the world. The foot of the human body has more worth than the eye of a pig or a dog, and even those parts through which the excrement of food and drink are discharged have greater importance than the head of an ass.

Here the Prophet, incidentally, exposes the reason why many men either do not enter the Church, or leave it, or, once ejected for a sin, are reluctant to return. Those who are puffed up by worldly success are unwilling to deflate their camel humps in order to pass through the lowly entrance.[170] We learn from accounts of the past that numerous heresiarchs were occasioned by the fact that they were not promoted to the augustness of a bishopric. They preferred to occupy first place among the dogs and the pigs rather than a modest spot among the sheep of Christ. This foolish ambition gave us a Basilides and a Marcion and other unlucky names. And what have these unhappy men attained? Among men, everlasting shame; as far as God is concerned, they have earned perdition. How much better to be the least noteworthy among the sheep of the Church if only you may have your name enrolled in the book of life.

Afflicted by a similar madness are those who, although they have deserved to be cast out of the fellowship of the Church for their great and manifest sins, still decline to express the penitence that would reconcile them with the Church. They consider it humiliating and degrading to be kept from entering, to stand bare-headed and bare-footed in the anteroom, to ask on bent knees for the prayers of those who are going in, to wear sackcloth instead of purple, to be smeared with ashes instead of ointments. Why? Because they do not see what a great dignity it is, what a great good fortune, what security to be situated in the vestibule of the Lord. What use, and how great the peril, on the other hand, to be outside the house of God even for an hour.

That man dear to God, the Emperor Theodosius,[171] understood this when he preferred to put aside all the confused noise of empire and enter into the humble role of penitent rather than not be in the house of the Lord. Those very penitents, miserable in garb, weakened by fasting, worn out by tears and remorse, who lie just like beggars on the threshold of God's house, are much more fortunate than those who, with Satan as master, are reigning in the tents of wickedness, inasmuch as these penitents, if they are sincere, can be outside the Church in body while inside it in mind or spirit.

What is it then which the Prophet longs for so ardently when he appeals to God by way of the countenance of Christ? That he be permitted to reside either in some out-of-the-way corner or on the threshold of the house of God, or that he be numbered among the very least of Christ's members, outside of whom there is no hope of salvation for anyone. But if we are either approaching or returning to the door-sill of the house of God, the Lord's mercy is ready to sustain our weakness so that we can go on to greater excellence. The truth of the Lord has been provided so that we may be rich in all spiritual understanding; the grace of the Lord has been prepared so that we may overflow in spiritual love; and, last of all, the glory of the Lord has been made ready to transform us into the likeness of Christ. Christ is truth; Christ is our righteousness, and if we follow His lead there happens what Isaiah speaks about: "And your justice will go before your face and the glory of the Lord will cover you." [172] His mercy pardons your mistakes, His truth illuminates your mind to keep you from falling back into error. His grace equips you with gifts of the Spirit so that when you have been transformed you can inspire your brothers and recover many men from sin. As the blessed David says after he had experienced the great mercy of God and had been restored to truth by Nathan: "I will teach the wicked your ways and the sinful will be converted to you." [173]

This is what this Prophet perceived. Because God esteems mercy and truth, the Master will give grace and glory. So it was that Paul, cured of the madness of persecution by means of the Lord's mercy and instructed in the way of the Lord through the truth of the Gospel and, finally, enriched by amazing powers through the grace of the Holy Spirit and made the vessel, the chosen instrument, for that reason succeeded in glorifying the Lord even in the midst of adversities.

Although this brief verse can be interpreted in a different fashion, according to the word of Jeremiah, chapter thirty-one, the fact that we are drawn to the cognition of truth is a function of divine mercy: "So, having mercy on you, I have led you." Truth, moreover, belongs to the man acknowledging his own sins and recognizing the gratuitous mercy of God. This is what Psalm 50 observes: "Behold, you have loved truth and have manifested to me the dark uncertainties of your own knowledge." As long as David concealed his sin, he was a liar, trying to deceive not only men but God. But God out of His mercy calls him back, through the Prophet Nathan, to the truth of confession, making clear that it is useless to hide evil in the presence of men since no one can fool the eyes of God.[174]

Grace and glory attend him who applies for mercy and avows the truth. When the stress of penitence has been endured and the members thus amended, just as formerly they had been subjected to harshness after harshness so, once made a temple of the Holy Spirit, they will be subject to mercy upon mercy. Thus it comes about that the Church can glory in the fact that where sin once was its grace is superabundant, and there is greater rejoicing among the angels over one sinner saved than over ninety-nine of the just.

Indeed, it is not a pointless remark of Augustine that truth is faith in the promises of God.[175] Only He is truthful when all men are liars, not because men are always deceitful but because in themselves they have no power to achieve what they promise and, being irresolute, will be overcome the next day. As long as we carry around this paltry body of mortality, vulnerable to many hurts and perils, His mercy encompasses us like a shield so that we will not sink back into our vices. The truth of God in His promises supports and cheers our minds so that, despising the goods of this life as much as its ills, we may be borne toward the celestial world.

Psalm 35 applies here: "Extend your mercy," it says, "to those who know you, and your righteousness to those of an upright heart." Justice gives to each one what is his, but what should God return to us when He owes nothing to any one? We have nothing that should not be credited to His benevolence. But justice and generosity are different things. The true nature of justice is to make good what you have voluntarily promised. By this reasoning God, in a sense, made Himself our debtor so that what we could not appeal to on the basis of our deserts we could plead on the basis of His promises. Therefore, if we are mindful of our duty He does not object to being called unjust if He should perform less than He has promised. "Come," he says, "and accuse me, says the Lord." David is referring to this justice of God when he says, "That you may be justified in your words, and triumph when you pronounce judgment." [176]

Sometimes God defers our expectation, but He never deceives. Meanwhile those who do not understand His truth murmur and have their doubts, just as did those two disciples when they said "We were in hopes that He was going to redeem Israel." [177] Great sorrow gripped them because, since they did not believe He would be resurrected, they thought they had been treated to empty talk.

The way Jerome and certain others translate from the Hebrew here differs from the Septuagint version in such a way that there seems not to be a discrepancy of that sort which frequently occurs because the same idea is being expressed in different ways, or because someone has read a different meaning into the same words; but rather, because there seem to have been variants in the manuscripts of the Hebrew scriptures. What they render from the Hebrew goes as follows: "Because the Lord God is my sun and my shield, the Lord will give grace and glory." This reading, if authentic, puts *sun* in place of *truth*, which is Christ, "who lights up every man coming into this world"; *shield* in place of the *mercy* sheltering believers against all the taunts of Satan.

So it is in Psalm 31: "Mercy will encompass him who hopes

in the Lord." Nevertheless Paul exhorts us to take up the shield of faith,[178] and another Psalm says, "His truth will enclose you with a shield and you will not quail with the terror by night." [179]

Do you wish, then, to be safe from all evil? You must not be tossed about by every wind of doctrine: let us hold fast with steady faith to what the Catholic Church has handed down to us from holy scriptures. Let us follow in simple obedience what it teaches and await in eager hope what it promises. To those who walk with straightforward openness, mercy will not be lacking, nor will truth or grace or any kind of good that is relevant to eternal blessedness. The following passage applies here: "The Lord will not deprive of," or "He will not cheat out of good things those who walk in innocence." [180] For this the Septuagint reads *en akakia*, which signifies "a simplicity free of all guile or malice." The Holy Spirit loves dovelike souls. Here and now it will give glory to the pure conscience; in time to come it will grant that unspeakable glory. In the meantime, content with so precious a pledge, await the blessings of the future, rejoicing in hope, so that you may say with the Prophet, and from the heart: "Lord of hosts, blessed is he whose hopes are in you."

This is the way a number of psalms conclude. That which has always to be fixed in our minds has to be repeated frequently. Thus the second psalm closes with the words "Blessed are all who trust in Him"; the fourth, "Because you, O Lord, have made me exceedingly resolute in hope." Twenty-six has this: "Wait for the Lord, act manfully, and let your heart be strengthened, all you who hope in the Lord"; the thirty-second, this: "We have hoped in His holy name"; thirty-three: "All those who hope in Him will not fail"; thirty-six: "He will save those who have hoped in Him." So it is in forty-one and forty-two: the psalmist urges us to the hope that clings to God. It is the same in both sixty-three and one hundred thirty.

Nor is that any commonplace hope which the sacred writings commend to us with such great energy. The farmer hopes to have from God an abundant harvest from his fields, the sailor a prosperous voyage, the expectant mother a successful delivery, the sick man convalescence. But it is the man of piety who truly hopes, that is, who fastens his entire expectation on the Lord, who in utter trust places his entire case in the hands of God, having been persuaded that whether happiness or sadness befalls him, whether life or death, everything will happen for good through the mercy of God, who in His inscrutable wisdom thus regulates the affairs of mortal men.

Therefore, Lord of Hosts, since man who has placed his full trust in you is blessed, and since this cannot happen except within your house, the Church, deign, I pray, to open our eyes so that seeing how lovely, how beautiful, how peaceful, how secure, how happy are your tabernacles—and, furthermore, how unlike these are the tabernacles of wickedness with their array of conjectures and their dissonance of passion—and seeing that we, as one in meaning and purpose, are engaged in that happy communion of all the saints, it can truly be said of us, "Look! how good and pleasant it is to live together as brothers." We will never grow into oneness unless we as one place our hope in Christ Jesus, King of Sion, and our Lord, and all look to Him alone.

Where ambition dominates, or love of money, or obstinacy, or blind partisanship, or blinder animosity, so that we stubbornly go on asseverating whatever we once said or wrote, where we commend to the bias of factions what we know ought not to be commended, or damn out of personal hatred what was spoken with sincere piety; finally, when each man looks to himself and the thin rope of contention is being tugged from every direction, affairs cannot be restored to peace. Let us reflect on the folly of so detesting the practices of certain popes or priests or monks that we ourselves become worse than they are; for anyone who abandons the fellowship of the Church and moves into heresy or schism is worse than one who leads an indecent life in sound beliefs. Likewise, it is exceedingly hurtful for us to be sharp-eyed as lynxes for the faults of others while we are blinder than moles about our own; for people carrying a beam in their own eye to see the mote in somebody else's.[181]

As human beings we are involved with human beings. Although I concede that they sin quite gravely who, once established in public authority, are not mindful of their obligations, nevertheless very often the intransigence of the people is responsible for the fact that those who rule are not the ones who should do so. So it was that the Israelites took arrogant Saul in place of gentle Samuel.[182] One will be more tolerant of others' mistakes if he has first assessed his own. A special occasion for discord is our scrutinizing the errant ways of our neighbors with only the left eye. Let that eye be closed, and the right eye then opened to their good points. If we have been honest appraisers of their virtues, we will be the more lightly distressed by their faults. Between brother and brother or husband and wife no friendly concord can exist unless they mutually shut their eyes to certain defects in each other.

How, then, will there be peace in the whole Church if everyone closes his eye to the virtues of the other fellow and has such an eye for his blemishes as are those mirrors which present an alleged image much enlarged and distorted? It is a matter for grief that there are so many monks who show very little evidence of religion beyond their vestments and their frigid ceremonialism, that there are so many priests who neither live chastely or know sacred letters, that there are even many abbots and bishops who differ very little from secular princes and satraps. But meanwhile we forget how many among them are men of piety, sobriety, learning, deserving well of the state, remaining poor in the midst of riches, humble in a post of authority, gentle in the possession of power. We do not consider how much more rapacious we might be if we were given access to unrestrained liberty in so many matters.

It is a good idea, therefore, for the generality of men who, disregarding the good qualities of the priesthood, see and exaggerate only their faults, to bring their own handbag from the rear to the front and inspect it.[183] How rarely do we see a laborer—to begin at the bottom—who is reliable in doing his job or reasonable in reckoning his pay. That well-known adage did not originate by accident: "Every artisan is a thief in his own profession."[184] What is there anywhere at all which those fellows won't spoil for the sake of profit? What tricks they have for cheating on the quality of wheat and flour, wine and beer, clothing and other textiles! I pass over now the lying promises, the arrogance and peevishness in trade, so that it is about as easy to deal with a king or a cardinal as with some stone-cutter who has scarcely enough for dinner at his place. What would people who are like this in menial and lowly work be if they were elevated to the position of those whose practices they cannot abide? The masses—on the pretext of violated vows, sacrilege, and impurity—magnify the dissoluteness of those initiated in sacred orders so that they may excuse their own baseness and license.

But let them make no mistake: no Christian has a license to sin. All of them have been bound by a most sacred sacrament—unless they think, perhaps, that what they avowed in baptism was all in sport. If those who abandon the principles of Benedict or Francis are called by that hard name of "apostate," how much more do those deserve this name who, having professed contempt for the world in baptism, nevertheless serve the world wholeheartedly and desert their Commander, Christ, for Satan!

Adultery, an offense by no means trifling and one which among pagans was punished by the sword, among the Jews by stoning, is nowadays somehow accounted a joke. If one looks very closely, indeed, he will find everything riddled with cheating, lying, and graft; so I need not remind you of what a Lerna of evils the shadow of war hides. There is no point in speaking here about those minor officials, or about those who want everything permitted to them by reason of a title of nobility, or about the rest of the princes. Wherever you look, good heavens, what rich occasion for lamentations!

But this is the nature of human behavior to pass off most of their own deeds as the way human beings behave, which exempts them from the category of evils. Man often changes his vices; he never gets rid of them. What recourse then but for each man to abandon his self, for us all to take refuge in the mercy of Christ? Some faults are too innocuous, relatively, to require the application of strong remedies. Some are glossed over with less strain put upon religion than when they are censured. Furthermore, those which are more serious than it is fitting to cover up require a skilled and instructed hand lest we bring about what customarily happens to inexperienced physicians who, when they apply their cures with too little skill, eliminate the patient instead of the disease, or render a rather slight ailment incurable.[185] And many steal upon us little by little as the occasion offers and have to be got rid of little by little as the occasion offers and if it can be done without a desperate upset. If not, they should be disregarded until the time itself offers a more favorable opportunity.

The same kind of adroitness must be used in dealing with dogmas. There are some who while they are feebly bleating "Heresy! Heresy! To the fire! To the fire!" and making the most sinister interpretation of any equivocal remark or distorting by misrepresentation what was said with piety, have won a large measure of sympathy for the very ones they were marking for extermination. Again, those who under the praiseworthy label of the

Gospel set in motion such things as are diametrically opposed to the Gospels, are vastly helpful to the sects of those very people whom they wanted to suppress. Therefore, when one group will permit no innovation at all, and the other side will suffer nothing established to remain, a virtually uncontrollable storm has been stirred up. And when the thin rope of contention has been pulled too taut on both sides, the result is that the rope snaps and both parties fall flat on their backsides.

Not that the Church may fall. Since it is built upon the indestructible rock, Christ, it is shaken by no hurricanes; but I am speaking of certain men who look after the cause of the Church with great—I will not say "mischief"—indeed with great zealousness, but not according to knowledge. The disease has not yet gone so far as to become incurable. The blaze can be put out if we remove the incendiary material. But the particular source of this turmoil is the irreligious moral habits of men. This is not a chance for some of us to cast the blame on others. It is the first example provided us by the parents of the human race, but as it was a bad one *per se* it is an unhappy one for us: "A woman beguiled me. A serpent beguiled me." [186] Since we have all aroused the wrath of God, it behooves us all together to be converted to Him with sincere hearts. As He is influenced by prayers, He in turn will be converted to us and will turn these disordered commotions of affairs to peace if we exert ourselves in that direction in proportion to our own powers, however trifling.

Just how, you ask, will this happen? Let every man personally be what he ought to be. Let popes be high priests who are vicars of Christ, caring sincerely for the Lord's flock. Let princes be ministers of divine justice who are going to render an account to God; the more immune they are to fear of men, the more they ought to fear Him. Let officials manage public affairs with good faith. Let monks demonstrate in their characters the excellence they profess to in their name. Let priests meditate day and night on the law of the Lord by which they can be the salt of the people. As for the laity, let them be what they are called: let them not dictate, but respectfully submit to their priests, faithfully obey the laws of their governors. Let each one in his own work try his own conscience before that highest *kardiognose*.

We would like to adapt the words of Saint Luke here: [187] if a man is a banker, let him be a trustworthy banker; if he is a builder, let him build honestly; if he is a baker, let him bake honestly; if he is a smith, let him be an honest smith; if he is a clothes dealer, let him be an honest dealer, trusting Him who does not desert those upright in heart. And the same thing must be said of the rest. Let no one smooth over his own faults with the excuse that "this is usual practice, everybody does it." Don't look around you, O you virtuous man, to see what others are doing, but what that supreme Judge, whose eye no one eludes and at whose tribunal we all must stand whether we be kings or destitute farmers, would expect you to do. There this subterfuge of "such is the custom, everybody acts this way" will avail you nothing.

Let your itch for advancement be put aside, and your obstinate determination to get the better of others; let biases depart along with personal grudges; let the heedless clamor of lunatic contention subside so that peace-making truth can be heard. Let that *sygkatabasis* draw near so that both factions may make some concessions to the other, without which no harmony can exist. Let yourselves yield up to this point, that *ta akinta* (inflexibility) may not be produced, and let human frailty be so far endured in order that man may be gradually brought to a more perfect state.

But it ought to be a deep conviction of everyone that it is neither safe nor helpful in fostering peace to brashly abandon those positions which have been established by the authority of our ancestors and confirmed by the practice and agreement of generation after generation. Nothing should be altered unless necessity compels the change or a signal advantage invites it. Argument over freedom of the will is more likely to produce briars than fruit.[188] If there is anything to be looked for here, let it be objectively discussed in the discourses of theologians. Meanwhile, it is sufficient to agree among ourselves that man can do nothing through his own powers; if he can do anything, he owes it all to the grace by whose gift we are whatever we are. Thus, in all matters we may recognize our own frailty and give the praise to the Lord's mercy. Let us agree that we must attribute very much to faith; still, let us acknowledge that this is the special gift of the Holy Spirit and is much more generously accessible than the general run of men believe, nor is it present in everybody who says, "I believe Christ suffered for me." Let us grant that we are justified by faith, that is, that the hearts of those who believe are made pure; but let us acknowledge that works of love are essential for attaining salvation. Real faith cannot be indifferent, since it is the fount and seedbed of all good works.

We should distinguish, as a matter of fact, between the righteousness which cleanses the inner abode of our mind, which you could accurately describe as "innocence," and the righteousness which adorns and enriches it with good works. God is really no one's debtor except perhaps out of His gratuitous promise, although it is through His generosity that we must meet this very condition of His promise. The word *merit* or *reward* ought not to be rejected, however, because God, who works in us and through us, receives and weighs us in accordance with His own goodness.

We should have no fierce contention over words, only an agreement upon the thing itself; the ears of the untutored crowd should not be assailed by such *paradoxa* as these: "It's of no importance what our works are like; if only you have faith enough you will be saved," and "Man, whatever he does, does nothing but sin." Things which may be true in one sense are nevertheless pounced upon by the uneducated in a different sense than is proper. Take, for example, those words "Christ has paid for our sins." Did He die for us that we might live in our sins, or, rather, that once washed by His blood we might keep free from every contamination? He died and rose from the grave in order that, emulating Him, we might die to sin and rise up in newness of life. He bore the cross for us, but He also declares that "he who does not bear his own cross every day is not worthy of me." [189] Besides, for those who daily crucify the Lord with their sins, since He is in them, His death will not benefit them so much as ensure a heavy increase of punishment.

Some devout people are disposed to believe that the prayers and good works of the living help the dead, especially if they were scrupulous about doing these things while the deceased were living. Let these people only be admonished that if they arrange for funeral processions and masses in order to achieve status, they are wasting their money; they are more likely to reap a benefit if they spend what the deceased willed to them on those who are alive and healthy. But as for those who do not believe in any of this, let them not make an uproar about the silliness of others; the more philanthropically they themselves relieve the plight of the poor and the more ardently they espouse good works, the less those others will believe that the dead are assisted by benefactions of the living.

There is also the conviction of some religious people that saints male and female—whom God created so little burdened by their corporeal bodies that in answer to their prayers He drove out devils and brought the dead back to life—even now have some influence with Him. As for those who hold firmly to a different belief—that one should pray with pure mind and devout faith to Father, Son, and Holy Spirit—let them not maliciously trouble these people if, short of superstition, they invoke the approbation of saints. Superstition, which I confess to be most evident in these cults of the saints, ought to be exposed; but devout and ingenuous feeling must be sustained, even if it is attended by a certain amount of error. Granting that the saints do not hear our prayers, nevertheless Christ, who loves childlike hearts, does answer them and will grant what we seek, if not through the agency of saints, certainly in place of them.

In my opinion, indeed, those people who have been infuriated by images of the saints have been spurred to this zealotry—intemperate, one must say—by something not altogether a fact. Idolatry—that is, image worship—is, of course, a heinous offense which, even though it has long since disappeared from human custom, is nevertheless a danger, lest through the wiles of the evil spirits those who are off guard bring it back. But since in the liberal arts sculpture and painting have this long time been considered as silent poetry,[190] sometimes depicting the human feelings more effectively than a man, however eloquent, could express in words; and since Plato, acknowledging that poetry has the utmost importance, for good or ill, in the education of a commonwealth, did not remove all poets from that state he invented—only Homer and those like him, who imputed to the gods and their offspring adultery, homosexuality, thieving, lying, unbridled rages, dishonesty, and other vices which no good governor of a republic could tolerate in his citizens or an upright head of the household in his wife, children, or servants—whatever superstition had crept in by way of their imitations had to be corrected. Public welfare had to be preserved.

Would that every wall of every chapel presented the life of Christ effectively portrayed. In churches, however, let it be as the African Council has decreed: "Just as nothing should be read except the canonical scriptures, so it is best to have no picture unless its subject is contained in the canons of scripture." In the courtyards, on the porches and shaded walks let them be permitted to picture other things drawn from human events; only let them make for good moral conduct. Paintings fatuous, or smutty, or inflammatory ought not only to be removed from churches but also from the whole commonweal. And just as it is a kind of blasphemy to twist sacred literature into silly and ribald jests, so those people deserve a stiff penalty who paint scriptural subjects but mix in some contemptible stuff of their own invention and unworthy of the saints. If they want to play the fool, let them go to Philostratus [191] for their material, although there are many subjects from pagan history which could be profitably presented to the eyes of laymen.

So, if one has been persuaded that the images of saints, being insentient, should receive no reverence, let him enjoy his own perceptiveness but not rail at those who, short of superstition, thus venerate images for love of those whom they represent, just as the new bride of an absent bridegroom fondly kisses a ring or a garment he has left behind or sent to her.[192] This emotional response, which springs from a certain overflowing of love—but is not superstition—cannot be displeasing to God.

In the same way we ought to regard those who, with like feelings, eagerly kiss the bones and other relics of saints. In these matters Paul, as I see it, conceded that "each one should be quiet in his own opinion." [193] I knew a theologian who, when he saw a certain man passing through a graveyard (for it was a public thoroughfare) without baring his head at the sign of the crucifix, not intentionally, really, but because he was engrossed in the talk of the companions he was strolling with, declared with astonishing conviction to those he was talking to, "I would be willing to swear that fellow is a Lutheran!"

That, surely, is an unsuitable attitude, just as the other side errs in hatefully denouncing, not a superstition, but the artlessly devout emotion of those who set some store by images. It is possible, without causing injury, to impress on everybody the fact that saints, male and female, are best reverenced by emulation of their lives.

Similarly, as to those not yet convinced that the sacramental confession of these times was ordained by Christ himself, they should consider it a beneficial practice, commendable for many uses and sanctioned by its observance for many ages; but it lies with us, largely, whether it becomes relatively valuable or of little importance. Obviously, if we select a priest who is honest, knowledgeable, and capable of keeping his mouth shut, we should not baffle him with vague, unintelligible talk, so that he has to interrogate us as if he were probing for crimes. Instead, just as if we were in the presence of God, we should open up precisely those faults which are assuredly deadly wounds. This kind includes adultery, homicide, theft, deep and willing drunkenness, malicious scandalmongering—which is a kind of murder or poisoning—perjury, fraud, looting, and other sins of that sort, whether actually committed or merely in the definite cast of one's mind. Those who have lacked only the opportunity have in effect already done the deed.

But avoid the superstition of repeating confessions; avoid the solicitous enumeration of everything you did and the attendant circumstances, or going over the whole confession before another priest if some detail escaped you the first time. Let us be quite sure that what we have admitted to we really abominate, and that we return to our pristine condition.[194] That is the chief point of all, to regulate our life in such a way as not to fall into any grievous sin. One who can do this is free from the burden of confessing. Avoiding even lesser faults is granted to scarcely anyone in this life, but with God's help it is not difficult for those who have been once rooted in God's love and faithful to it to shun the major offenses.

This groundwork, then, should be established and consolidated in our hearts before everything else. If we should happen to slip into error it is not necessary to run forthwith to the priest, but one does need to flee to God. It is His favor you must return to; you can wait for a convenient time to confess to a priest also. The question is, whether the faults you are hesitant about are really deadly or not, when there is an opportunity to report to a priest. I should say it is like the matter of contracts, the legality of which you are in doubt about. Many knotty problems come up in the life of mortal men—about lending money, for instance, or about marriage, or debts to be paid, or religious pledges. If some people believe that this practice of confession has been ordained by Christ, let them observe it all the more devoutly; but let them also allow others to rest peacefully in their own conviction until such time as a most holy synod makes some explicit pronouncement on the subject. With this agreement it will come about that neither will Christian peace be shattered nor the morals of the unstable degenerate into total license.

As to the Mass, if any superstition or vulgarity has entered into it, it is only reasonable to make improvements. But why we should execrate the Mass itself to such an extent, I do not understand. It consists of psalmody, or *Introit*, glorifying of God, prayers, sacred songs, the reading of words of the Prophets or the Apostles, called the Epistles, the reading of the Gospel, the profession of the Catholic faith, the giving of thanks called the *Eucharist*, and the reverent commemoration of the death of the Lord, more prayers, including the Lord's Prayer. Then follows a token of Christian peace; next, Communion, a sacred canticle again, and more prayer. At the conclusion the priest with his benediction entrusts to God all the people received into his care and urges them to persist in spirit of piety and mutual charity. What is there here that is not good and worthy of veneration?

Those who are disgusted by the dirty mob of mercenary performers of the Mass should get rid of what is unworthy, keep what is good. Those who are displeased by the "proses," especially the crude ones, can omit them.[195] The Roman Church knew no proses. By the same token, it would be possible to omit, with no loss to religion, those chants which are now done in some churches after the consecration of the Lord's body and blood, for peace, or against the plague, or for an abundant harvest. These were all superimposed upon the traditional practice. At that time people did not scurry about to see what kind of a show a priest was giving, but with bodies prostrate on the ground and souls lifted on high they gave thanks to Christ, the Saviour, who washed us in His blood and redeemed us by His death.

In the early days the Roman Church knew nothing of such practices as these. The sanctuary of the Pontiff contains only a single altar and a single religious rite. Today, in fact, many churches following the Roman model do not permit private masses to be served, at least when the most solemn rites are being performed. Theirs is a deplorable insolence who during a most solemn mass stroll around exchanging chitchat about trivialities, or demand a personal priest to serve them privately, or at vespers seize upon any priest they meet to do the even-song praises for them alone, even if he has already completed his service, and who are so infuriated by a refusal that he is liable to get their fists in his face. To such an extent whatever is public is despised, and everyone wants individual attention.

If people do not like the sound of instruments in church or that kind of music accompanied by instruments, they can be dispensed with without any sacrifice of religious devotion; if they do like them, they should see to it that the music is appropriate to the temple of God. It is too bad that in some churches nowadays some excellent features are either left out or abbreviated on account of the ensemble of musicians or instruments. Nearly an hour is taken up by the "proses," and even the symbol of faith is curtailed and the Lord's prayer omitted. Those cadences drawn out to great length on every line [196] take up no small part of the time. It preserved the solemnity of worship, however, if there was nothing superfluous to make it tedious.

So many particularized subjects for masses also tend toward superstition: a mass of the crown of thorns, a mass of the three nails, a mass of the foreskin of Christ, a mass for sailors, for pedestrians, for travelers by horseback, for the barren, for the pregnant, for those in labor, one for the victims of quartan ague, and one for the three-day patients. But this problem and many like it can easily be either endured or corrected. It was not necessary to get rid of the Mass, accepted for so many centuries, as if it were something wicked and pernicious.

Those questions, also, which some have concerned themselves with—about qualification, about "primary" and "secondary merit," about *opere operante* and *opere operato* [197]—could be set aside as matters of opinion until a synod could make a pronouncement on these too, or leave each one to his own preference.

The early fathers of the Church did not cringe at the words *sacrifice* or *immolation*. I agree that once Christ was dead He did not die again; but that unique Sacrifice is recreated every day, so to speak, in mystical rites as long as we draw upon that inexhaustible fountain for a grace continually new for us. We are offering a sacrifice for both the living and the dead as long as, on their behalf, we appeal to the Father through the death of the Son. Finally, since every prayer or any rendering of praise and gratitude is rightly termed *sacrifice*, the name is especially appropriate to the mass, which more ritualistically incorporates all of these things.[198]

There are those who lament the absence of communion in the Mass. This, I admit, is the way it was originated by Christ and in former times was customarily observed, but the fact that this mutual participation has dwindled is hardly the fault of the priesthood but of the laity, in whom charity, alas, has grown cold. That holy food should not be thrust upon those who do not want it or upon the squeamish; it will not be denied to those eagerly seeking it. What mutual participation is possible these days when in some places churches are almost empty at the time of communion. Some leave the sanctuary as soon as they have been sprinkled and make their exit before the Introit. Others retreat after hearing—without understanding—the Gospel.

It is after the priest has said "Lift up your hearts" and "Let us give thanks" that those special parts designed for the people come, when, with the priest silent, each person speaks privately with God. But by that time they are gossiping on the street or having a drink in some dive. Even these people, however, behave with more propriety, I must say, than those who throughout the whole sacrament are exchanging jokes inside the church.

To sum up, even if there is no sharing of sacramental tokens between the one serving and those in attendance—and in early times this communion was not for everybody—there is, nevertheless, a sharing of the sacred doctrine: the exhortation to piety, the prayers, the giving of praise and thanks. So, what is life-giving is mutually participated in; the part that is not means nothing anyway without those other things.

Some, of course, are uneasy about the adoration. If the whole Christ is in the Eucharist, why should He not be adored? But even if Christ is in the sacrament in the form of food and drink so that He may be taken up with deepest purity of heart, He should not be made a spectacle of or paraded around in public sports and processions, or carried around the countryside on horseback. This has no precedent at all in ancient practice, but vulgar tastes are catered to far too often in this matter. Some people think they are being wonderfully pious if, whenever the priest allows the body of the Lord to be seen, they rush up on all sides and stare fixedly at close quarters. How much more reverent was the tax collector who kept far back from the chancel-rail and, prostrate on the ground, made his supplications to the crucifix in his heart.[199] No one is so stupid as to worship the human nature of Christ in place of the divine, or the bread and wine in place of Christ. However, since no one but the priest himself is certain whether he has really consecrated it, no one adores Christ there except by a tacit assumption, and yet that which is properly worshipped in Christ is never absent.

Consider also the fact that there is no sacrament so commonplace that we should not stand with bared heads when it is administered, as for example in baptism or the confirmation of children. What are they thinking of, then, who consider it idolatrous to uncover their head before this sacrament, even if the body and blood of Christ are present only in a symbolical sense? Furthermore, how many brands of sacramentarians [200] do we see! How many times have they themselves changed their minds? How often have they rejected another point of view?

Just recently there has appeared a fellow who has concocted so irreligious an opinion concerning this sacrament that it would subvert the whole rite. That does not deserve to be called a sacrament which is observed only in thought, not in any external tokens. Do people behaving this way seem to themselves to be investigating these very serious matters, or making a joke of such things? But if they are in doubt, as is evident on the face of it, how much more satisfactory to stay with that which the Catholic Church has bequeathed us. It has taught that the body and blood of the Lord was truly there, unquestionably living. If we believe that the divine nature did not depart from the lifeless body of the Lord in the tomb, how much more credible it is that this divine nature is not dissevered from the living body in the sacrament! Therefore, if we agreed upon this point, the other questions which are causing anxiety—such as, precisely how it comes about that the Lord's body and blood are there in the substance of bread or in the guise of bread and wine, and what happens to the body once it has been received, and like problems—they could be settled by a synod. Nowadays, when everyone invents whatever notion he pleases about such important subjects, are we not to a certain extent making nauseous that very special comfort and joy of devout minds?

Devout people themselves would willingly see a reduction of the vast number of feast days which have been introduced either by bishops catering to popular caprice or ordained for inadequate reasons by Roman pontiffs. Of this sort is the Feast of the Conception and Nativity of the Virgin Mother, as well as the Feast of Presentation in the Temple. I am not sure that it would not be a good idea to set up no feast days at all that had no justification in sacred letters—always excepting the Lord's Day. The sincerely religious would be quite content with fewer festivals, observing with greater devoutness the ones which were left. It is a day by no means unholy when, by lawful labor and without dishonesty, one manages to feed his wife and children and to relieve the need of his neighbors. Feasts which confraternities set up by private authority for their own gain ought to be abolished by the magistrate, along with the societies themselves. They are no better than the routs of Comus and Bacchus.[201]

The Church did not institute fast-days or a selectivity of foods except for bodily and spiritual health. Those who run a risk in eating fish or perceive that by fasting their physical strength and mental vigor are impaired are in no way bound by the injunction of the Church. But for those who see that abstaining from meat or fasting makes them feel better physically and mentally, what kind of obstinacy, I should like to know, would make them—out of hatred for the Church—abandon a practice which benefits them so much? In this matter, then, let no one decide for someone else: the person who eats has no business reviling those who fast; those who fast should not condemn those who eat, even if the reason is not apparent. "They stand or fall to their own Master." [202]

I feel the same way about other regulations of the bishops which, if they are conducive to piety, if they serve a purpose, if they are fair, ought to be kept because they are of such a nature. If the word *rule* makes us uneasy, let us embrace them simply as wholesome counsel. If a slave purchased at auction gives you useful advice, you pay attention to it and follow it, not because a slave gave it but because it is to your advantage to do so. Shall we then snub the advice of those who stand high in public eminence and who act as our fathers and teachers?

We direct these remarks to this end, not that we want everything we say to be held as gospel certainty or that we would dictate to the Church what decisions she should make, but that until such time as a synod is provided we do not do to anyone else what we would cry to high heaven about if it were done to us, or that we may not force anyone into a new form of worship which he does not agree with. The most equitable policy is for those who themselves don't want to be coerced because of their religion to avoid coercing others, especially when the position of those maintaining themselves by the sanction of long tradition is also the better one. This advice applies to both sides: if temperate *sygkatabasis* will mitigate this convulsion of dissident factions, then it will come about that the healing relief of the synod will work more efficiently for peace. Thus physicians, before they make use of a powerful drug, get the body ready for it with certain agreeably gentle little potions they call syrups. Would that we would all follow their example! But I am afraid that there are those who, either because of lack of judgment or concern with their own self-interest, will rush to make everything worse, so that a synod will convene in vain.

But what evil genius has bewitched the miserable Anabaptists? I hear that they are more deluded by error than inspired by malice as they rush to speedy destruction the way they do. Isn't the baptism which has sufficed the Catholic Church for fourteen hundred years good enough for them? In the time of Augustine the custom of sprinkling infants was already so ancient that the originator of this practice was unknown, and it is more than likely that it was started by the Apostles themselves. Although it is not made explicit in Scripture that the Apostles did baptize infants, nevertheless, there is room for permissible inferences. Paul admits that he baptized three families, those of Crispus, Caius, and Stephen; [203] and at Philippi he baptized at night the jailer and his whole family.[204] And in the tenth chapter of Acts, Peter baptized not only the family of Cornelius but also his kinsmen and relatives whom he had called together at the arrival of Peter. It is probable that several children or infants were included in these families.

Christ says, "Give to Caesar those things which are Caesar's." [205] And Peter and Paul, the chief of the Apostles, were careful to advise Christian citizens to obey their kings and governors, even the idolators.[206] They would have the baptized slave [207] serve his master even more faithfully than before: do such people as these, then, balk at obeying princes bathed at the same font, professing the same religion?

They are said to require of their own people communal ownership of all property, but this practice existed only for a while at the time of the Apostles, in the very early days of the Church and not even then among all Christians. When the gospel had spread more widely, common property could not be preserved; it clearly was going to lead to dissension. It is more conducive to harmony that personal property and the right of managing it belong to the rightful masters; charity will assuredly lead to sharing.

And now we hear that a new brand of Jews, called the Sabbatarians,[208] has sprung up in Bohemia. They observe the Sabbath with such credulous literal-mindedness that if something gets in their eye on that day they will not remove it, as if the kind of Lord's Day which was holy even for the Apostles did not suffice as Sabbath for them, or as if Christ had not made it abundantly clear what should be accorded to the Sabbath day! Saint Paul would curse an angel who presented a different gospel message from heaven than he himself had taught.[209] Now we see the minds of many vacillating to such an extent that if the most insignificant little nobody offered a new doctrine, however inane, it would find disciples.

What is the cause of such wavering in the minds of the Germans, who have always surpassed other peoples in their reputation for constancy and staunchness? What could be a greater blessing for us than to put aside our quarrels to work harmoniously together in the house of the Lord? The Emperor Charles works for this with the highest enthusiasm, as does Ferdinand, King of Rome, Hungary, and Bohemia, a prince possessed of unusual devoutness. The Most Christian King of France is going to live up to his title in this matter, nor will the King of England forget that not so long ago he himself earned the impressive title of "Defender of the Catholic Faith."

Those well acquainted with the character of Pope Clement assure us that he will agree to the most equitable terms if only peace can be restored to the Church. The moderation of the learned cardinals will not be lacking. Under Christ's direction the matter will have a happy outcome if other princes and states also direct their energies to that end.

Far too long now have we found excuses for brawling; perhaps in sheer exhaustion we will seek peace. If the gentleness of the Lord encourages unrestrained presumptuousness on our part when it ought to invite penitence, it is to be feared that "His wrath will be kindled when His patience has been too often tried" [210] and, as Paul wrote concerning the Jews, "The wrath of God will fall on us without measure." [211] It is not even a good idea to abuse the clemency of kings. They are not ignorant of their own strength, but in the name of mildness prefer if possible to amend this evil by gentler remedies than cauterizing or surgery. Perhaps we think the emperor is asleep, but he is no doubt vigilant in this business. He is comparatively lenient—as it befits a prince in possession of extraordinary power not to be impetuous in what he does—but, nevertheless he eventually does whatever he once has resolved upon.

The integrity and quite philosophic spirit of Ferdinand—the kind Plato insists on in a prince—does not deserve contempt but fuller respect and more devoted obedience. The boldness and ill-advised rashness of a Cyclops has never had a happy outcome, but as that most perceptive of poets has so aptly put it

> Strength without wisdom collapses in ruins
> from its own weight.[212]

A tempered power, however, the gods elevate to something greater.

If, therefore, with moderate counsels and passions controlled we concentrate upon restoring peace in the Church, what Isaiah prophesied will come to pass: "My people will sit in the beauty of peace, in the tabernacles of faith and the fullness of rest," [213] and mutually rejoicing one with another we shall all say with a single voice, "How lovely are your tabernacles, O Lord of Hosts."

NOTES

1. Number 84 in KJ, which divides the Vulgate's Psalm 9 into two, resulting in a difference by one in the numbering of all succeeding psalms. The numbering in the text is that of the Vulgate; those cited in the notes following are numbered according to KJ.

2. Cf. Phil. 4:7.

3. Cf. Rom. 10:3-12.

4. 1 Cor. 9:24-26.

5. E.g., Rom. 8:13; Col. 3:5.

6. Cf. 2 Cor. 10:3-5; 1 Tim. 1:18; James 4:1-2.

7. Migne, *Patrologia Latina*, XXXVII, 1055 ff., "Enarratio in Psalmum LXXXIII."

8. *Epist.* 1.7.13.

9. Exod. 40:34-38.

10. Exod. 16:13ff. and 17:3-6.

11. Cf. Matt. 6:28 and 10:29-31; Luke 12:6-27.

12. *Adagia* 387C.

13. Cf. Eccles. 3:1-8.

14. Heb. 1:3.

15. Matt. 23:37.

16. Cf. Isa. 65:2.

17. Cf. Ps. 95:10. Erasmus differs from the Vulgate 94's "offensus fui . . . generationi illi et dixi: Semper hi errant corde": he has "*proximus* fui . . . *huic* et semper dixi. . . ." KJ follows the Vulgate here.

18. Acts 7:51.

19. In the Vulgate. Cf. Chron. 26 in KJ.

20. Ps. 83:5-7.

21. Ps. 2:2.

22. 1 Cor. 7:17.

23. The Sadducees were considered infidels in the opinion of orthodox Judaism for denying the truth of certain beliefs which the Pharisees held to be implicitly contained in Scripture: e.g., everlasting life and the existence of angels. The Herodians, mentioned on two or three occasions in the New Testament (Mark 3:6 and 12:13; Matt. 22:16) as having manifested an unfriendly disposition toward Christ, were generally held to be more a political party than a religious, presumably friendly to Herod the Great and his dynasty.

24. A second-century sect particularly offensive to orthodox Christians as tending to dishonor the Creator, who was equated with evil, against good, represented by the serpent. Christ was not a part of the Ophite Trinity but the offspring of the female Holy Spirit by the so-called "First Man" and the "Second Man" of the Trinity.

25. Another second-century sect who treated Cain and other wicked Scriptural characters as saints.

26. An early Gnostic sect which cultivated immorality as a method of demonstrating superiority to everything fleshly. During the Middle Ages "Nicolaitanism" was a word applied to clergy suspected of immoral practices.

27. An obscure sect flourishing in North Africa during the second and third centuries. Its members pretended that they were re-established in Adam's prelapsarian innocence, rejecting marriage, therefore, and living in absolute lawlessness, holding that their actions could be neither good nor bad.

28. One of the exponents of Gnosticism in second-century Alexandria. He seems to have assumed the existence of two warring principles, Light and Darkness, not derivable from each other, and with Darkness making itself master. The material world was thus essentially a creation of the powers of evil, not of a good God.

29. A follower of Valentinus (second-century Gnostic teacher) about whom little is known.

30. A fourth-century Spanish theologian, advocate of an asceticism so rigorous his followers were severely persecuted for heresy. He came in conflict with the authorities on the question of total continence in, if not the renunciation of, marriage. Charged with practicing magic and conducting licentious orgies, he was burned in 385. Augustine was one of those responsible for accusing him of heresy, though later review pretty well established his doctrinal orthodoxy.

31. A second-century reformer of the Christian Church. Convinced

100 / ERASMUS AND THE SEAMLESS COAT OF JESUS

that Christianity was already being corrupted by false Jewish doctrines, he advocated (not unlike the Christian humanists fourteen centuries later) a return to pure gospel and the authentic institutes of Christ, especially the teachings of Paul, whom Marcion considered to be the only Apostle who had rightly understood the teachings of Jesus. He came to an assumption of two Gods, one of the Old Testament and one of the New, the first a just deity of Jewish law and the second the good God, Father of Christ. False Jewish Christianity had subverted Paul's teachings of the true gospel which Marcion had been raised up by the *good* God to restore.

32.   Beginning in the third century, the doctrines espoused by Mani, who professed to have blended Christian teachings with old Persian Magism. Like the Ophites, Manicheeism advanced a rigidly dualistic system with Light (good) and Darkness (evil) conceived of as beings. The heresy also recruited from the Marcionites and became widespread in spite of persecution, including many adherents even among the clergy.

33.   Sabellius, of the third century, held that Father, Son, and Holy Spirit were merely three names for the same Person. God also was not Father, Son, and Spirit at one and the same time. Rather, He had merely been active in three different manifestations or energies—as Creator and Law-giver, as Redeemer, and as Giver of Life.

34.   Perhaps the best-known of the anti-Trinitarian heresies and one of the most widely spread, though it was denounced in the Council of Nicaea in 325 and Arius, along with other followers, excommunicated. Arius held that Christ, however much He surpassed other created beings, remained himself a created being, to whom the Father, before all time, had given an existence formed out of not-being. The doctrine thus reduced Christ to something of the status of a pagan demi-god.

35.   Followers of a fourth-century bishop and leader of an extreme form of Arianism which held that God, being Unbegotten, was an "absolutely simple Being." Hence the assumption of generation (in the Trinity) involved a contradiction of His essence by introducing duality into Godhead.

36.   Fourth-century Bishop of Alexandria, saint, and great opponent of Arian and other espousers of Unitarian beliefs. The episode Erasmus refers to here took place in 335.

37.   The Donatists, of the fourth century, held that the mark of the true Church was its guarding the essential predicate of holiness by the exclusion of everybody guilty of mortal sin, the Catholic position being that essential holiness was not destroyed by the presence of unworthy members in the Church. The Circumcellions were bands of fugitive slaves, vagrants, debtors, and malcontents who attached themselves to the Donatists, reacting with violence against the persecution of the Donatist sect and threatening civil war within the Church.

38.   E.g., in Ep. 23.7, *Psalmus Contra Partem Donati,* and *Liber Contra Donatistas post Collationem.*

39. 1 Cor. 13:12.

40. Matt. 18:20.

41. Num. 24:5.

42. Num. 23:10.

43. Ps. 133:1. The "Song of Degrees" or "Song of Ascents" *(canticum graduum)* appears in the superscriptions of Pss. 120-134. *The Interpreter's Bible* (IV, 638) offers a number of differing explanations of this heading but considers it most likely that the fifteen psalms included formed a collection for the use of pilgrims coming up to Jerusalem to be present at the great feasts.

44. Matt. 17:4; Mark 9:5; Luke 9:33.

45. See Rom. 7:24: "Who shall deliver me from the body of this death?"

46. Verse 8, after the Vulgate. KJ had "his eye" for "pupillam oculi mei."

47. Acts 9:4, 22:7, 26:14.

48. Cf. Matt. 25:40.

49. 2 Kings 6:17.

50. Cf. John 10:28.

51. Ps. 127:1.

52. Rom. 8:31.

53. Rom 8:38-9. Erasmus omits the phrase "neque virtutes" of the Vulgate and varies slightly in other respects.

54. Cf. Luke 12:32. Here again Erasmus does not quote exactly the Vulgate's wording.

55. John 16:33.

56. Cf. Matt. 12:29; Mark 3:27.

57. Cf. Acts 8:32.

58. II Cor. 10:4-5.

59. Ps. 45:11 ff.

60. Cf. I Cor. 2:9 and Isaiah 64:4.

61. See Seneca's *Hippolytus,* 585-586.

62. Ps. 118:81-2. A marginal gloss in *Opera Omnia* mistakenly cites 108.

63. Song of Songs 2:5.

64. Pliny, *Natural History,* VI.35.181.

65. With a play on the verb *capio*: "quando ego non te capio tu capies me." Lorenzo Valla uses the same legend in his "Dialogue on Free Will." See C.E. Trinkhaus tr. in *The Renaissance Philosophy of Man* (Chicago, 1965), p. 181.

66. Prov. 25:27, Vulgate, which has ". . . qui scrutator est majestatis, opprimetur a gloria." *Opera Omnia* has *opprimitur.* As the KJ has it: ". . . for men to search their own glory is not glory."

67. Cf. Isa. 40:23, Vulgate. KJ has "that bringeth the princes to nothing."

68. Cf. Rom. 12:4-5; 1 Cor. 6:15.

69. *Serm.* 1.6.56-7.

70. 1 Cor. 2:14.

71. James 3:15.

72. 1 Cor. 15:50.

73. Cf. Gen. 6:13 ff.

74. Jude 19.

75. 1 Cor. 2:9.

76. 2 Cor. 5:17.

77. 1 Cor. 15:44.

78. 1 Cor. 1:29-31, 3:21; 2 Cor. 11:30-31.

79. John 14:6.

80. Cf. Rom. 6:6; Eph. 4:22; Col. 3:9.

81. See Gen. 17:15-17; 21:1-7; Rom. 4:19-21.

82. Cf. Matt. 10:27-9; Luke (12:6) lowers the price, making it five sparrows instead of two for a penny.

83. Pliny (*Natural History* X.52.107) notes the "salaciousness" of the sparrow and its relative shortness of life compared to pigeons and turtle doves.

84. Matt. 10:27-9.

85. Song of Songs 2:12.

86. 2 Cor. 5:4.

87. Cf. 1 Cor. 4:13 and 15:8-9.

88. Phil. 4:13.

89. Heb. 11:37-38.

90. Ps. 22:6.

91. Phil. 2:10.

92. Literally "from the lime-kiln into the charcoal furnace" (*a calcaria in carbonariam*) *Adagia,* 550f.

93. Cf. 1 Thess. 4:4; 2 Tim. 2:20.

94. 1 Cor. 13:9.

95. Cf. Eccles. 1:18.

96. For the story of Lot see Gen. 19.

97. Rom. 7:24.

98. 2 Cor. 7:4.

99. Cf. John 17:3.

100. For *sexcentos mundos,* a phrase frequently used by Erasmus to indicate an indefinitely large number.

101. Rom. 1:21.

102. *Carmina,* 3.16.17.

103. I have been unable to find this passage in Horace. Tilley (*Dictionary of the Proverbs in England in the Sixteenth and Seventeenth Centuries,* G306) cites a seventeenth-century proverb, "The more goods the more greed," but no such saying is included in the *Adagia.*

104. The general practice among churchmen of using their benefices only as stepping-stones to higher ones, with greater prestige and higher revenues, had long been a target of reformers. In his convocation sermon of 1512, for example, Colet reproached the assembled clerics for their "pride of lyfe: howe moche gredynes and appetite of honour and dignitie is nowe a dayes in men of the churche? Howe ronne they, ye almost out of brethe, from one benefice to an other; from the lesse to the more, from the lower to the hygher? Who seeth nat this? Who seynge this sorowethe nat? More ouer these that are in the same dignities, the moost parte of them doth go with so stately a countenance and with so hygh lokes, that they seme nat to be put in the humble bysshoprike of Christe, but rather in the high lordship and power of the worlde . . ." (In J. H. Lupton, *A Life of John Colet* [Connecticut, 1961] p. 295).

105. Julius II, pope from 1503-1513, and one of Erasmus's favorite *bete noires. Julius Exclusus,* a satirical colloquy picturing the pope's unsuccessful petition to Saint Peter at the gates of heaven, is generally conceded to be the work of Erasmus although he never admitted it.

106. Migne, *PL,* XXXVII, 1061.

107. The ultra-Jewish party in the early Christian Church; they rejected the Pauline books and, in some cases, the virgin birth of Christ.

108. A fourth-century cult with extravagant mystical techniques, practiced by both male and female votaries. They were called "Enthusiasts" by some.

109. The *Adagia,* 343E, cites the first proverb in slightly more laconic form, "mali corvi malum ovum." It does not include the second.

110. Ps. 4:8.

111. Matt. 11:28-29.

112. *Adagia,* 499B.

113. A rather cryptic abridgement of Christ's words in John 2:19: "destroy this temple and in three days I will raise it up."

114. Migne, *PL,* XXXVII, 1061.

115. Cf. Col. 3:5; Isa. 1:11. For an earlier expansion of this theme see the *Enchiridion Militis Christiani* (*LB*, V, 36C-37B; pp. 123-125 in Himelick translation).

116. Isa. 1:13.

117. 1 Cor. 10:31.

118. Matt. 11:25-26.

119. Ps. 33:12.

120. Dan. 3:51 ff., Vulgate. KJ omits the passage.

121. A commonplace, of course, in Renaissance cosmology. For a handy redaction of these theories see E.M.W. Tillyard, *The Elizabethan World Picture* (London, 1948), Chapter 5 especially, or Hardin Craig, *The Enchanted Glass* (New York, 1936), Chapter 1.

122. 1 Cor. 6:20.

123. 2 Cor. 5:13.

124. Migne, *PL*, XXXVII, 1063. I translate Augustine's *assumtio* as *adoption*.

125. *The Interpreter's Bible* (IV, 638) notes that there were fifteen steps leading from the women's court to the men's court in the temple. Jerome's theory of the "song of degrees" was that the fifteen psalms were sung by the Levites on those steps.

126. 2 Cor. 1:24 (23 in the Vulgate).

127. Rom. 11:20.

128. Cf. 1 Pet. 5:8-9.

129. Isa. 26:1.

130. Isa. 30:15.

131. An adaptation of 2 Tim. 2:9-10.

132. Cf. Rev. 11:2. Although Erasmus refers to "quadraginta et duo *mansiones*" (delays, continuances), the Vulgate, speaking of a court which is outside the temple and given over to the Gentiles, has "et civitatem sanctam calcabunt *mensibus* quadraginta duobus." In KJ "the holy city shall they tread underfoot forty and two months."

133. Phil. 2:13.

134. Gen. 19:26.

135. 1 Cor. 2:2-6.

136. Cf. 2 Cor. 9:6. Erasmus's "Qui seminat in benedictionibus, de benedictionibus metet vitam aeternam" is an expansion of the Vulgate's "de benedictionibus et metet."

137. Cf. Matt. 10:37-38 and Luke 14:26-27. Erasmus seems to have been thinking of the latter, although he does not tally exactly with either Vulgate version of the Gospels.

138. Gen. 3:17-18.

139. Cf. Gen. 1:22.

140. Isa. 60:4, following the Vulgate's "filiae tuae *surgent*" rather than Jerome's *lac sugent*, which KJ seems to have adopted.

141. Isa. 39:3. (The Vulgate has *viri* rather than *filii*.)

142. One is reminded of More's remark to his son-in-law two years later: "'Son Roper, I thank Our Lord, the field is won.' What he meant thereby I then wist not, yet loath to seem ignorant, I answered 'Sir, I am thereof glad.' But as I conjectured afterwards, it was for that the love he had to God wrought in him so effectually that it conquered all his carnal affections utterly." (William Roper and Nicholas Harpsfield, *Lives of Saint Thomas More*, Everyman ed., [London, 1963], p. 36)

143. A marginal gloss in the *Opera Omnia* text cites Bernard here.

144. Cf. Ps. 80:30.

145. John 14:8.

146. Matt. 5:8.

147. Cf. 2 Cor. 5:10.

148. Apparently a fusion of James 1:12 and Matt. 25:21.

149. 2 Kings 20:30; Isa. 38:3.

150. 2 Cor. 12:19.

151. 2 Cor. 4:2.

152. 2 Tim. 4:7-8.

153. Cf. Gen. 32:24-29.

154. Ps. 27:1.

155. Ps. 5:12, Vulgate. KJ changes the tense of the verb and the person of the direct object.

156. Cf. Deut. 32:10.

157. 1 Pet. 2:9.

158. Isa. 9:6.

159. Ps. 110:4.

160. Ps. 45:7.

161. Matt. 3:17; Mark 1:11; Luke 3:22; 2 Peter 1:17.

162. James 3:2.

163. Reading *taedebant* instead of *taedebat*, as in the *Opera Omnia* text.

164. Heb. 9:1.

165. Zech. 14:6-7, Vulgate. KJ does not refer to the temperature.

166. Rev. 21:22-23. Erasmus telescopes the two verses.

167. Isa. 60:2-3.

168. John 8:12.

169. John 14:2.

170. Matt. 19:24; Mark 10:25; Luke 18:25.

171. There were three emperors of the Eastern Roman Empire by this name. Erasmus apparently refers to the third, a usurper who reigned only a year (716-717) before being deposed by another usurper and then retiring to a monastery.

172. Isa. 58:8.

173. Ps. 51:13.

174. Cf. 2 Sam. 12:1-13.

175. Migne, *PL*, XXXVII.

176. Ps. 51:4.

177. Luke 24:21.

178. Eph. 6:16.

179. Ps. 91:4-5.

180. Cf. Vulgate, Ps 83:13. Erasmus employs both the *privabit* of the Vulgate and his own insertion, *fraudabit*.

181. Cf. Matt. 7:4-5; Luke 6:41-42.

182. The story is told in 1 Sam., chapters 9-11.

183. *Adagia*, 256B. Tracing the proverb to Aesop, Erasmus cites uses of it in Catullus, Horace, Perseus, and Jerome. His explanation follows the sense of the passage here: "Non videmus nostra ipsorum vitia, cum aliena curiosis oculis perspiciamus."

184. This "well-known adage" ("In sua quemque artificem arte furem esse") seems to have eluded Erasmus' collection in *Adagia*.

185. Cf. the letter to Jodocus Jonas of 1521 (EE, IV, 1202): "Responsible physicians don't rush immediately to drastic remedies. They first treat the ailing body with milder medicines, and regulate the dosage in such a way as to heal it, not bury it."

186. Cf. Gen. 3:12-13.

187. Perhaps an adaptation of Luke 16:10: "He that is faithful in that which is least is faithful also in much."

188. An echo, one suspects, of the debate with Luther, increasingly bitter in tone, which began in 1524 with the publication of Erasmus' *De libero arbitrio (On the Freedom of the Will)*. As Preserved Smith pointed out, what was a matter of life and death to Luther, was scarcely more than a subject of interesting conversation to Erasmus (*Erasmus* [New York, 1923], p. 351).

189. Luke 14:27; Matt. 10:38. Erasmus fuses the two verses.

190. As poetry was a "speaking picture." The source of this sixteenth-century commonplace would seem to be Horace's *Ars Poetica*, 361: "ut pictura poesis: erit quae si propius stes te capiat magis, et quaedam se longius abstes."

191. Although there were three sophists by this name, Erasmus was probably referring to Philostratus the Athenian, author of a long Greek romance called *Apollonius of Tyre,* as well as a collection of letters.

192. Erasmus uses very much the same simile in "A Fish Diet": "An engaged girl, before marriage, comforts herself with her fiance's letters; she kisses the gifts that come from him; she embraces pictures of him. But when she possesses him in person, she neglects the things formerly loved for the sake of the lover." (Craig Thompson, *The Colloquies of Erasmus* [Chicago, 1965], p. 321)

193. Apparently a reference to Rom. 14:5; the Vulgate, however, has *abundet,* not *acquiescat* as in Erasmus.

194. For a similar expression of Erasmus's views on confession, see the colloquy "The Whole Duty of Youth," pp. 38-39 in Thompson's translation, where Gaspar points out the advisability of finding as confessor "a man of some learning, dignity, demonstrated integrity, and a sober tongue." Many years before, Erasmus had made the distinction between the genuine and a merely formal confession: "I would rather that you loathe, inwardly and genuinely, your bad habits than that you should deprecate them verbally over and over again before a priest." (*The Enchiridion of Erasmus,* tr. Raymond Himelick [Bloomington, Indiana, 1963], p. 128)

More's views resemble those of Erasmus. In *A Dialogue of Comfort* he speaks of "the scrupulous person which frameth himself many times double the fear that he hath cause, and many times a great fear where there is no cause at all, and of that that is indeed no sin maketh a venial, and that that is venial imagineth to be deadly, and yet for all that falleth in them, being namely of their nature such as no man long liveth without. And then he feareth that he be never full confessed nor never full contrite, and then that his sins be never full forgiven him; and then he confesseth and confesseth again, and cumbreth himself and his confessor both." (Everyman ed. [London, 1962], II:244.)

195. First introduced into the celebration of the Mass in the tenth and eleventh centuries, "prose" was originally the name attached to any versicle or strophe introduced into, or supplementary to, the other ecclesiastical chants. Earliest proses were without rhyme or assonance and followed traditional patterns of neumes; they later departed, however, for these traditional patterns to become more melodious and popular in character and quite regular in metrics. As proses proliferated, quality declined, especially in northern Europe, and many were considered an encumbrance to the Divine Office, being composed in, or translated into, the vernacular tongues and sung by the people on every possible occasion. Ultimately Pius V and the Council of Trent reduced to four those to be used as part of the Mass: the *Victimae Paschali, the Veni Sancte Spiritus,* the *Lauda Sion Salvatorem,* and the *Dies Irae.* In the early eighteenth century the *Stabat Mater* was added. (*Dictionary of Hymnology,* ed. John Julian, I)

196. ". . . Vocum caudae, ad singulos versus in longum productae." It is possible that Erasmus is referring to the increasingly florid use of *melisma* in liturgical music, the process whereby a single syllable might be spun out through many notes. This technique seems to have gone hand in hand with more and more involved counterpoint until many of the devout found the sacred texts too much obscured by the settings, another practice which the Council of Trent felt obliged to take up.

His *Ecclesiastes* registers a similar complaint against both, proses and *vocum caudae*. The prayers of the service were being mingled with, or even displaced by, songs that were too often crude and silly, wholly inappropriate for divine worship. Sometimes as much as the whole half-hour was given over to the singing of proses understood by no one, while the *caudae* were as long as, or longer than, the song itself (cf. LB, V, 859B-C).

The growing use of instrumental music in churches also culminated in strictures and regulations by the council. Edward Lowinsky, ("Music in Renaissance Culture," *JHI*, XV [1954]), notes contemporary records of masses performed with two alternating choirs of woodwind and brass instruments and tambourines. The result of this "secular gaiety invading the sacred sphere" was a chorus of increasingly bitter complaints about the profanation of church music throughout the sixteenth century.

Something of this was in More's mind, no doubt, when Hythloday is made to say of his Utopians, "But in one thing doubtless they go exceeding far beyond us. For all their music, both that they play upon instruments and that they sing with man's voice, doth so resemble and express natural affections, the sound and tune is so applied and made agreeable to the thing, that whether it be a prayer or else a ditty of gladness, of patience, of trouble, of mourning, or of anger, the fashion of the melody doth so represent the meaning of the thing, that it doth wonderfully move, stir, pierce, and inflame the hearers' minds." (Everyman ed., II: 129).

197. Two phrases which, according to a modern theologian, "crystallize the antithesis between the Roman and Reforming positions." *Ex opere operantis* ("from the work of the doer") lays all the emphasis in the sacrament of the Eucharist upon the recipient's moral condition in causing or receiving sacramental grace. *Ex opere operato* ("by the work done") lays the emphasis upon the doing of the action, expressing the dogma that this grace is caused by the sacramental rite validly performed and not by the merits of the recipient or the minister. The first position, by stressing the doer and his faith tends to relegate the liturgy to reflection upon, and commemoration of, those principles of truth which it embodies, an essentially Protestant position. (See Cyril C. Richardson, "The Eucharistic Sacrifice," *Anglican Theological Review* 32 [1950]: 61.)

198. Richardson (*ibid.*, pp. 54-66) points out that the sixteenth-century conflict between Rome and Protestant elements began over the mode of presentation of the Lord's Supper, the Romanist view holding

that the Mass is not only a sacrifice of praise and thanksgiving, a "bare commemoration of the sacrifice consummated on the Cross, but also a propitiatory sacrifice for the living and the dead," with the Reforming groups agreeing in a flat denial of this position, maintaining that no real sacrifice is made, only a "commemoration of the Cross," and a "spiritual oblation" of praise to God for His sacrifice. Thus in their revisions of the Roman Mass the Reformers deleted all the sacrificial references (e.g., "altar") and thus "attenuated or even abolished the themes of offering and destruction which properly precede the Communion."

199. See Luke 18:13.

200. Broadly, those who denied the Real Presence of Christ in the Eucharist, holding that the bread and wine were the Body and Blood of Christ only in a "sacramental" (i.e., metaphorical) sense. Among the Reformers themselves, however, as Erasmus suggests here, there was less than total agreement. Luther seems to have given the name "Sacramentarian" to theologians like Zwingli and Oecolampadius, who differed from his own theory of "consubstantiation." For an account of disagreement among English Reformers see, for example, C. W. Dugmore, *The Mass and the English Reformers* (London, 1958), pp. 87-97.

201. In 1512 the Spanish ambassadors were instructed to ask the Lateran Council to reduce, because of abuses, the number of feasts to those of Christ, the Blessed Virgin Mary, the Apostles, and a few others. In 1523 Cuthbert Tunstall, Bishop of London, ordered all feasts for the dedication of churches to be transferred to and celebrated on October 3, since these feasts habitually gave rise, not to prayer, fasting, and meditation, but drinking, dancing, brawling, even murder (see Edward L. Surtz, *The Praise of Wisdom* [Chicago, 1957], pp. 187-188).

202. Rom. 14:4.

203. 1 Cor. 1:14-16.

204. Acts 16:27-33.

205. Matt. 22:21; Mark 12:17; Luke 20:25.

206. Cf. 1 Pet. 2:13-14; Heb. 13:7.

207. Eph. 6:5.

208. Originally a movement identifying the Lord's Day with the Jewish Sabbath. The medieval doctrine was rejected by the Reformers but revived by English Puritans, though applied to Sunday, which was held to be a day of sermons, meditation, and sobriety. The movement seems to have become more powerful after Erasmus's day.

209. Gal. 1:8.

210. *Adagia*, 209A.

211. 1 Thess. 2:16.

212. Horace, *Carmina* 3.4.65.

213. Isa. 32:18.

SELECTIONS FROM
THE LETTERS

*This letter to Paul Volz, abbot of a Bene-
dictine monastery near Schlettstadt, in
Alsace, first appeared as a preface to
an edition of the* Enchiridion Militis
Christiani *which Froben published in 1518.
An anonymous English translation appeared in 1533, and is now believed to
have been written by William Tyndale in
the early twenties. A vernacular version
did not appear until Henry VIII was
willing to offend Rome. The Latin text
(EE,III, 858) contained an additional
paragraph on early monasticism which
Erasmus wrote for his 1529* Opus Epistolarum. *Not included in Tyndale's translation, it appears in modern language in
John C. Olin,* Christian Humanism and the
Reformation *(New York, 1957), 109-133.*

ALBEIT, MOST VIRTUOUS father, that the little book to the
which I have given this name or title *Enchiridion Militis Christiani,* which many a day ago I made for myself only and for a certain friend of mine being utterly unlearned,[1] hath begun to mislike
and displease me the less, for as much as I do see that it is allowed
of you and other virtuous and learned men such as you be, of whom
(as ye are indeed endued with godly learning, and also with learned
godliness) I know nothing to be approved but that which is both

110

holy and also clerkly; yet it hath begun well nigh also to please alike me now, when I see it (after that it hath been so often times printed) yet still to be desired and greatly called for, as if it were a new work made of late—if so be the printers do not lie to flatter me withal. But again there is another thing which often times grieveth me in my mind, that a certain well learned friend of mine long ago said, very properly and sharply checking me, that there was more holiness seen in the little book than in the whole author and maker thereof.

Indeed he spake these words in his jesting, bourdingly,[2] but would to God he had not spoken so truly as he bourded bitterly. And that grieveth me so much the more because the same thing hath chanced to come likewise to pass in him for the changing of whose manners principally I took upon me this labor and travail, for he also not only hath not withdrawn himself from the court, but is daily much deeper drowned therein than he was afore time, for what good purpose I cannot tell, but as he professeth himself with much great misery.[3] And yet, for all that, I do not greatly pity my friend, because that peradventure adversity of fortune may teach him once to repent himself and to amend, seeing that he would not follow and do after my counsel and admonitions. And verily, though I—enforcing me to the same thing and purpose—have been turned and tossed with so many chances and tempests that Ulysses, a man living ever in trouble (which Homer speaketh of) might be counted in comparison to me even Polycrates, which ever lived in prosperity, without any manner trouble, I do not utterly repente me of my labor, seeing it hath moved and provoked so many unto the study of godly virtue; nor I myself am not utterly to be blamed and rebuked although my living be not in all points agreeing to mine own precept and counsels. It is some part of godliness when one with all his heart desireth and is willing to be made good & virtuous; nor such a mind so well intending I suppose is not to be cast away, although his purpose be not ever luckily performed. To this we ought to endeavor ourself all our life long, and no doubt but by the reason that we so often times shall attempt it, once at the last we shall attain it. Also he hath dispatched a good piece of a doubtful journey which hath learned well of the journey the way.

Therefore am I nothing moved with the mocks of certain persons which despise this little book as nothing erudite & clerkly, saying that it might have been made of a child that learned his A, b, c,

because it entreateth nothing of Dunce's [4] questions, as though
nothing without those could be done with learning. I do not care
if it be not so quick, so it be godly; let it not make them instructed
& ready to disputations in schools, so that it make them apt to
keep Christ's peace. Let it not be profitable or helping for the disputation in divinity, so it make for a divine life. For what good
should it do to entreat of that thing that every man intermeddleth
with? Who hath not in handling questions of divinity, or what else
do all our swarms of school men? There be almost as many commentaries upon the master of the *Sentence* [5] as be names of divines.
There is neither measure nor number of summularies,[6] which, after
the manner of apothecaries, mingle often times sundry things together and make of old things new, of new things old, of one thing
many, of many things one.

How can it be that these great volumes instruct us to live well
and after a Christian manner, which a man in all his life can have
leisure once to look over? In like manner as if a physician should
prescribe unto him that lieth sick in peril of death to read Jacobus'
de Partibus,[7] or such other huge volumes, saying that there he
should find remedy for his disease; but in the meantime the patient
dieth, wanting present remedy wherewith he might be helped.

In such a fugitive life it is necessary to have a ready medicine
at the hand. How many volumes have they made of restitution, of
confession, of slander, and other things innumerable! And though
they bolt and search out by piecemeal everything by itself, and
so define everything as if they mistrusted all other men's wits, yea
as though they mistrusted the goodness & mercy of God while they
do prescribe how He ought to punish & reward every fact, either
good or bad, yet they agree not amongst themselves, nor yet sometimes do open the thing plainly, if a man would look near upon it,
so much diversity both of wits and circumstances is there.

Moreover, although it were so that they had determined all things
well and truly, yet besides this that they handle and treat of these
things after a barbarous and unpleasant fashion, there is not one
amongst a thousand that can have any leisure to read over these
volumes. Or who is able to bear about with him *Secundam se-
cunda*,[8] the work of Saint Thomas? And yet there is no man but he
ought to use a good life, to the which Christ would that the way
should be plain and open for every man, and that not by inexplic-
able crooks of disputations not able to be resolved, but by a true

and a sincere faith & charity not feigned, whom hope doth follow which is never ashamed.

And finally let the great doctors, which must needs be but few in comparison to all other men, study & busy themself in those great volumes. And yet, nevertheless, the unlearned and rude multitude which Christ died for ought to be provided for; and he hath taught a great portion of Christian virtue which hath inflamed men unto the love thereof. The wise king when he did teach his son true wisdom took much more pain in exhorting him thereunto than in teaching him, as who should say that to love wisdom were in a manner to have attained it. It is a great shame and rebuke both for lawyers & also physicians, that they have of a set purpose, and for the nonce, made their art and science full of difficulty and hard to be attained or come by, to the intent that both their gaines and advantage might be the more plentiful & their glory and praise among the unlearned people the greater. But it is a much more shameful thing to do the same in the philosophy of Christ. But rather contrariwise, we ought to endeavor ourselves with all our strengths to make it so easy as can be, and plain to every man. Nor let not this be our study, to appear learned ourselves, but to allure very many to a Christian man's life.

Preparation and ordinance is made now for war to be made against the Turks, which for whatsoever purpose it is begun, we ought to pray, not that it may turn to the profit of a few certain persons but that it may be to the common & general profit of all men. But what think you should come of it if to such of them as shall be overcome (for I do not suppose that they shall all be killed with weapons) we shall lay the works of Occam, Durandus, Duns, Gabriel, Alvarus, or any such schoolmen, for the intent to bring them in mind to take Christ's profession upon them? What shall they imagine and think in their minds (for surely even they, though they be naught else, are men and have wit & reason) when they shall hear those thorny & cumbrous, inextricable, subtle imaginations of instances, of formalities, of quiddities, of relation: namely, when they shall see these great doctors & teachers of religion & holiness so far disagreeing and of so sundry opinions among themself & often times they dispute & reason so long one with another until they change color & be pale and revile one another, spitting each at other and finally dealing buffets & blows each to other? When they shall see the Black Friars fight & scold for their

Thomas, & then the Gray Friars matched with them,[9] defending on the other party their subtle and fervent hot doctors, which they call seraphicos, some speaking as reals, some as nominals?[10] When they shall also see the thing to be of so great difficulty that they can never discuss sufficiently with what words they may speak of Christ—as though one did deal or had to do with a wayward spirit which he had raised up unto his own destruction if he did fail never so little in the prescript words of conjuring, & not rather with our most merciful Saviour, which desireth nothing else of us but a pure life and a simple?

I beseech thee for the love of God show me what shall we bring about with all these reckonings, especially if our manners & our life be like to the proud doctrine & learning? And if they shall see & well perceive our ambition & desirousness of honor by our gorgeousness, more than ever any tyrant did use, our avarice & covetousness by our bribing and polling,[11] our lecherousness by the defiling of maidens & wives, our cruelness by th'oppressions done of us—with what face or how for shame shall we offer to them the doctrine of Christ, which is far away contrary to all these things?

The best way and most effectual to overcome & win the Turks should be if they shall perceive the thing which Christ taught and expressed in His living, to shine in us. If they shall perceive that we do not highly gape for their empires, do not desire their gold and good, do not covet their possession, but that we seek nothing else but only their souls' health & the glory of God. This is that right true & effectuous divinity, the which in time past subdued unto Christ arrogant and proud philosophers, and also the mighty & invincible princes. And if we thus do, then shall Christ ever be present & help us. For truly it is not meet nor convenient to declare ourselves Christian men by this proof or token, if we kill very many, but rather if we save very many; not if we send thousands of heathen people to hell, but if we make many infidels faithful; not if we cruelly curse & excommunicate them, but if we with devout prayers & with all our hearts desire their health, and pray unto God to send them better minds.

If this be not our intent it shall sooner come to pass that we shall degenerate & turn into Turks ourselves than that we shall cause them to become Christian men. And although the chance of war, which is ever doubtful & uncertain, should fall so luckily to that we had gotten the victory so should it be brought to pass that the Pope's dominion & his cardinals' might be enlarged, but not the kingdom of Christ, which finally flourisheth and is in prosperity if faith, love, peace, & chastity be quick and strong, which thing I trust shall be brought to pass by the good governance and provision of the Pope Leo the Tenth, unless the great trouble and rage of worldly business pluck him from his very good purpose another way.

Christ doth profess to be primate & head himself in the heavenly kingdom, which never doth flourish but when celestial things be advanced. Nor Christ did not die for this purpose, that goods of the world—that riches, that armour, & the rest of the ruffling fashion of the world—should be now in the hands & rule of certain priests, which things were wont to be in the hands of the gentiles, or at least amongst lay princes not much differing from gentiles. But in my mind it were the best, before we should try them in battle, to attempt them with epistles and some little books. But with what manner of epistles? Not with threatening epistles, or with books full of tyranny, but with those which might show fatherly charity & resemble the very heart and mind of Peter and Paul, & which should not only pretend and show outwardly the title of the apostles, but which also should savor and taste of the efficacy and strength of the apostles. Not because I do not know that all the true fountain and vein of Christ's philosophy is hid in the gospel and the epistles of the apostles, but the strange manner of phrase, and often times the troublous speaking of diverse crooked figures & tropes, be of so great difficulty that often times we ourself also must labor right sore before we can perceive them. Therefore, in mine opinion the best were that some both well learned men and good of living should have this office assigned and put unto them, to make a collection and to gather the sum of Christ's philosophy out of the pure fountain of the gospel and the epistles and most approved interpreters, and so plainly that yet it might be clerkly and erudite, and so briefly that it might also be plain.

Those things which concern faith or belief, let them be contained in a few articles. Those also that appertain to the manner of living, let them be showed and taught in few words, and that after such fashion that they may perceive the yoke of Christ to be pleasant and easy, and not grievous and painful, so that they may perceive that they have gotten fathers and not tyrants, feeders and not robbers, pillers nor pollers, & that they be called to their souls' health and not compelled to servitude.

Undoubted they also be men; neither their hearts be of so hard iron or adamant but that they may be mollified and won with benefits and kindness, wherewith even very wild beasts be woxen gentle and tame. And the most effectuous thing is the true verity of Christ. But let the Pope also command them whom he appointeth to this business that they never swerve nor go from the true pattern and example of Christ, nor in any place have any respect to the carnal affects and desires of men.

And such a thing my mind was about to bring to pass as well as I could when I made this book of *Enchiridion*. I did see the common people of Christendom, not only in effect, but also in opinions to be corrupted. I considered the most part of those which profess them selves to be pastors and doctors to abuse the titles of Christ to their proper [12] advantage. And yet will I make no mention of those men after whose will and pleasure the world is ruled and turned up and down, whose vices, though they be never so manifest, a man may scarcely once wince. And in such great darkness, in such great troublous ruffling of the world, in so great diversity of men's opinions, whither should we rather fly for succour than to the very great and sure anchor of Christ's doctrine, which is the gospel? Who, being a good man indeed, doth not see and lament this marvelous corrupt world? When was there ever more tyranny? When did avarice reign more largely, and less punished? When were ceremonies at any time more in estimation? When did our iniquity so largely show with more liberty? When was ever charity so cold? What is brought, what is read, what is decreed or determined, but it tasteth and savoreth of ambition and lucre?

Oh, how infortunate were we if Christ had not left some sparks of His doctrine unto us &, as it were, lively and everlasting veins of His Godly mind. Hereto, therefore, we must enforce ourself to know these sparks, leaving the coals of men's fantasies. Let us seek these veins until we find fresh water which springeth into everlasting life. We delve and dig the ground marvelously deep for to pluck out riches, which nourisheth vice; and shall we not labor then the rich earth of Christ to get out that thing which is our souls' health? There was never no storm of vices that did so overcome and quench the heat of charity but it might be restored again at this flint stone. Christ is a stone, but this stone hath sparks of celestial fire and veins of lively water.

In time past Abraham in every land did dig pits and holes, searching in every place the veins of lively water; but those same being stopped up again by the Philistines with earth, Isaac and his servants did delve again, and not being only content to restore the old, did also make new. But then the Philistines did scold and chide, yet he did not cease from digging.[13] And in this our time we have Philistines which do prefer the naughty earth to the lively fountain, even those which be worldly wise and have their respect to earthly things, and wring and wrest God's doctrine and His gospel to their carnal affections, making it serve to their ambition, bolstering up therewith their fifthy lucre & tyranny. And if now any Isaac or any of his family should dig and find some true and pure vein, by and by they brabble and cry against him; perceiving right well that that vein shall hurt their ambition although it make never so much for the glory of Christ, straightways they cast in naughty earth, and with a corrupt interpretation they stop up the vein and drive away the digger. Or at the least they make it so muddy with clay & filthiness that whosoever drinketh thereof shall draw unto him more slime & naughtiness than he shall good liquor. They will not have those which thirst & desire righteousness to drink of the pure liquor, but they bring them unto their old worn & all too trodden cisterns, which have broken stones and mortar—but water they have none.

But yet, for all this, the very true children of Isaac, that is, the true worshippers of Christ, must not be wearied & driven away from this labor; for verily even they which thrust naughty earth into the fountain of the gospel would be counted the very worshippers of Christ. So that indeed nothing nowadays is more perilous than to teach truly Christ's learning. So greatly have the Philistines prevailed, fighting for their earth, preaching earthly things for celestiall and men's inventions for God's commandments, that is to say, not teaching those things which make for the glory of Christ but those things which be for their own advantage, which be pardons, compositions, & such like pelfare.[14] And this they do so much more perilously, because they cloak their covetousness with the titles & names of great princes, of the Pope of Rome, yea, of Christ also Himself. But there is no man that doth more for the

Pope's profit or business than he that teacheth Christ's learning purely & truly, whereof He is the chief teacher. There is no man that doth more good to princes, or deserveth more of them, than he which endeavoreth himself that the people may be wealthy & in prosperity.

But some of the flock of schoolmen will here speak against me, saying it is easy to any man to give general precepts: what is to be desired and what is to be eschewed; but what shall be answered then to those that ask counsel for so many fortunes & chances?

First, I answer that there be more diverse kinds of such worldly business than that any living person can give direct and sure answer to each one of them. Secondarily, there is such diversity of circumstances, which if a man do not know, it is not well possible to make an answer. In conclusion, I doubt greatly whether they themselves have any sure answer that they may make, seeing they differ in so many things amongst themselves. And they also which amongst them be of the wiser sort do not thus answer, "This, ye shall do, this ye shall not do," but of this manner: "This, in mine opinion were the better; this I suppose to be intolerable."

But if we have that simple and bright eye which the gospel speaketh of, if the house of our mind have in it the candle of pure faith set up a candlestick, all these trifles shall easily be put away and avoided, as it were clouds or mists. If we have the rule & pattern of Christ's charity, to it we may apply & make meet all other things right easily.

But what will ye do when this rule doth not agree with those things which hath been communly used so many hundred years, and which be ordained and established by the laws of princes? For this thing chanceth very oft. Ye must not condemn that thing which princes do in executing their office, but again do not corrupt & defile the heavenly philosophy with men's deeds. Let Christ continue & abide—as He is indeed—a very center or middle point unmoved, having certain circles going round about Him. Move not the mark out of his own place. Those which be in the first circle, next to the center (that is to say, next to Christ), as priests, bishops, cardinals, popes, and such, to whom it belongeth to follow the lamb whithersoever He shall go—let them embrace & hold fast that most pure part &, so far forth as they may, let them communicate & plenteously give the same unto their next neighbors. In the second circle let all temporal and lay princes be, which in keeping war & making laws, after a certain manner do service to Christ either when with rightful battle they drive away their enemies & defend & maintain the public peace and tranquillity of the commonwealth, or else when with punishment according to the laws they punish malefactors & evildoers.

And yet, because they can not choose but of necessity be occupied and busied in such things as be joined with the most vile dregs & filth of the earth & with the business of the world, it is jeopardous lest they fall somewhat further off from the center & mark, lest they make sometimes war for their own pleasure & not for the commonwealth, lest—under the pretext of justice—they use cruelty upon those whom they might reform with mercy, lest—under the title of lordship—they pill & poll those people whose goods they ought to defend.

And moreover, as Christ, like the fountain of everlasting fire, doth draw next unto Him the order of priests, & maketh them of like nature—that is to say, pure & clean from all corruption of worldly dregs and filthiness—so in like case it is the office of priests, & especially of the highest, so much as they can, to call & draw unto them those that be princes and have power and authority. And if it fortune at any time that war do rise suddenly in any place, let the bishops endeavor themselves, so much as in them is, either to end the strives and variances without shedding of blood. Or, if that cannot be brought to pass, by reason of the great storms of worldly business, yet let them so do that as little blood as may be be shed and that the war may shortly be brought to an end.

In times past the bishops' authority had place even in just punishments, and hath gotten divers times (as Saint Augustine plainly in his epistle doth testify) the malefactor from the hands of temporal judges. For some things there be so necessary unto the order of the commonwealth that partly yet Christ did dissimule at them, and partly he put them from Him, and partly neither approving nor disallowing them, did in a manner wink and look beside them. He would not know the money of Caesar, nor the scripture [15] upon it. The tribute He commanded to be paid if it were due & debt, as though it little pertained to Him, so that God had His duty. The woman taken and found in adultery He neither openly absolved, but only did bid her that she should no more do so. Of those which were condemned of Pilate, whose blood he intermingled amongst their sacrifices,[16] He neither said it was well done nor evil, but only threatened every man that they should be punished with a like destruction if they did not amend. Moreover, when He was desired to divide the inheritance between the two brethren, He plainly refused it, as an unworthy thing for Him to give judgment of such gross matters, which did teach things heavenly.[17]

And also, of the other part, there be certain things which He openly abhorred, as the covetous pharisees, the hypocrites, the proud rich folks—saying unto them, "Woe be unto you."[18] He never rebuked the Apostles more sharply than when they would have been avenged, or when they were ambitious. When they asked Him whether they should command fire to be sent down from heaven to burn up the city from whence they were shut forth, He answered and said to them, "Ye know not of what spirit ye are."[19] When Peter was about to call Him unto the world from His passion suffering, He called him an Adversary.[20] When they contended about the preëminence, which of them should be the best, how often & how many ways doth He call them back to a contrary mind? And other things there be which He teacheth and commandeth openly to be observed: as not to resist evil, to do good to thine enemies, to use meekness of mind, and other like. These must be departed in sunder, & every of them set in order in his own place.

Let us not, therefore, straightways make Christ an author of all things which be done by princes & temporall officers; nor defend it (as we call it) to be done by God's law. They deal & meddle with many things which be low and gross, not altogether of the very pureness of a Christian man; yet they be not to be rebuked, inasmuch as they be necessary to the maintenance of order to be observed. Nor we be not by the ministering of their office made good, albeit that by them it is caused that we be less evil & that they which be evil do less hurt and noyance to the commonwealth. And therefore they also ought to have their honor, because they do somewhat serve the justice of God and the public & common tranquillity, without the which sometimes those things be troubled and vexed which belong to godly holiness. They must be honored when they do their office; and if sometimes they use their power for their own pleasure or profit, yet peradventure it were the best to suffer them, lest more hurt should spring thereof. For there appeareth an image, or rather a shadow, of the divine justice in them, which justice yet ought to shine more evidently, and more purely, in the living & laws of priests. An image both of another manner shows in a mirror of glass than it doth in iron.

And in the third circle must all the common people be, as the most gross part of all this world, but not yet so gross but that they pertain unto the mystical body of Christ; for the eyes be not only members of the body, but also the legs, the feet, and the privy parts. And those which be in the third circle we ought to suffer in their infirmity that, as much as is possible, we do call them unto those things which be more approved of Christ. For in the mystical body he that but late was the foot, may be the eye. And like as the princes, if they be not all the best, must not with chiding be exasperate, lest (as Saint Augustine saith)[21] when they be moved, they stir up more perilous tragedies, so the weak people—like as Christ suffered His Apostles and nourished them—must be suffered and after a fatherly manner cherished until they wax aged and strong in Christ. For godliness also hath his infancy, it hath mean age, it hath full strength and perfect age.

Yet all men after their degree must endeavor themselves to attain & come unto Christ. The elements have every one his proper place, but the fire, which hath the highest place, by little and little draweth all the other unto him and, so much as he can, turneth them into his nature. The clear water he turneth into the air, and the air clarified he transformeth into his own nature. Saint Paul doth in many things suffer and pardon the Corinthians, but in the mean season putting difference between those things which he did proffer in the name of his Lord unto them that were perfect, and those things which he did pardon, that were written in his own name unto them that were yet weak & young in Christ; but ever on this trust, that they should profit and go forward to more strength and perfection. And also he travaileth again to bring forth the Galatians until Christ be fashioned in them.

Now if any man will think this circle to be more convenient for princes, I will not strive greatly with him. But whatsoever is without the third circle is at all times and in all points to be hated and refused: as ambition, and desire of money, lechery, ire, vengeance, envy, backbiting, and such other pestilences, which then only be made incurable when they, disguised with the visor and cloak of holiness & virtue, do creep into the circle afore spoken: that is, when under the pretext of executing the law and justice, we use our tyranny, when by the occasion of religion we provide for great lucre, when under the title of defending the church we hunt for worldly power and authority, and whensoever those things be commended as things pertaining unto Christ which be disagreeing much from His learning.

Therefore, the mark must be set before every man which they ought to shoot at; and there is but one mark, which is Christ, and His most pure learning. If thou set forth a worldly mark in the stead of a celestial mark, then shall there be nothing whereunto a man ought justly enforce himself which laboreth to profit and go forward. Every man ought to enforce himself to that which is best and most perfect, that at the least we may attain and come to the mean things.

And there is no cause why we should put away any kind or manner of living from this mark. The perfection of Christ consisteth only in the affects [22] & not in the manner or kind of living; it consisteth in the minds, & not in the garments, or in meats and drinks. There be among the monks which be scarce able to be put in the third circle, and yet I speak of those which be good but yet weak, and not perfect. There be amongst these that have had two wives which Christ thinketh worthy for the first circle.

Nor yet in the meantime I do no wrong to any manner living, or profession, though I propone and set forth afore every man that thing which is best and most perfect—unless ye would think Plato to have done injury against all cities because in his book of the governing of a city, or a commonwealth he feigned such example of a commonwealth as yet never any man could see. Or except ye do think that Quintilian hath hurt the whole order of orators because he feigned such an example of an orator as yet never was. And though thou be far from the principal and chief pattern, Christ, thou art not yet therefore cast away, but extimulate & moved to go forward and profit. Art thou near the mark? Then art thou monished & counseled to approach more near; for there was never yet any man that went so far forward but that he might have gone much more near the mark.

There is no kind of living but it hath some perilous points annexed unto it to cause men to degenerate from the truth. And whosoever showeth those jeopardous & dangerous points doth not derogate or minish the honor of the order, nor speak against it, but rather is for the profit thereof. As the felicity of princes is in danger to fall into tyranny, is in danger & jeopardy of foolishness and flattering, now whosoever showeth those dangers to be eschewed doth deserve thanks of the order of princes. Nor he doth not speak against their majesty, wherein they glory, which doth show in what things their very majesty doth consist, which also doth put them in remembrance—whereto they were sworn when they took their authority—what is their duty unto their people and what they ought to do unto their officers.

The heads and rulers of the Church have, in a manner, affinity with two pestilent vices, avarice and ambition, which well perceiving, Saint Peter, the chief pastor next unto Christ, doth monish the bishops to feed their flock, and not to pill, poll, and flay them; [23] nor that they should not feed them because of any filthy advantage, but of their free and ready will; nor that they should use themself as lords upon them, but that by the example of life they should provoke them to godliness, rather than by threatening and power. Doth he then speak against the order of priests, which doth show by what means and how the bishops may truly be great, mighty, and rich?

Moreover, the kind of religious men is accompanied most commonly (besides other enormities) with superstition, pride, hypocrisy, and backbiting. He doth not straight condemn their manner of living which doth show & admonish them in what things most true religion doth stand or rest, and how much the true godliness of a Christian man is away from pride, and how far true charity is from all feigning and deceit, how much backbiting and slandering and venomousness of tongue is contrary to pure and true holiness. And specially, if he show what is to be eschewed, after such sober and discreet manner that he do neither name any man nor touch any order.

What thing is that in this mortal life so fortunate and prosperous but it hath some pestilent things annexed unto it? Therefore, like as he doth not noy [24] the health of the body, helpeth it, whosoever showeth what things corrupteth health and what things preserveth it, so he doth not dissuade men from religion but exhorteth them rather unto it, which showeth the corruptous infections thereof and also the remedies.

For I am informed that there be divers which so judgeth of this book, as though the precepts thereof did withdraw and turn away men's minds from the life of religious men because they do not so much praise and allow ceremonies, neither yet man's constitutions, as some would which indeed overmuch regard them. And there can be nothing so circumspectly spoken but that thereof lewd and evil persons do take occasion either of quarreling or else of sinning, so that it is dangerful nowadays to any man to teach anything well. If a man should dissuade from much war and battle, which now of long time hath been used—worse than ever any amongst the gentiles [25]—for things of no value, he should be noted by and by of the pickquarrels to be one of those which think that no war is lawful for a Christian man. For these which were the bringers up and authors of this sentence we have made heretics because a pope—I wot not who—doth seem to approve and allow war. And yet he is not suspected nor noted of heresy which doth provoke and stir up men to battle, and bloweth the trumpet thereunto for every trifling matter, against the doctrine both of Christ & of His Apostles.

If a man admonish that this is a deed truly belonging to the successor of an Apostle, to bring the Turks unto religion with Christ's help rather than with war, anon he is suspected, as though he affirmed not to be lawful for Christian men to withstand the Turks when they invade us. If a man show & praise the temperance that was in the Apostles, and speak anything against the great superfluity that is used nowadays, there be that note him for a favorer of the Ebionites. And if a man exhort diligently that these which be married should rather be joined together by the consents and agreeing of their minds than by the embracings of their bodies, & so purely to use matrimony that as much as might be, it were made like to virginity, he is anon suspected to think that every act of matrimony were sin and unlawful, as the Marcionites did. If a man do admonish that in exercise and disputations, specially of divinity, there should be no ambitious pertinacy to overcome his fellows in defending his own opinion, nor no ambition to show what they can do in commonplaces, he is wrongfully accused, as though he did condemn utterly all school learning. For Saint Augustine, when he giveth warning to the logicians that they should beware of lust to brawl and chide, doth not condemn logic, but showeth the pestilence thereof that it might be eschewed.

Also, if a man note or reprove the preposterous & wrong judgment of the common people, which among virtues esteem those to be of most great value & chiefest which be of the lowest sort; and contrary, which also among vices most sore hateth and abhorreth those which be the smallest & lightest, and clene cam [26] when they be most abominable & grievous, anon he is accused, as though he should favor those vices which he showeth to be more grievous than other, and as though he should condemn those good deeds and benefits to whom he preferreth other more holy and better. As if a man did admonish and give us warning that it is more sure to trust unto good deeds than to trust to the Pope's pardons, but preferreth that which by Christ's learning & doctrine is of more certainty.

Also if a man do teach those for to do better which tarry at home and provide for their wife and children than those which go to see Rome, Jerusalem, or Saint James; & that money which they should spend in that long & perilous journey to be better & more devoutly spent upon poor folks,[27] yet condemneth not he their good intent, but preferreth that which is more near to very godliness. And this is a thing not only used now in our time, but also in times heretofore past, to abhor some vices as though there were none other, fawning upon the rest as they were no vices at all, when in very deed, they be more detestable than those which we so hate & abhor.

Saint Augustine doth complain in his epistles [28] that lasciviousness of the flesh is only imputed unto the priests of Africa as a vice, and that the vice of covetousness and drunkenness be taken well nigh for a praise. This specially we speak most against and cry out upon and exaggerate for an exceeding abominable fact, if one touch the body of Christ with the same hands wherewith he hath touched the body of an harlot. And there be some over-raging bold that be not afraid openly to affirm that it is less sin for a woman to commit carnal acts with a brute beast than to lie with a priest. Now he that something rebuketh their unshamefastness doth not therefore favor the naughtiness of priests, but showeth that they regard not those offenses which be a great deal more to be cried out upon.

But if a priest be a dicer, a fighter, a brawler, all unlearned, drowned and wrapped in temporal business, all given to the evil service of evil princes—yet against him they cry nothing at all, which, altogether worldly and polluted, doth handle and intermeddle with holy mysteries. When a priest is a flatterer or a pick-quarrel which with his bitter tongue and false lies doth hurt the names of those which never offended him, but rather hath done him pleasure, why do we not now cry out? Oh what an horrible sin is this, to receive the Lord God, which suffered His passion for sinners, with that tongue which is full of poison of hell & with that mouth wherewith thou killest & flayest an innocent! But this evil and ungraciousness we set so little by that in a manner those men are even praised for it which profess themselves to be the most religious amongst religious men. There is no man that denieth but they be to be reprehended & sore rebuked which nourish and keep at home concubines, to the evil example of all the common people; but yet these other evil vices be more hateful to God. Nor he doth therefore say that butter is naught which saith that honey is better, and more to be preferred, nor yet doth not approve the fever that counseleth the frenzy more to be avoided.

And it is hard to tell & express how great infection of manners and disposition doth spring of these perverse & wrong judgments. There be diverse things nowadays received into the order of virtues which rather have the visor and appearance of godliness than the nature and strength of it, insomuch that unless we look well unto them, and take good heed of them, they do quench and utterly destroy virtue. If it had been but a little pestilence of religion which in ceremonies doth lie covered, Paul would never so sharply have spoken against them in all his epistles. And yet do not we condemn in any place ceremonies that be moderately observed, but that all holiness should be ascribed unto them we cannot suffer.

Saint Augustine did prohibit those of the clergy which were in house with him to use any notable vesture but, if they would be commended of the people, that they should rather bring that to pass by their manners & virtuous living than by any sundry fashions of raiment.[29] But nowadays it is a world for to see what new and wonderful fashions of apparel and vesture there be. But yet I speak not against that; but this I marvel of, that those things are so overmuch regarded and set by which peradventure might be right be reprehended. And again that those things be so little regarded which we should only behold and regard.

I do not rail against the Gray Friars & Black Monks that they make much of their own rule, but because certain of them regard more their own rules than they do the gospel, which thing would to God were not found in the most part of them. I do not speak against this: that some eat fish, some live with herbs, others with eggs; but I admonish those to err & to be far out of the way which will of these things justify themselves, after the manner of the Jews thinking themselves better and preferring themselves to other for such trifles of men's invention, and take it for no default at all to hurt another man's good name with false lies.

Of the diversity of meat and drink Christ never commanded anything, nor the Apostles; but Paul often times did dissuade us from it. Christ curseth bitter slandering, which also all the Apostles doth detest and abhor; and yet, that not withstanding, we will appear religious in such using of meats, and in hurting men's fame we be bold and hardy. I pray, think you that he which doth admonish these both in general—not touching any man, and also lovingly— doth hurt religion? Who is so mad that he would be accounted eloquent for showing and bringing to light the vices that belong to monks? But these peradventure fear lest their covents & brethren would be less obedient, & lest also there would not so many desire to be shaven into their order. Yet verily, no man is more obedient to his head than he which, inspired with the Holy Ghost, is free and at liberty.[30]

True and very charity taketh all things well in worth & suffereth all things, refuseth nothing, is obedient unto rulers, not only to those that be sober and gentle, but also to those that be sharp & rough. But yet rulers must be wise of this, that they do not turn the obedience of other men into their own tyranny, and that they had liefer, therefore, to have them superstitious than holy & virtuous, whereby they might be more obedient at every beck. They have pleasure to be called "Fathers," but what carnal father is there that would have his children ever infants & young because he might use his power upon them at his own pleasure?

And of the other part, all those that purpose to profit in the liberty of Christ, of this they must beware, lest, as Saint Paul doth admonish, they make their liberty a cloak or cover to their carnal living;[31] or, as Saint Peter teacheth, with their liberty they make a cover & cloak to maliciousness.[32] And be it that one or two do abuse this liberty, yet it is not right forthwith that all other, therefore, should be ever kept in superstitiousness & bondage of ceremonies, like unto the Jews. And whosoever will mark it shall perceive that amongst these religious men no man causeth the ceremonies to be more straitly observed than they which, under the precepts thereof, be as kings over other, & servants to their own bellies rather than to Christ.

Moreover, they need not to be afraid lest such kind of Essenes be not enough spread abroad in so great diversity of men's natures, whereby it is caused that nothing is so unreasonable but divers & many will love & desire it, although their selves ought more to desire that they had true professors of religion, rather than many.

But would to God that it were provided & ordained by a law that no man should be taken in such snares afore he were xxx years of age, before he something knew himself, or knew what the nature & virtue of true religion is. But these which, like unto the Pharisees, doing their own business & providing for their own profit, wander about to make novices both by sea and land, shall never fail of young men lacking experience whom they may allure into their bails and nets, & also deceive. There be a great number of fools and simple souls in every place.

But I desire even with all my heart—and I doubt not but so do all that be very good men—that the religion of the gospel might be so pleasant to every man that they, being contented therewith, should not desire the religion of Black Monks or Grey Friars. And I doubt not but so would Saint Benedict & Francis themselves. Moses did rejoice that his own honor was defaced and dimmed with the glory of Christ; & so should those other be glad if, for the love of Christ's law, we set nothing by man's constitutions. I would that all Christian men did so live that these which now be called only religious should appear little religious, which thing even at this day is of truth, & that in many; for why should I dissimule that thing that is so manifest? And yet in the old time the beginning of the monastical life was nothing else but a going aside into a secret place from the cruelness of the idolators. And anon after, the manner of living of religious men which followed them was nothing else but a reformation & calling again to Christ; for the courts of princes in the old time showed & declared their Christendom in their titles, rather than in their living.

The bishops anon after were corrupt with ambition & covetousness, & the common people also fainted & waxed cold from that charity which was in the primitive Church; and for this purpose did Saint Benedict seek a solitary life, and then—after him— Bernard, & after that divers other did associate themselves together for this intent only, that they might use the pure & simple life of Christian men. Then after in process of time, when their riches and ceremonies did increase, their true godliness and simpleness did abate and decrease. And now, although we see men of religion to be overmuch out of good order and to use manners like unto gentiles, yet is the world filled with new institutions and kinds of religion, as though they should not fall to the same point hereafter that other have done afore them.

In times past (as I said) a religious life was nothing but a solitary life. And now these be called religious which be altogether drowned in worldly business, using plainly certain tyranny in worldly matters. And yet these, for their apparel & title (I cannot tell what) doth challenge such holiness to themselves that they accompt all other in comparison no Christian men at all. Why do we make so strait and narrow Christ's religion, which He would have so large? If we be moved with magnifical and high terms, I pray you, what thing else is a city but a great monastery? Monks be obedient to their abbot and governors; the citizens obey the bishops and curates whom Christ Himself made rulers, and not the authority of man. The monks live in idleness and be fed of other men's liberality, possessing that amongst themself in common which they never labored or sweat for (yet speak I nothing of them that be vicious). The citizens bestow that which they have gotten with their great labor and travail to them that have need, every man as he is of ability and power.

Now, as concerning the vow of chastity, I dare not be bold to express what difference is betwixt the religious man unmarried and the chaste matrimony of the other. And, to be short, he shall not very greatly lack those three vows of man's invention that doth keep and observe purely and sincerely that first only vow which we all solemnly make unto Christ—and not unto man—when we receive our baptism. And if we compare those that be evil of one kind with those that be evil of the other, without doubt the temporal men be much better. But if we compare those that be good of the one sort with those that be good of the other, there is little difference—if there be any at all—saving that those appear to be more religious which keep their religion & duty with less coaction.[33]

The rest is, therefore, that no man foolishly stand in his own conceit, neither for his diversity of living from other men nor despise or condemn the rule or order of other men's living. But in every kind of living let this be our common study, that every man according to his power endeavor himself to attain unto the mark of Christ, which is set open to all men; and that every man do exhort other to it, & also help other, neither envying them that over run us in this course nor disdaining them that be weak and cannot yet overtake us.

In conclusion, when every man hath done that he can, let him not be like unto the Pharisee whom the gospel maketh mention of which doth boast his good deeds unto God, saying, "I fast twice in the week, I pay all my tithes," & such forth. But, after Christ's counsel, let him speak from the heart and to himself, and not to other, saying, "I am an unprofitable servant, for I have done no more than I ought to do." There is no man that better trusteth than he that so distrusteth. There is no man further from true religion than he that thinketh himself to be very religious. Nor Christ's godliness is never at worse point than when that thing which is worldly is writhen [34] unto Christ, and the authority of man is preferred unto the authority of God.

We must all hang of that Head, if we will be true Christian men. Moreover, whosoever is obedient to a man which doth persuade & call him unto Christ, he is obedient unto Christ and not unto man. And whosoever doth tolerate and suffer those men which be subtle, cruel, and imperious, teaching that thing which maketh not for religion, but for their tyranny—he useth the patience meet for a Christian man so that these things which they command be not utterly wicked and contrary to Christ's doctrine. For then it shall be convenient to have that answer of the Apostles at hand: "We must rather be obedient unto God than to any man."

But we have long ago passed the measure & quantity of an epistle, so greatly the time deceiveth us whiles we commune & talk most pleasantly with our well beloved friend. This book is sent unto you in Frobenius' print as though it were new born again, much more ornate & better corrected than it was before. I have put unto it certain fragments of mine old study in times past. We thought it most convenient to dedicate this edition (such as it is) unto you, that whosoever shall take any precepts to live well of Erasmus should have an example ready at hand of our father Volzius.

Our Lord preserve you, good Father, the honor and worship of all religion. I pray you counsel Sapidus [35] that he be wise: that is, that he go forth as he hath begun. To Wimpfeling [36] ye shall speak also, that he prepare all his armor to fight shortly with the Turks for as much as he hath kept war long enough with keepers of concubines. And I have great hope and trust to see him once a bishop, and to ride upon a mule and to be set high in honor, with a miter and cross.

But in earnest, I pray you commend me heartily both unto them and unto Ruserus [37] and the rest of my friends; and in your devout prayers made to God I pray you remember Erasmus and pray for his soul's health.

At Basel, the even of the Assumption of Our Lady, in the year of our Lord God MCCCCC and xviii.

NOTES

1.   Presumably one John de Trazegnies, a dissolute soldier, whose wife had prevailed upon Erasmus to set down some notes that would restore her husband to some sense of religion. The "notes" developed into the *Enchiridion*.

2.   Playfully.

3.   A letter to a "Master John" in 1516 makes the same complaint to, inferentially, the recipient of the notes (Allen, III, 698).

4.   Duns Scotus. The pun is Tyndale's: Erasmus's phrase is *Scoticarum quaestionum*.

5.   A reference to Peter Lombard's compilation of opinions of the Fathers (twelfth century), *Sententiarum libri quattuor*, sometimes called the *Book of the Sentence*.

6.   *Summularies* seems to be Tyndale's slightly Anglicized version of Erasmus's *summulariorum*, a pejorative diminutive meaning literally a dealer in petty sums.

7.   Jacobus was James Despars, fifteenth-century editor of the work of Avicenna, medieval Arabic physician (Allen, p. 363n.).

8.   Erasmus has *Secundae secundam*. Allen notes that *partis partem* should be understood here; i.e., the reference is to a part of the *Summa*.

9.   Dominicans and Franciscans, respectively. Erasmus, however, has only *Praedicatores* (the Dominicans were a preaching order) and *Minoritas*.

10.   I.e., Realists and Nominalists.

11.   Plundering, extortion. Often combined with *pill*, as with Tyndale later in the letter. *Poll* originally denoted a hair trim (cf. Skeat and Mayhew, *Tudor and Stuart Glossary* [Oxford, 1914], p. 300).

12.   I.e., personal.

13.   See Gen. 26:18.

14.   Tyndale's translation of *cauponationes*. *Huckstering* would be a reasonably close present-day equivalent.

15. I.e., inscription.

16. Luke 13:1.

17. Luke 12:13.

18. Matt. 23:13-15; Luke 6:24.

19. Luke 9:55.

20. Matt. 16:23; Mark 5:33.

21. Ep. 134.

22. I.e., the inward state.

23. 1 Pet. 5:2-3.

24. Harm.

25. Pagans or unbelievers.

26. I.e., completely askew, the reverse of what their moral values should be.

27. Cf. the Colloquy "A Pilgrimage for Religion's Sake," as well as pp. 99-100 in *The Enchiridion* (Himelick tr.).

28. E.g., no. 22.2-3. Cited by Allen, p. 372n.

29. Ep. 447.515-8 (Allen, 373n).

30. Titus 3:1.

31. Gal. 5:13.

32. 1 Pet. 2:16.

33. Coercion.

34. Twisted, distorted.

35. John Witz, a scholar and teacher at Schlettstadt, near the monastery of Abbot Volz.

36. One of the German humanists, a former rector of the University of Heidelberg.

37. John Ruserus was a priest at Schlettstadt.

*From a letter to Albert of Brand-
enburg, Archbishop of Mainz, from
Louvain, October 19, 1519 (EE, IV, 1033).
A complete translation may be found
in John C. Olin,* Christian Humanism and
the Reformation *(New York, 1965),
pp. 135-145.*

I DISAPPROVED OF THE publication of Luther's books, and
when certain of his treatises first began to be showed around,
I vigorously opposed their publication because I was afraid of the
uproar they might cause. Luther had written me a very Christian
letter, it seemed to me, and I replied, urging him, in the course of
it, not to write anything seditious or anything against the Roman
Pope, and not to write with too much arrogance or asperity, but
to set forth the teaching of the Gospel in a sincere spirit and with
all mildness. I did this in a courteous manner in order to better
achieve my purpose. I added that there were people here who were
sympathetic with him, so that he would the more readily make
concessions to their judgment.

Certain dolts have interpreted these things to mean that I favor
Luther—although not one of those persons has admonished Luther
as yet. I alone have done so. I am neither Luther's prosecutor nor
his defender nor his ally. I would not presume to pass judgment
upon the spirit of the man, a very difficult task, especially for purpose of hurting him. And even if I were to favor him as a good
man—as his enemies concede him to be—or as a defendant—as
the law allows even to those sworn in as judges, or as a man
harried by these persons who are really exerting themselves against
good letters behind a façade of bogus piety, why should they
resent it as long as I did not attach myself to his cause? In short, I
think it is a Christian act to thus countenance Luther as, if he is
innocent, I should not want him oppressed by a party of scoundrels;
if he is guilty of error, I want him to be brought back to the path,
not destroyed. This policy is more compatible with the example of

133

Christ, who, as the Prophet says, did not extinguish the smoking flax or break the bruised reed.[1]

I should prefer that that heart which appears to contain some bright sparks of gospel teaching not be stifled, but instead corrected and called to preach the glory of Christ. Nowadays some theologians I know neither admonish Luther nor instruct him. They merely abuse the man with rabid outcries in front of the people and rip him apart with the most savage and vicious detractions, talking of nothing but heresies and heretics. There is no question but that tumult has been raised most objectionably here among the commons by those who have yet to see a book of Luther. It is a fact that some people have condemned in detail specifically those things they have not understood. For example: Luther had written that we are not obliged to confess mortal sins unless they are manifest, thinking of *manifest* as those known to us when we are confessing. A certain Carmelite theologian,[2] reading *manifest* as meaning sins which had been openly committed, raised an extraordinary fuss about something he did not understand. It is certain that what has been condemned as heretical in the books of Luther is considered orthodox, or even pious, in the works of Bernard and Augustine.

I have counseled these people from the beginning to abstain from outbursts of this sort, but instead to handle the matter by writing and debating. In the first place, they ought not to publicly condemn what they have not read, and assuredly what they have not pondered over (I won't say, what they have not understood). In the second place, I pointed out that it was not fitting for theologians, whose judgment ought to be most influential, to carry on any affair in a tumultuous uproar, and most especially they should not revile a man whose life was considered blameless by everyone. Finally, I suggested that perhaps it was not safe to touch upon such matters before the common crowd, where there are many people to whom the confession of secret sins is extremely offensive. If these people hear that there are theologians who think it unnecessary to confess all sins, they will quickly pounce upon this and, as a result, fall into error.

Although to any reasonable man this seemed quite reasonable— as it did to me—nevertheless, from this friendly advice they arrived at the conviction that Luther's books were largely mine, and had been conceived at Louvain, even though not one bit in them is mine, nor were they published with my knowledge or by my will. Even so, relying on this completely false suspicion and without any request for explanation, they stirred up many calamitous situations here, more rabid than any I have seen before. Moreover, although the proper job of theologians is to enlighten, today we see many who are doing nothing but restrict or crush or extinguish, unlike Augustine, who did not approve of those who only coerce without instructing—even in regard to the Donatists, who were not only heretics, but savage robbers as well.

The men whom mercy especially becomes seem to thirst for nothing but human blood and long for nothing so much as to see Luther seized and destroyed. But this is to play the hangman, not theologian. If they want to show themselves great divines, let them convert the Jews, let them convert those who are strangers to Christ, let them improve the public morals of Christians, unsurpassed in corruptness even among the Turks. By what principle is it reasonable to seize for punishment one who first of all proposed for discussion points which theologians have debated, and even questioned, in all the schools? Why should they strike at him who submits himself to the decision of the Apostolic See, who yields himself to the judgment of the universities? It is not surprising if he does not put himself in the hands of those who would rather destroy him than correct him.

First of all, we must examine the origins of this evil. The world has been overwhelmed by human regulations. It has been burdened by scholastic notions and dogma. It has been oppressed by the tyranny of mendicant friars who, although they are subordinates of the Roman See, have nevertheless arrived at such power and numbers that they intimidate the Roman Pontiff and even kings themselves. When the Pope acts in their favor, he is greater than God; whatever serves to their disadvantage, though, is as ineffectual as a dream.

I am not condemning them all, but a great many are of the sort who for profit and power take pains to ensnare the consciences of men. Casting shame to the winds, they had now undertaken, without regard to Christ, to preach nothing but their own novel and increasingly impudent dogmas. About indulgences they talked in such a way that even the uneducated could not bear it. As a result of this and many practices of a like nature, the life of Gospel teaching was, little by little, ebbing away. And, with matters always growing worse the probability was becoming more and more likely that that spark of Christian piety from which a dead charity could be revived would eventually be totally extinguished. The highest perfection of religious worship bordered on a ceremonialism more pronounced than that of the Jews. Good men sigh and deplore these things. Even the theologians who are not monks—as well as some monks—admit to this state of affairs in private conversation.

These things, I think, were what first moved Luther to dare to oppose the unbearable effrontery of some of these men. What else am I to think about one who is ambitious for neither honors nor money? The articles they object to in Luther I am not debating at the moment, only the kind and the cause. Luther has dared to question indulgences, but others had first made claims too immodest for them. He dared to speak rather moderately about the authority of the Roman Pontiff, but those people had already written with very little moderation about it, especially three preachers: Alvarus, Sylvester, and the Cardinal of San Sisto.[3] He dared to belittle the principles of Thomas, but these preachers had virtually set them above the Gospels. He dared to brush aside several niggling little points about the nature of confession, but in this matter the monks are endlessly entangling the consciences of men. He dared to disregard, in part, principles of the school men, but they themselves at one and the same time attach too much weight to them and disagree with one another about them. Ultimately, they keep changing their minds and inventing new ones to replace the old ones.

It was troubling to devout minds to hear almost no talk about gospel teaching in the universities and find that the sacred writers once approved by the Church were now considered out of date: to hear, even in sermons, very little about Christ, but almost everything about papal power and the opinions of the moderns; to hear the whole discourse manifestly betraying self-interest, obsequiousness, ambition, and hypocrisy. To whatever extent Luther has written rather harshly, these conditions, I think, must also be blamed.

Whoever believes in the teachings of the Gospels also believes in the Roman Pontiff, who is the first spokesman of the Gospels, just as other bishops are heralds of the same Gospel. All bishops serve as vicars of Christ, but among these bishops the Roman Pope is preeminent. We must believe of him that he favors nothing more than the glory of Christ, whose representative he glories in being. Those people who in fawning servility attribute to him that which he himself disclaims, and which does not serve the interests of his Christian flock, deserve the least of him. Indeed, some who are responsible for these lamentable agitations are not acting out of zeal for the pope but are abusing his authority for the sake of their own interests and power. We have, it seems to me, a good pontiff. In such a flood of events, however, there is much he is unaware of. Certain things he cannot accomplish, even if he wants to. As Virgil says:

> The charioteer is swept along by the horse,
> Nor is the chariot controlled by his reins.

Therefore, anyone who speaks up for those things which are peculiarly compatible with Christ is a support to papal godliness. It is plain, though, that there are those who are stirring up His Holiness against Luther, and even against everyone who dares to mutter a word against their dogmas. But the chief princes ought to be considering what the consistent policy of the pope is seeking rather than a complaisance exacted by self-interest.

Now, I could show very precisely just what kind of people the promoters of this commotion are, except that I am afraid of seeming slanderous even while I am proceeding in sober truth. I have known many of them intimately; many have revealed what they are in the books they have brought out, and the reflection of mind and life shows up there more clearly than in any mirror. Would that those who take for themselves the rod of the censor, with which they scourge out of the company of Christians whomever they want to, had drunk more deeply of the teaching and spirit of Christ. This teaching does not reach any except those whose hearts have been cleansed of all filth of worldly desire. Whether those people are of this sort anyone who has business with them that involves self-aggrandizement, glory, or revenge, will soon find out. Would that I could explain to Your Highness what I have perceived and discovered about these matters, but it behooves me to be mindful of Christian propriety.

I speak of these things the more freely because I have nothing whatever to do with the case of Reuchlin [4] and Luther. I myself do not wish to write in such a manner, nor do I associate myself with that teaching; as a result, I feel no need to defend their writings from others. I do not hesitate, however, to expose the secret that those people [5] are aiming at something quite different from what they say they are. For a long time they have taken it hard that good letters are flourishing, that languages are flourishing, that the ancient authors who, buried up to now under the dust were only food for worms, are coming to life again and that the world is being brought back to the well-springs themselves. They fear for their own deficiencies, they don't want to seem to know nothing, they are afraid that something may shrink their august dignity.

Although they have covered up this ulcer for a long time, recently it has burst, and the resultant pain has been too much for conceal-ment. Before Luther's books came out, they were already working assiduously, especially the Dominicans and Carmelites; one could wish that most of them were not more rascally, even, than they were ignorant. When Luther's books appeared, having lighted upon a handle, as it were, they undertook to bundle together the case of languages, of learning, of Reuchlin, and Luther and even my own—making not only an inept presentation but a clumsy division as well.[6] In the first place, what have liberal studies to do with the question of faith? In the second, what have I to do with the case of Reuchlin and Luther? But by this device they linked to-gether all students of good letters in such a way as to harass them with the same charge.

Furthermore, one can infer that the business was not handled sincerely from this fact: when they themselves admitted that there were no writers, either ancient or modern, in whom no errors were to be found, even those that would make them heretical if anyone were to obstinately defend them, why—overlooking all the others —do they scrutinize this one or that one with such malevolence? They do not deny that Alvarus erred in many points, that the Cardinal of San Sisto did, that Sylvester Prieras did. About these there is no concern, for they are Dominicans. Reuchlin is singled out for fuming against because he is versed in languages, and Luther because those fellows consider him to be possessed of our learning, although he has made only modest achievements here.

Luther has written much that is more ill-advised than impious; they are much distressed that he has little respect for Thomas, that he threatens the profit from indulgences, that he has small regard for the mendicant orders, that he is less respectful of scho-lastic dogma than of the Gospels, that he disregards the wire-drawn subtleties of the debaters. These, no doubt, are the heresies they find intolerable. But, camouflaging all this, cunning men who are united only for the purpose of doing harm hide their envious malice from the pope.

There was a time when a heretic was listened to attentively and absolved if he gave satisfaction; but if, having been convicted, he persisted, the ultimate punishment was his exclusion from the orthodox communion of the Church. Nowadays the crime of heresy is another matter, and yet—on whatever trifling occasion you please—people are immediately ready to shout, "This is heresy, this is heresy." At one time a heretic was held to be anyone who dissented from the Gospels or from articles of faith or those points considered to carry an equivalent weight. But now if anyone ever differs from Thomas he is called a heretic, or even if he differs from a specious argument just now contrived by some sophist in the schools.

Whatever displeases, whatever they know nothing about—that is heresy. To know Greek is a heresy. To speak in a polished manner is a heresy. Whatever they themselves do not do is a heresy. I admit that the offense of a corrupted faith is a serious one, but one ought not translate simply anything he wishes into a question of faith. And those who deal with matters of faith ought to be far removed from any semblance of ambition, self-interest, malice, or vengefulness.

But who does not see what those people are manifesting, the direction they are heading in? As soon as the curbs are removed from their unbridled passions they will begin to lash out at random at every good man; finally they will become a threat to the bishops themselves and even to the Roman Pontiff. I do not hesitate to say what would seem unlikely except that we see it already being done by certain men. What the Dominican order has dared to do Savonarola and the atrocious affair at Berne [7] ought to warn us—not to mention anything else. I am not rehearsing the disgraceful matter of the order, but I am warning about what we have to look out for if those men succeed in what they are boldly attempting.

What we have said thus far is aside from the case of Luther. We are talking only about a dangerous method of handling it. The Roman Pontiff has taken the case of Reuchlin upon himself. The affair of Luther has been turned over to the universities. Whatever decision they make will present no danger to me. I have always been careful not to write anything scurrilous or seditious or out of keeping with the teaching of Christ. I will never knowingly be the teacher of error or the cause of disruption; I will suffer anything rather than stir up dissension.

Nevertheless, I wanted Your Highness to be informed about the state of things: not that I would advise or command, but so that, if the foes of good letters try to take advantage of the protection of your eminent position, it can be more readily determined what it would be best to do about these affairs. In my opinion, the more one stays free of this business the more effectively he preserves his own equanimity.

NOTES

1. Cf. Isa. 42:3.

2. Nicolaus Egmondanus, an intransigent conservative and critic of Erasmus. He had detected heresies in the *Colloquies,* too (cf. Allen, V, 86 and 88).

3. I.e., Dominicans, who were a preaching order, *praedicatores.* Erasmus' memory is at fault, however. Alvarus, a fourteenth-century theologian, was not a Dominican (Allen, p. 103n).

4. Reuchlin was a German scholar under attack for heresy because of his Hebrew studies. The satirical *Letters of Obscure Men,* supporting Reuchlin, grew out of this controversy.

5. I. e., the Dominicans and other reactionary elements.

6. Perhaps an ironic application of terms for the structuring of an argument, here the *propositio* and *divisio.*

7. Savonarola was later to be claimed by the Reformers as their own, but Erasmus here takes the papal point of view about his death, as did Reuchlin. The Berne affair alludes to an effort of the Dominicans to defeat the Franciscans in a theological dispute. They made a series of bogus apparitions appear to one John Jetzer and then tried to poison their dupe (see Allen, p. 106n).

From a letter to John Slechta (EE, IV, 1039), written from Louvain in 1519. Slechta was a powerful noble of Bohemia, a man of education and means. See P. S. Allen, Age of Erasmus (Oxford, 1914), pp. 281-286, for a fuller account of the relationship between him and Erasmus.

I WILL REPLY TO your long letter only briefly now, my dear Slechta, so that you may rest assured that it was delivered to me and carefully read; I am too busy to do anything more at present. To the words of disparaging critics—even when they are cloaked with kindness—I have long since turned a deaf ear. I once thought I possessed a modest knowledge of human affairs, since I knew the customs of various sorts of men in widely different regions, but I have found such monsters among Christians as I would never have believed possible if I had not found them out to my own great sorrow. But these people, of course, can't be anything but what they are. We will strive to be what we are, and we will not cease to deserve well of everybody in proportion to the talent which we have. Perhaps God supposes thus, that in this way we may expiate those deeds of ours by which we have frequently offended Him. I shall forgive those people so that He may in turn forgive me, for the holiness of life which your words credit me with, may Christ, the author of all holiness, sometime in his blessed kindness also attribute to me.

Because you fill your spare time agreeably with our lucubrations you are certainly doing a friendly thing and will even be doing a useful one if you read our thoughts judiciously, for we are not expounding dogma. Accordingly, you will pick up Erasmus at a time when an abundance of better books is not at hand. But indeed you certainly depict that whole area so very clearly that I can see more definitely from your words how I would have regarded it if I had spent several years where you are.

The fact that your Germany is infested far and wide with brigands I take in part to be the inheritance of ancient ferocity, in

141

part the result of the fact that the region has been cut up into so many autonomous states under petty princes, not one of whom is willing to give in to another, partly because no people more frequently wages war for money. So they prepare themselves for war by practicing highway robbery, and those who have been discharged from service keep in practice for the duration. As a matter of fact, since no situation is so disagreeable that it cannot be quite useful to someone else who can make a profit in kidnaping foreigners or merchants, they not infrequently arrange for a trip to be unsafe so that their help will be necessary. In my opinion, though, it would be more advisable to meet evils of this sort with prudent policies calculated to prevent their commission than to punish them afterwards. Wherever travel back and forth was most common the road could be cleared of dense forests, and fortified by hamlets, farmhouses and guard posts. It certainly seems odd to me that German cities and princes don't furnish in their territories what the Swiss, relying upon democratic policy, furnish in their own. But perhaps our Prince Charles, when he becomes the supreme ruler and thus the most important champion of justice,[1] will correct these ills.

As for the rest concerning the disagreements in matters of faith, the disaster would be less complete, in my opinion, if delusion were not afflicting everyone in the same way. A large part of you not only part company with the Catholic Church but in sundry aberrations you differ sharply with one another. What you consider Judaic adulteration is probably common to parts of Italy and Germany, but especially to Spain. Who would believe, however, that there are still those who profess that nonsense of Epicurus, denying that our souls survive us after death? It is common enough to see people living as if they did not believe there were any life after death, but not to see anyone so mad as to want to be the propounder of this doctrine, or even associated with it. Similarly, you may see a good many Nicolaitans, sharing their wives with many others, but no profession of such a dogma as this even if Plato, a revered author, did not disdain the doctrine. But pray tell me, my dear Slechta, whether those people are not ashamed to be called heretics. Nothing is more abhorred than this label of which, strictly speaking, they seem undeserving. What *does* one believe if he denies the immortality of the soul? Or what has one got from the Gospel if he want wives to be common property?

I am always amazed that there is no notion so absurd that it will not find its followers. Pythagoras enjoined people not to eat beans, and he found those who would give them up. There have been those who preached that it was filial piety to do away with an aged parent, and people have been found who ritually did so. There have been those who argued that it was wicked for anyone to own personal property; and people appeared, as Saint Augustine points out in his catalog of heresiarchs, who, reveling in idleness, lived by begging, while they excluded from any contact with themselves those other sinful persons who were feeding their wives and children by working. There were those who credited Judas the betrayer with the salvation of the world, and disciples were not lacking to worship him as the saintliest of saints. There have been those who intoned aloud innumerable psalms all day long, without doing anything else in between psalms. And proponents of this idiocy were never wanting. There have been those who declared that anyone who lived a chaste married life was sinful, more wicked than those who insisted on wife-sharing, and these have been able to provide their own flock with a pretext. There have been those who argued that it was an act of piety for parents to burn their own children alive, and people have been found to subscribe to such an unholy doctrine.

So entirely gullible is the human race, and so various the possibilities of character. As a matter of fact, I am of the opinion that if someone should appear now to preach that ritual solemnity required men and women to dance together in the nude on the public square, the cult would not lack patrons and members. Those who are in authority, therefore, ought to be all the more careful not to teach or practice anything that does not square with the principles of Christ.

But passing over absurdities of this sort, as is only right, you point out that the whole state of Bohemia and even the frontiers of Moravia have been divided into three sects.[2] I wish, my dear Slechta, that some holy artisan could make a monad of that triad. However, as long as each group pursues its own individual advantage, neither public nor private good will be served and hardly anyone is considered except as he appeals to popular tastes; these matters, as they say, are handled more moderately among the Turks than among us. I am not talking about the articles we insist on for faith, but of those matters from which evangelical piety pours, as it were, like a fountain, namely, the contempt for money and high place, the restraint of passions such as wrath, hatred, and jealousy. If anyone is a slave to these feelings, what good, I ask you, is a profession of faith? If greed or ambition or a more criminal lechery, a fiercer hatred, a more pernicious spite, a more venomous detraction is what is really important to us, what good does it do to profess Christ, who created man for the purpose of winning us away from these things? If anyone wants to upbraid me for speaking so, let him upbraid the Apostle James, who carefully and fully sets these matters out in his Epistle.

Therefore, the sect which you rate as of first importance [3] I should prefer to be first, or even the only one of its kind. What comes nearer to a likeness to the heavenly hierarchy than that out of divided ranks the supremacy should return to one? What would be more effective in expunging the dissonance in the world? If any prince should attempt a despotic rule, let him be quieted by prayers, exhortation, teaching, and authority of the Roman pontiff. If some bishop plays the tyrant, it will be from that quarter that the people should seek help. If someone introduces devilish doctrines, the shepherd of Rome, who out of the pure springs of evangelic philosophy can draw what is worthy of the steward and vicar of Christ, will be sufficient. If it should happen on occasion that the supreme head does not satisfy, it cannot be supposed from the outset that he who presides over everybody will please everybody. Ultimately it is up to us to put the best construction on everything, insofar as it can be done. Afterwards we ought to impute a good part of those things which happen, not to the pope himself but to those whom he of necessity has relied on. In this situation it is sensible to keep in mind that the one who rules over men is but a man, nor can we long have mutual harmony unless, just as his mildness indulges us in many respects, so we in turn should accommoderate ourselves to him on occasion, especially since apostolic teaching holds that we should obey even unjust and wayward princes insofar as obedience accords with godly integrity.

But in this respect it seems to me that the second faction [4] errs more seriously because of its vexing rejection of the judgment and tradition of the Roman Church than because of its belief that piety requires partaking of the Eucharist in both kinds. If what your letter reports is true, would that this Eugene had preferred to concern himself with public tranquillity rather than with his own personal feelings. Nevertheless, if the Bohemians were to follow my advice, it would be that even if their views on this subject are defensible, even so they should conform rather than dissent, especially since most of Christendom does not follow this practice. Even if—to speak my mind candidly—I am astonished that a practice instituted by Christ has been changed and the causes alleged for the change don't seem completely convincing.

Of course it is little wonder that the Pyghard sect is furthest removed from the rule of Gospel concord when, as you write, it was created by a disreputable founder. If the Roman papacy is the Antichrist just because there sometimes happens to be an impious pope, or if the Roman Church is corrupt just because it sometimes has bad cardinals or bishops, or officials bad in other respects, by the same argument we should obey no bishops, no pastors, no rulers. To say nothing of the fact that, once this breach had been opened, disliking this or that would be synonymous with considering it wicked. How much more plausible is the opinion of Augustine that the gift of God is not spoiled by the character of its minister, since it is conferred upon us by the sacrament—even though those priests who by their irreligious habits cause the worshipful name of our Lord Jesus Christ to be wrongly applied to by the laity and the untutored are going to suffer the heaviest of punishments. But if those sectarians go on being blatantly wrong in exceeding the limits of all decency so that they have to be restrained in some way, it is not for just anyone to reproach them, nor should there be recourse to arms, lest the policy of violence, once established, hurt even the innocent.

The fact that they choose their own priests and bishops is not inconsonant with the practice of the early Church. Thus was Saint Nicolaus chosen, and Ambrose; but regulations for choosing officials had then not yet been formulated. Similarly, kings were at one time selected by the people. Finally the numerous popular disturbances resulted in the matter being handled by the decision of a few men. Still, the fact that the Pyghards choose men unlearned and innocent of all letters is rather more tolerable if only holiness of life makes up for lack of education. There is a two-fold disaster for the people though if they are not less wicked than ignorant.

As for the fact that they call one another brother and sister, I don't see anything reprehensible in that practice. I could wish that the same suggestion of mutual charity evinced itself in all Christians

—provided that their actions were not inconsistent with the words! And as for their having less respect for theologians than for Scripture, their instincts are right; but to reject their authority in every respect is as bad as to swallow it wholesale. Moreover, even if it is not inconsonant with fact that Christ and the Apostles conducted sacred worship in everyday garb, it is nevertheless wrong to despise what was essentially a wholesome practice instituted later by the Fathers. These are ceremonies, but in such ceremonial rites holy mysteries are made agreeable to the people.

For that matter, what purpose is served by squabbling over this point, which can be complied with without raising any crucial issues? [5] Unless, that is, the Roman Pontiff were to allow them to use their own rites conforming to the memory of the early Church, as he permitted the Greeks and the Milanese their own ritual, quite different from ours. And if the Lord's Prayer pleases these people so much, this is also a part of our service. Just as it is foolish to admit nothing but one prayer to a sacred rite, though, those people who scramble together prayers and popular tunes are just as absurd.

Those things they believe about the sacraments are too silly for the devout to consider, except for the fact that we can glean this much good from such errors—that we do not pervert things which were well instituted into a means of making a profit or achieving empty glory, or even despotism. I can't imagine why they condemn vigils and moderate fasting, when these acts are so many times recommended to us in the words of the Apostles, but I should prefer that men be exhorted rather than coerced.

Furthermore, as far as feast days are concerned, their opinion is not much different from that of the time of Jerome. Nowadays the multitude of feasts has ballooned enormously, but on no days does the general populace commit more sins; and—what is most barbarous—those who have no way of feeding their wives and children, or perhaps their parents also, except by daily labor have to give over whole days to idleness. To proclaim a holiday and not give them anything, what is this but to make sure that they're hungry? Let there be abundant feasts, but in churches; let the affluent come, but let the poor live. In any event, things should be handled in such a way that, once the sacred ceremonies have been performed, they could go back to their holy work. For what is more holy than manual labor for the welfare of children and family?

Now, a feast day is ordained to satisfy the superstitious disposition of anyone you please; indeed, we commonly see some bishops animated by this desire, so that every one adds several feast days to the calendar to commemorate his term in office by this mark. But just as it is the duty of the people to observe what ecclesiastical leaders ordain, by the same token it is up to the leaders' common sense not to rashly burden the people with regulations of this sort or to have little regard for the public morals.

Up to this point we have learned about a sickness from your letters. Would to God a trustworthy, workable medicine could now be discovered! And I think it could be, if only grave and good men directed all their efforts in this direction, especially since we have Charles as an emperor entirely disposed to favor those things which pertain to the Christian religion and since we have a Leo who is especially mild and reasonable. Unity will be happily restored if only each side will give in a little to the other.

Perhaps the complaints of neighboring regions cause many of those people of yours to shrink away from the control of the Roman Pope, because these neighbors vociferously claim to have been harshly plundered and oppressed by the brutality of those who manage papal affairs. But if I am not clearly mistaken, the disposition of Leo, as clement as it is pious, will lead him to pass over the involved problems of former times and, in the future, avoid intransigence as much as possible in dealing with those who dissent, especially if with sincere hearts they entrust themselves to him as they would to their father. He will consider it reward enough if, having quieted controversy, he will have made way for peace and concord. The power of the emperor will lend itself to this program; he is a monarch, I think, whom Bohemia does not understand. As for the rest of it, that which has to do with ordinances and sacraments ought in no way to be dissonant with the rest of orthodoxy. But perhaps some things will be relaxed in regard to the definitions of recent times. As far as ritual is concerned, anything will be readily condoned, although I should prefer that Christians everywhere made use of the same rites and prayers. Nowadays the diversity is extravagant, as long as everybody improvises these according to his own fancy and each person adds something to those already in use.

In my opinion, indeed, the fact is that the pope would win over most peoples to the Roman Church, where they are now assembled so to speak under a certain head, if everything under the sun were not precisely defined in terms of matters of faith, but only those things which have been plainly laid out in Scripture or without which the basis of our salvation is not made clear. A few principles would suffice for this purpose, and a few are more persuasive than many. Now we divide a single article into six hundred parts, some of which are of the sort that could remain unknown or debated without peril to Christian piety. It is the nature of man that, once something has been spelled out, he grimly insists upon it. Furthermore, the essence of the Christian philosophy consists of this, that we understand that our whole hope resides in God, who freely bestows on us all things through His Son Jesus. By His death we have been redeemed; on His body we have been ingrafted through baptism, so that, once dead to the lusts of this world, we may live in accordance with His teaching and example in such a way that not only are we guiltless of sin but also serve Him well in every way; and if misfortune befalls us we bear up stoutly in the expectation of the coming reward which unequivocally awaits all good men at the coming of Christ, and continually advance from virtue into virtue in such a way that we attribute nothing to ourselves, but give God credit for anything good.

These things must above all be so impressed upon the hearts of men as to transform his nature, as it were. Accordingly, those who scurry about quibbling over the divine nature of Christ or His human nature or some of the more arcane sacraments, by which process the more they elevate the mind into a rarefied atmosphere the more they detach it from more modest problems, should draw the line at immediately coercing everyone else into accepting what has been perceived only by this or that person. Just as controversy is more quickly born of wordy legal documents, so debate thrives upon too much defining.

We need not blush to answer certain questions this way: God knows how this happens; it is enough for me to believe that it does happen. I know that the body of Christ and His pure blood had to be taken in purity from purity; He wished this to be a most holy sign and warranty both of His love for us and of the harmony of Christians one with another. Let me examine myself, then, as to what there might be in me that is incompatible with Christ, what there is that is conducive to discord.

As for the rest, just how the ten categories come about and how bread can change its substance through the words of consecration, or how the same body can be present in such tiny form and in different places—in my judgment these matters have little to do with the attainment of piety. I know I am going to be raised from the dead; this is something Christ, who was the first to rise from death, has promised everybody. But as to just what my body will be like, or how that can be the same which has so many times been changed in one way or another, just as I would not summarily reject even a restrained consideration of these questions at the proper time, by the same token giving excessive attention to them contributes very little to real goodness. Nowadays, as a result of these and countless other disputations of the sort, in which certain men are showing off, the minds of men are distracted from those principles which alone pertain to the heart of the matter.

Finally, world peace will most effectually be strengthened if secular leaders, but especially the Roman Pontiff, divorce themselves from every vestige of tyranny and greed. Men quickly recoil when they see that bondage lies in store, when they know that they are not being summoned to godliness but seized as booty. If they see that we are blameless, that we are generous, they will most readily consider themselves of our faith.

NOTES

1. Charles I of Spain, crowned Charles V as Roman Emperor in 1520.
2. Orthodox Romanists, Utraquists, and the Brethren (Pyghards). See P. S. Allen, *Age of Erasmus*, pp. 281-286.
3. The orthodox party.
4. The Utraquists, who also read Scripture in the vernacular in their services.
5. For *citra negocium*.

From a letter to Lorenzo Campeggio, written from Louvain in 1520. Campeggio, cardinal and patron of letters, was advised by Erasmus from time to time on such matters as policy toward Luther. In EE, IV, 1167.

O F ALL OF Luther's books I have not read twelve pages, and even these only perfunctorily. Nevertheless, from these pages, sampled—to put it more accurately—rather than read, I received an impression of rare natural endowments and a talent beautifully suited to the explication, in accordance with the method of the Fathers, of obscure passages, to the fanning of the spark of gospel teaching, from which general moral behavior both of the world and of the schools—too much preoccupied with niggling little subtleties rather than essential questions—seems to have radically departed. I have heard distinguished men of unexceptionable doctrine and devoutness congratulate themselves for having happened upon the books of this man. I have noticed that whoever was most upright in character and closest to pure Gospel was least outraged by Luther. Besides his life was commended even by those who did not like what he taught. As for the essential spirit of the man, something only God can judge, I have chosen, quite properly, to look at it from the good side rather than the bad. Finally, the world—sick, as it were, of this doctrinalism which makes too much of either polite little exegeses or piddling little rules—seemed to be thirsting for that pure juice to be imbibed from evangelic and apostolic veins. For advancing this cause he seemed to me both fitted by nature and inspired by his studies.

This is the way, then, that I have supported Luther; I have supported the good I saw, or believed I saw, in him. Rather, I should say that I was not supporting him but the glory of Christ. Yet I also saw something that inspired some anxiety and doubt in me. Moreover, when he gratuitously challenged me in his letters, I at once seized the opportunity to carefully suggest what I hoped he would shun so that his talent, controlled and purified, might fruitfully and to the glory and benefit of Christ restore to us the evangelic philosophy now almost disregarded. If he had performed this service, I had no doubt that he would have Leo himself as the principal sponsor of his task; I think there is nothing more important to him than the glory of Christ, whose vicar he is, and the spiritual health of the flock entrusted to him. Ask yourself if you please whether this is a letter of support for a Luther who was writing in opposition to Christian doctrine and piety.

Since in his writings he had offended a grimly inflexible somebody or other—having too slight a regard for the gentleness of the gospel spirit—I suggested that in accordance with the example of Christ and the Apostles he teach those things which pertain to true piety. Since it was to his advantage, I advised him to be mild in his treatment of the Roman Pontiff, whose authority it was best to consider inviolable, and that he deal gently with those lofty eminences who when assaulted with violent reproaches or scolded too vehemently not only would not be reformed but, once angered, would stir up a great many more pernicious uproars. The result of such a policy as his would be that the teacher loses his influence and along with it the vital effectiveness of his teaching. Even though it is never permissible to deny a truth, it is nevertheless sometimes advisable to pass over it when occasion demands. The essential thing is to bring it to light at the right time and in as fitting and restrained a manner as possible. Some things which theologians admit to one another it would be injudicious to air before laymen, and often a seasonable admonition, courteous and temperate, straightens out people whom an irascible and wholesale denunciation would utterly lose. I don't want to imply what Plato seems to have believed, that an uncritical and ignorant commons cannot be kept in line except by occasional judicious hoodwinking and deceit; but just as this business calls for an honest man, so it also demands an especially canny one.

I have advised him not to damn without reservation all school men or monastic orders, but to point out gently what ought to be changed. These practices which have grown out of long habit more than rational judgment he should handle with close, cogent argument rather than heat. And, since I was not unacquainted with the German character and was not unaware that he was most incensed by the carking criticism from certain quarters, I urged him not to answer insult with insult but either to ignore them entirely or to reply with evidence, and to refrain altogether from polemical vituperation. Since I was fearful that so much intemperance at this point would only result in chaotic upheaval, I admonished him not to say or do anything in an arrogant or factious manner. Finally, he was to look into his own heart—something I could not judge— to see whether it was in any way tainted by anger or insolence or empty pride, which have a way of ensnaring us even when we are busily pursuing the work of God. Anyone guilty of these feelings did not seem a very plausible representative of the philosophy of Christ.

Now I ask you, what did I leave out that Luther should have been warned against?

I wrote all these things in a friendly, open spirit but people weren't lacking among the Germans to interpret this letter to Luther as an attack upon his teachings, while at the same time another bunch was assaulting it as the views of one of his faction. Some were shaken up by the fact that I had replied to the man— as if I should have, so to speak, shunned him like a vice—although I would have replied to the sultan if he had written to me. Besides, Luther had communicated none of his dogma to me. Others took it badly that I had answered him so civilly. But those people don't take into account how everyone is flattered by his own natural bent and how disagreeable being admonished at all is by its very nature. I did not know Luther personally, as I still do not. With the exception of a few pages, I had had no contact with his books. And things had not yet reached this contentious state. A few people were making a great deal of noise, but everybody suspected them of serving their own interests. Disputation was being encouraged; judges were being appealed to. How would I have looked had I— in the first place a stranger, in the second with no authority, and, finally, of wide rather than narrow experience—taken a haughtily critical attitude toward him? What hope would there have been that he would deign to listen to me, or what could I have expected to accomplish except that by abusing him I would in the long run ensure his acerbity when he answered me? The very fact that I was giving gratuitous advice where it was not asked was in itself not very polite. Nor was I unaware of how much more we ordinarily accomplish by courteous and mild suggestion than by harsh condemnation.

I am not so smug about my own talents and learning that I

presume to make pronouncements about somebody else's faith unless it is obviously at variance with the most widely accepted tenets. Let other people account for their own presumptions. There are those who think I am nothing but a philologist. Whether I am or not I will not argue now; that they are something else is beyond dispute.

But back to the matter at hand. Would those fellows have tolerated a philologist's talk about heresy? Even if my erudition were clearly up to it, I wouldn't have been able to refute his books without reading them again and again, or without investigating passages in those writers from whom he had imbibed his doctrines. And he imbibed a good deal from the early Fathers; if he had footnoted them carefully by name he would have escaped a good deal of the wrath he aroused. But I scarcely had time to read my own things, and if I had any leisure I preferred—to speak frankly—to spend it in expounding those Fathers. Since many learned men, as well as the scholastics, had already taken upon themselves the job of refuting Luther, wouldn't it have been effrontery on my part to have suddenly rushed in to snatch from others both the prerogative of damning him and the glory of victory?

As for the rest, what offended some—some for example, the fact that after the conventional form of instruction I tossed in an "I do not admonish you to do these things but to go on doing what you are doing"—suggests their total ignorance of the rhetorical civilities by which we are accustomed to soften the severity of criticism. Who has not learned these devices?

But I am reminding someone who already remembers, teaching someone who already knows—the pig instructing Minerva.[1] No doubt I was only day-dreaming when I imagined that Luther, of his own accord, was doing what I wanted done. Besides, if there hadn't been something about him to make me uneasy, it would have been stupid of me to prescribe in such detail another mode of writing. Still, those fellows we have been talking about insist on interpreting my advice as "Write seditiously, write heretically." Now, even if Luther had been even then disposed in that direction, not even he could have understood what I was saying as anything but a suggested form. But they are giving a twisted interpretation of what I appended both here and in England—that not a few people were well-disposed toward his books—as if I were trying to encourage his audacity, when I actually did this to urge upon him a more moderate and temperate approach by which he would be more acceptable to the judgment of good men, and to write—with restraint—those things which would merit the lasting approval of the devout and the learned. So we applaud wrestlers, not to dull their competitive spirit with our cheers but so they respond to the encouragement of their well-wishers. Several, meanwhile, do not adequately take into account the fact that in the same letter I am making two points: one concerns the outcry against good letters and their practitioners; the other has to do with attacks upon Luther. On the first point I disagree totally and unequivocally with the critics. On the second, I do not appoint myself judge, either hostile or favorable. I only suggest what I should like for Luther to avoid.

In a letter to the Most Reverend and Learned Cardinal of Mainz,[2] what do I urge except that Luther should not be forcibly silenced when his case has not been studied, that such an opportunity not be presented to certain people wanting to condemn what they do not confute and—for all I can tell—do not even understand. To this extent I was supporting Luther: I did not want him consigned to the tender mercies of certain people who—whatever they pretended to be doing—were really working for the ruin of good letters; but I did not so sympathize with him that I was not willing to be convinced by the evidence of holy scripture, or won over by argument, if he deserved to be refuted. Finer natures want to be taught, but they can't stand to be coerced. It is the job of theologians to teach; only tyrants compel. Thus I was well disposed toward Luther insofar as to prefer his amendment to his destruction, to bring him back into the fold if he had strayed in some way, not get rid of him. And everybody who has written anything has gone astray, excepting only the canonical scriptures.

In this spirit I think that all true theologians today are well disposed toward Luther. In fact, I perceive that Pope Leo himself is of this disposition. Cyprian loved the work and the character of Tertullian although He did not agree with his doctrines. Jerome loved the genius of Origen while rejecting his censured ideas. Augustine seems to have been delighted by the books and the character of Tychonius while at the same time avoiding that man's party.

I do not, however, want to injure Luther. I am not tagging him with any label; he has his own judges. Just as my commendation was of no help, by the same token I should not like to see him penalized if I look at him differently. I wish only to show how far I am from being what people think I am. From the first I suspected that his books would stir up dissension. From the first I objected to their being produced at Basel; indeed, I did so in no uncertain terms, first by direct oral warnings when I was there and then by my letters when I was gone. Over and over again I painstakingly advised, now by letter, again by friends, what I wished he would avoid. I did this with such candor that I was admonished in letters from my friends not to write such things as I was saying here and there for fear of alienating from myself the hearts of many Germans. The clerics who think they are opposing Luther so stoutly now were doing nothing of this sort then. No one advised the man in the spirit of brotherhood, no one discouraged him, no one instructed him, no one refuted him. They were too busy agonizing over the appearance of a new heretic who was teaching that confession of every misdemeanor as if it were a capital sin was something less than essential: Antichrist would soon be here!

I have never pronounced verdict on his case, except to the extent that I deplored the ill-judged, unbecoming, vituperative and unconstructive way he was attacked. Does it mean someone favors parricide if he refuses to pass sentence before the person charged with parricide has come to trial? Or is one in league with the enemy if he shows how that enemy could be contained with a minimal expenditure of troops? Or if he suggests, actually, exploring the possibility of reducing the enemy to surrender without the risk of warfare? If a person has the best interests of the state at heart when he would rather save a foe than destroy him, what kind of effrontery is this to censure someone who would expect as much from theologians?

I say these things, assuming what I did not know for certain at the time, that Luther is a teacher of error. Nevertheless, I advised him as it seemed to me best, in such a way as to leave him no less free than anyone else to use his own judgment if he so preferred. I saw that probing this sore spot before an uncritical populace, many of whom did not take kindly to the requirement of confession, was not without its risks. They would discard nothing more readily if they saw a divine, a man of blameless life, of such opinions. Still, it is uncertain even now whether, in his own writings, Luther understood this. Finally, what other result was achieved but that they publicized his books—previously known only to a very few—by uproars of this sort and incited people to read them who never would have otherwise, to the great profit of the booksellers, who, the more impotently those people raged, the more merrily sold his books. In the meantime they were instructing neither the people nor Luther. Why are they invested with the title of *doctor* except that they are to teach?

Whatever kind of a man Luther was, certainly it was a more decent act to correct him than to destroy him. In times past the authority of bishops was employed on behalf even of convicted criminals; they ought to be at least as unwilling to do away with a man of the church. To prevent their capital punishment, Augustine interceded with the imperial judges on behalf of the Donatists, whom I hardly know whether to label detestable heretics or savage thugs, although he knew they were plotting against his own life. One of the best of men, surely, he wanted them to come to their senses, not to die. He wanted those who could be so restored to live, and he wanted them to live even at the risk of his own life.

At one time a heretic was listened to, even with respect, as is made quite clear in the works of Augustine. At that time the punishment of one convicted of heresy and persisting in error was no more than removal from the communion of the orthodox. But nowadays nothing is more savagely impugned than the crime of heresy. Nevertheless, those people—I don't know who they are—who arrogate to themselves the function of bishops talk of nothing more loosely. Some of them I am sure are of the type who, to speak bluntly, would make me feel uneasy if they labeled me as orthodox.

It was a praiseworthy policy of certain wise men who wanted to ignore even the most criminal acts on the grounds that they ought not to waste time on those for whose deeds no really suitable punishment could be devised, but instead should consider only what the dignity of the name *Roman* demanded and the public welfare encouraged. Paul everywhere spares the pseudo-apostles lest those who had been exasperated by them should lash out even more violently at a still young and unfamiliar gospel teaching. How much less appropriate to so excoriate one whose life was praised by everybody, whose writings delighted so many distinguished men, so many of the learned, so many of the devout!

Now, if Luther had indeed been the kind of person they wanted

to make him out to be, no policy could be devised so well calculated to make him worse—and enhance the triumph of the theologians. They wanted Luther totally destroyed. But if either the
man's error or his stubbornness deserved drastic measures—which
are ordinarily applied only to members who are irrevocably lost
and after everything else has been tried—Luther could, of course,
be completely eliminated by this method. Provided, that is, he had
first been eradicated from the minds of men and then also from
libraries—and all this done without reducing all Christendom to
chaos. He could have been eradicated from men's minds if those
whom exceptional learning commended and visible integrity of
character vindicated from every suspicion of moral taint had
answered his dogma with sound argument and the testimony of
holy scripture.

Among all Christians the authority of the Roman Pontiff is great,
as it ought to be, but the more weight this carries the more care
should be taken that he not give too much rein to the personal
passions of certain people, and the less he should ignore the silent
judgments of the learned and devout. I will not hestitate to say
that, to speak pointedly, no one obstructs papal influence more
than those who defend it either stupidly or perversely. Who does
not know that the Pope of Rome can either crush or intimidate
anyone he wishes to? But what power was ever so invulnerable that
fear alone assured its perpetuity? God himself wanted to be loved,
not just feared. Accordingly, as I had started to say, where papal
influence is patently more weighty and extensive, the more awe-
some is the responsibility and the more mildly and temperately, in
my opinion, it should be applied.

Even if I had been the only one to argue thus, I should not, I
think, be condemned for it. But now I see that those who are
judicious agree with me on this point, not only here but even at
Rome, not just among the laity but even among the clergy, even
among the Dominicans themselves. Those whom it pleased to have
Luther condemned it did not please to have it done in this way.
I will not dilate here upon what kind of people pushed through
this very significant business; I will not recount, in terms of the
censured dogmas of Luther, just how they were described to us.
Perhaps, human affairs being what they are, it was relatively ex-
pedient; but if one considers the question of evangelical holiness,

it was absolutely reprehensible. Even those clerics who in other respects assail Luther with every kind of stratagem do not go along with these.

To this extent only, then, is my policy favorable to Luther: that he should not be harassed beyond his deserts, not beyond justice, not by violent uproar, not by a world-wide upheaval. My policy seems much more compatible with the dignity of the Roman Pontiff and the authority of the theological orders. Their decisions ought to be the most reasoned, their character especially moderate and free from every hint of folly, jealousy, greed, ambition, hatred, fawning obsequiousness, and the other carnal passions which deprive us of sound judgment. Just as no one helps the Roman Papacy less than those who support it recklessly and heedlessly, so no one is more detrimental to the reputation of theology than those who act in such a way as to turn divines into either toadies or bullies.

Moses did not hesitate to follow the counsel of Jethro, his father-in-law, and they are furious with me because of loyal advice which they were not obliged to take. If we are eager to listen, however, each one should be free to speak his mind and we should be tolerant of one who counsels us wrongly so long as he does so in an earnest spirit. If his reward is a rope, a heavy penalty, what chance do we have of discovering truth? Out of a large number of universities two so far have condemned several of Luther's contradictory doctrines.[3] And these two do not agree completely with each other; indeed, the theologians within both schools are not in total agreement with one another. The opinion of the University of Paris, which in matters of theology has always held an authoritative position analogous to the pre-eminence of Rome as the seat of Christianity, was awaited. Since its decision was being waited for, would I have been committing a crime even if I had come out in favor of certain teachings of Luther? Now, I have never defended any of his dogmas even when it was permissible; I only deplored the unconsidered and demagogic judgments of those people who were dissatisfied with the ones who were opposing Luther.

What a new Lutheranism this is! I first unequivocally censured the books of Luther because they seemed to have an upheaval in mind, a course I have always and consistently shunned. I was the first to object to the publication of his lucubrations. I am almost unique in not having read his books, in never having tried to defend anything of his—not even while drinking, when idle chatter has a way of being scribbled in wine. I have always urged those who were qualified to dispute with Luther, to write against Luther. When Louvain began doing this, I steadily approved what I should have liked them to handle less ineptly.

A precedent has been set by the two universities in contending with Luther. A frightful Bull has come out over the signature of the Roman Pope. Luther's books have been burned. People are in an uproar. Hardly anything more deplorable could be done. The Bull seemed to everyone to be too harsh to be consonant with the mildness of our Leo; nevertheless, its rigor did not suffice for these persons who administered it. Meanwhile no one saw Erasmus disquieted or more heartsick than usual.

What Sylvester Prieras wrote in opposition to Luther I have heard nobody commend so far, even those to whom Luther is most detestable. Augustine the Minorite was even less satisfactory than Sylvester. I will say nothing about Thomas Radinus because I have merely glanced at him. There was a man at Louvain named John of Turenhout who was neither badly trained in scholastic theology nor ignorant of that of the Fathers. He lectured publicly for many days against some of the arguments of Luther—and lectured as befits a theologian, without invective. He also wrote a treatise on this debate, and I have no doubt that he wrote as temperately as he spoke. No one worked more vigorously for the publication of this treatise than I. Would one do this if he sided with the errors of Luther?

What connection have I with Luther? What would I, who am unwilling to battle with my own particular bishop, hope to gain from him that I should want to side with him against the teaching of the Gospel, or against the Church of Rome, which I consider no different from the Catholic, or against the Roman Pontiff, who is chief of the whole Church? I am not so irreligious as to dissent from the Catholic Church, nor such an ingrate as to oppose Leo, whose kindness and favor I have experienced in no uncommon manner. Finally, I am not so incautious as to oppose one whom not even kings safely oppose and to do so even when Luther's cause was not very convincing, and especially when there was no prospect of a fruitful outcome.

If the immoral practices of the Roman Curia demand some sweeping and immediate reform, certainly it is not my concern or of those like myself to take this task upon ourselves. I prefer this state of human affairs, whatever it is, to the stirring up of new disorders which again and again lead to schism, and that is the way it seemed. Those who let the sea into new ditches are often deceived, for once admitted it doesn't flow where it was intended but rushes ahead wherever it pleases, to the considerable distress of those living nearby. I have not—nor will I, knowingly—be a purveyor of error, nor will I be either a sharer in or leader of agitation. Let others court martyrdom. I don't consider myself worthy of this distinction. I know that I am anathema to some—not because I am a Lutheran, for they are indignant at the very fact that I am not—but to those people who find favor with nobody but silly little females, with the ignorant, with the gullible. To put it baldly, Erasmus disturbs none except those who are disturbed by good letters and evangelical truth, which is to say those who are growing fat and rich on the folly of the people.

NOTES

1. Cf. *Adagia.*
2. Albert of Brandenburg (cf. Ep. 1033, *EE*, IV).
3. Cologne and Louvain (Allen, p. 409n).

*From a letter to Louis Marlian, from
Louvain, in 1520 or 21 (EE, IV, 1195),
Marlian was a native of Milan and a
physician who also wrote against Luther.*

E VEN IN THE beginning, before I saw where Luther was heading, I did not approve of seditious agitation among the people.
I urged that the learned discuss the matter in their books. I preferred to have Luther corrected rather than silenced or, if he had
to be put down, to bring that about without producing utter chaos
in the world. This policy the Roman Pontiff would even now favor
if he fully understood how to go about it and realized the fervor with
which many nations endorse Luther. But it has been the fiction of
certain monks—loving me about as much as they love good letters—
to tie me in willy-nilly with the Lutheran movement.

Those who seem to favor Luther have tried in every way possible
to draw me into their party. Those who rail at Luther have tried to
drive me into his faction by the indiscriminate abuse they bestow
on me in public sermons, if anything more hatefully than upon
Luther himself. There is no way, however, that I can be swayed
from the position I take. I acknowledge Christ, I am not acquainted
with Luther, I accept the Roman Church, which in my opinion is
not incompatible with the Catholic one. Nor will death estrange
me from her until she is patently out of harmony with Christ. I
have always abhorred sedition. Would that Luther and all Germans
were of the same mind! In many Cisalpine districts I note a good
many people who are backing Luther because of some external
pressure. Ironically, though, the fact is that Luther's enemies are
strengthening Luther's hand and he in turn is strengthening theirs,
as if they had some kind of mutual agreement with each other! No
one has done more damage to Luther than he himself has repeatedly done in his most recent and more offensive tracts. By the
same token, some people are raving so stupidly and ignorantly
and intemperately before the public that they are making themselves repugnant to everybody and endearing Luther to the hearts

161

of men. They embarrass the cause of the papacy in precisely the same way that an inept lawyer hurts the case of his client.

I praise those who support the Roman Pope, whom every devout person does support. Who would not support the one who in the closest imitation of Christ devotes himself wholly to the salvation of Christian people? I could wish, however, that he had wiser advocates. Those fellows want only to devour Luther, and as far as I can see they don't care whether they have him boiled or roasted. Certainly, the fact that they identify me with a movement I have no connection with is not only wicked behavior, it is also bungling policy; they could take care of Luther more expeditiously if they left me out of it.

THEY ALLEGE that Luther drew upon my books for much of his teaching. What lie could be more brazen, since his very first article[1] exposes their palpable nonsense? Where do I declare that anything we do is sin—not to mention innumerable other places where nothing of the sort can be found, even in jest? For all that, of course, there was a time when heretics did draw their poisons even from the words of the Gospels and the Apostles. I am speaking now on the assumption that he did write something heretical and had got it from my works. They say that he doesn't acknowledge some of his tracts. Maybe he would be wise not to acknowledge any of them, if he could be so persuaded; but whatever help he had in his writing, in all the books circulating under his name there is positively not one syllable of mine. I would not hesitate to swear to this by any sacred oath you please.

For many years now I have not only been aware of your extraordinary common sense but have also been conscious of your open and friendly attitude toward myself. And everybody knows well the extent of your influence. Accordingly, I beg of you to defend my innocence against malicious slanders of such a nature as this. Even those things which in the most private of letters I have confided to the intimacy of friends are being spread around, perhaps more readily than is ordinarily possible because of my own ingenuousness. They are broadcasting remarks which we have a way of blurting out between drinks. Nothing is going to be dug up except that I hoped that Luther would be set right rather than crushed while there was still hope that he would change for the better. Even now I should prefer to have the situation toned down rather than exacerbated to the point of a worldwide upheaval. I would rather make distinctions between what is good and what is bad than to see what is very good canceled out in the hatred for certain things which seem bad. In sum, I am urging that we avoid the Lutheran Scylla in such a way as not to be pushed headlong into the Charybdis of belligerent sectarianism.

If these opinions seem deserving of punishment, the defendant pleads guilty. I assuredly had nothing in mind but the consideration of both the best interests of the Roman Pontiff and theologians and the general accord of Christian authority. So far I have read no book of Luther's, however small, all the way through. I have never defended any doctrine of his, even as a joke. I do not approve of the ignorant and mutinous disturbances of certain people, nor does anybody else in his right mind. I see what they are aiming at—the eradication of all liberal studies, obviously, and the establishment of their own authoritarianism. So, I shun Luther but I do not side with these fellows. They are few in number, but they inflame many. I am not condemning the Order; [2] they, however, are the ones who perform the greatest disservice to their own Order.

You have, most revered patron, the whole picture of my mind. Whatever is being bruited about which is of a nature inconsonant with the Christian religion, which would shatter public peace, which would belittle the dignity of the Roman Church—consider it more than certain that it did not come from Erasmus, whatever label is being attached to it. Some day, at the proper time, he will make his position clear, holding nothing back; in the meantime I am willing to attest by any evidence you please that I don't want to depart a finger's breadth from those who agree with the Catholic Church. I know that anything is preferable to making the general condition of the world even worse; I know that it is sometimes an act of goodness to let a truth stay hidden, that this truth is not something to be waved about regardless of the place, the time, the audience, or the manner. Nor has it escaped any educated man that there are certain prescribed forms, gradually acquired either through custom or through the obsequiousness of recent advocates or the reckless exegeses of schoolmen or the policy and craft of princes, which we would be better off without. It is a matter of Christian common sense, however, not to apply a remedy in such a way that the sickness being treated is aggravated rather than cured and a quick death takes the place of the illness. I would not go so far, of course, as to suggest that Christians should by any means subscribe to the opinion of Plato, who permits those wise guardians of his to deceive the people for their own good, on the grounds that the common run of men cannot be prevented from becoming worse by rational, philosophic truth.

I have always been on guard against becoming the fomenter of dissension or the propounder of a new dogma. I have been urged by many important men to align myself with Luther; I have told them that I would be for Luther when he was for Catholicism. They have pressed me to assert the rule of faith; I have answered that I know no faith other than that of the Catholic Church. I have urged them to make their peace with the Roman Pontiff, and I have taken the force from their complaints. I was the first of all to oppose the writing of Luther's tracts. Soon after that I advised the man to avoid seditious utterances, for I have always dreaded this eventuality. I would have exerted more pressure except that, more than anything else, a kind of scrupulousness deterred me, lest perhaps I inadvertently be inconsonant with the spirit of Christ.

I have exhorted, and still do exhort, many to shun defamatory pamphlets, especially the anonymous ones; these only inflame the minds of men, doing ill service not only to Christian peace but also to the man they seem to be supporting. I can advise; I cannot compel. The world is full of print shops, full of scribblers, full of speech-ifiers. As to what those fellows are raising a fuss about—since it is out of my hands, it would be most unfair to blame me for somebody else's recklessness.

NOTES

1. Article I of Luther's *Assertio* maintains the doctrine of justification by faith to which Erasmus never subscribed (Allen, 460n).
2. The Dominican order (Allen, p. 461n).

From a letter to Jodocus Jonas, from Louvain, May 1521. Jonas was a professor at the University of Erfurt and a disciple of Luther (EE, IV, 1202) This letter is translated in its entirety in John C. Olin, Christian Humanism and the Reformation (New York, 1957), pp. 151-163.

I DO NOT KNOW whether the leaders of the Church have ever so eagerly and so openly as we see today thirsted for the worldly goods which Christ taught us to despise. Nor had the study of Holy Scripture suffered any less than morality. Divine literature was made to support human desires and popular credulity was used for the profit of the few. Devout minds, to whom nothing is more important than the glory of Christ, were grieved at these conditions. This situation resulted in the fact that in the beginning Luther inspired as much approval everywhere as, I think, any man had received in ages.

Indeed, as we readily believe what we very much want to believe, people thought a man had arisen who, free from all the lusts of this world, would be able to provide some remedy for such great evils. Nor did I immediately give up hope, although at the first scanning of the pamphlets which began to appear under Luther's name I was quite fearful that the affair would result in tumult and public dissension throughout the world. Therefore I have warned not only Luther himself by letters, but also those of his friends whose influence on him I thought would be considerable. What kind of advice they have given I don't know; certainly the matter has been handled in such a way that there is a danger of the evil becoming twice as great from the ineptness of the remedies that have been applied.

I very much wonder, my dear Jonas, what god has so vexed the heart of Luther that he inveighs with such an indiscriminate pen against the Roman Pontiff, against all the universities, against philosophy, against the mendicant orders. Even if everything were true—and those who are directing the attack upon his writing say

165

it is far from true—when so many have been antagonized, what outcome other than the one we see could be expected?

Thus far I have not had time to read Luther's books, but from the ones I have dipped into and from what I have now and then casually inferred from what others have said, although it was not for my modest capacity, perhaps, to pass judgment on the truth of the opinions he advanced, assuredly the manner and method of achieving the purpose was not at all agreeable to me. When an issue is in itself a bitter truth to many, when a situation disruptive in itself is can be expected to become critical if it drags on, it would be better policy to smooth out a situation prickly by nature through mild courtesy of treatment rather than to add hatred to hatreds.

What good did it do, then, to act in a different way, and to set forth certain points in such a way that at first blush they were even more obnoxious than when looked at more closely and coolly? Some things are vexatious, even when kept in the dark, so to speak. What purpose was served by denouncing in such violent terms those people? If he hoped to reform them, it would have to be set down as an imprudence, but if his intention was to incite them to evil all over the world, such a method should be defined as irreligious. Furthermore, even though it is the job of the careful housekeeper to present an honest accounting, that is, to bring it forward when the occasion calls for it, and to bring out a sufficient amount of it and what is appropriate for each account, Luther has erupted with everything at once in so many pamphlets, keeping still about nothing and making public even to cobblers what is usually reserved for the learned as *mystika kai aporreta*.[1] And frequently, as I see it, he is swept beyond what is right by a kind of uncontrolled impetuosity. For example, although it was enough to have admonished the theologians that they were too much preoccupied with Peripatetic, or rather Sophist, philosophy, he calls the whole philosophy of Aristotle the death of the soul.

That evangelical spirit of Christ has its own good sense, its own peculiar courtesy and mildness. Thus even Christ adapted himself to the feelings of the Jews. He spoke in one way to the relatively uncouth crowds, in another way to the Disciples; and, bearing with them for a long time, he gradually brought those very men to an understanding of the heavenly philosophy. Using this strategy he commands his Disciples to preach first of penance and the kingdom of God near at hand, but to be silent about Christ.

So it was that Peter, in the Acts of the Apostles, speaking not abusively but gently and in words full of love, added so great a throng as the first harvest of the Church. He did not cry out against those who had killed Christ, or stress in belligerent words their ungodly madness, even though there probably were people in that crowd who had brought Christ to His death. Instead, consoling them, as it were, he says this was brought to pass in such a way by a divine purpose; then, even the wickedness of the crime he blames upon the age itself: "Save yourself," he says, "from this corrupt generation." [2] He does not cast back abuse on those by whom they had been accused of being tipsy on new wine,[3] but answers in equable terms that it was the effect of a new spirit, not of wine. He presents the testimony of Joel,[4] which he knew would carry a great deal of weight with them. But he does not yet proclaim Christ as God and man; this mystery he held back for the proper time. For the time being he calls Him a just man,[5] he proclaims Him Lord and Messiah, and he does this on the authority of God, whom those men devoutly worshiped, so that he might win favor for the Son from the Father they had already accepted. And when he pointed out that what they interpreted as something said about David really referred to Christ rather than David, he softened the language that would be offensive, saying, "Men and brothers, let me speak freely to you about the patriarch David." [6]

Similarly, Paul becomes all things to all men in order to win all to Christ, instructing his followers to teach with all mildness, alienating no one by roughness of manner and speech, but winning over even the surly and the rude with gentleness.[7] With what courtesy he preached Christ to the Athenians, attributing their faults to the age itself: "The times of this ignorance God winked at." In a becoming and pleasing introduction he calls them "men of Athens." He does not savagely excoriate their impious reverence for demons, but with courteous speech charges them with an excessive devotion in venerating them more than they ought. He turns an inscription seen by chance on an altar into an argument for faith, but changing and also excising some of the words; but he does not as yet call Christ other than a man through whom God had elected to bestow salvation on the whole human race.[8] And he does not bring up the testimony of the prophets, something of very little weight with them, but uses that of Aratus.[9] And in what a civilized way he pleads his case before Festus and Agrippa.

In like manner does Augustine refute the raving Donatists and the worse-than-mad Manichaeans, so that he both expresses a wrath compatible with what the case deserved and mitigates it everywhere with the sweetness of charity, yearning for their salvation, not their destruction. This gentleness in teaching, this sensibleness in the dispensing of divine instruction captured the world and sent it under the yoke of Christ—something no arms, no philosophical subtlety, no rhetorical skill, no human force or art could do.

So much the more should we, if we wish to do good, refrain from all invective, especially if those we are opposing are of considerable public eminence. Paul wanted honor to be granted to magistrates, even the pagan ones, and he *palinodei*,[10] so to speak, because he had execrated the openly wicked Mosaic High Priest.[11] He wished for slaves who had been converted to Christ to obey their pagan masters even more scrupulously than they had done before. He wanted wives, as the result of their profession of Christ, to be even more compliant to their irreligious husbands, for no other reason but that by their agreeableness of behavior they might draw all men to the love of the gospel teaching.[12] Anyone who has a pious mind assuredly wishes nothing more than to do good, either going ahead in silence if there is no hope, or publishing and disseminating the truth in such a way as not to make the sickness worse instead of curing it.

Brutus is critical of Cicero, who in his speeches and writing angered those whom, once angered, he could not cope with. Feigning and dissimulation in the philosopher-prince of a republic do not displease Plato as long as he uses his guile for the public good. It is fitting, I know, that a Christian be free of all deceit; it sometimes happens, nevertheless, that truth is best left unspoken, and everywhere the important thing is when, where, and how it is revealed. Responsible physicians don't rush immediately to drastic remedies. They first treat the ailing body with milder medicines, and regulate the dosage in such a way as to heal it, not bury it.

Nor do I agree with those who say that the sickness of these times is too critical to be cured by mild remedies. As the Greek proverb has it, it is better to let an evil be as it is than make it worse by inept treatment.[13]

I do not deny, of course, that God sometimes amends His flock by means of wars, pestilence and afflictions, but it is not the role of good men to bring on war and unrighteous suffering, even if

God does sometimes convert the wretchedness of others into His own good. The cross of Christ brought salvation to the world, but still we abominate those who brought Him to the cross. The death of martyrs both enhanced and strengthened God's Church; nevertheless, we condemn the wickedness of those through whom this good has come to us. Many would be less evil if they were relieved of their riches. No honest man, however, has a right to take any person's money in order to improve his character. Furthermore, since everything new gives rise to disruption, even when it leads to better things; if anything is at odds with accepted practice it had better be advanced under the appearance of seeming as little different as possible.

But people say that Luther, even when he is teaching what others teach, nevertheless frequently tries by the very language he uses, it appears, to seem to be advocating something radically different. Besides, as the characters of men have a natural bent for the worse, their vices have to be remedied in such a way as not to offer others an excuse for sinning more freely. Paul preaches evangelical liberty, as against the deadly bondage of the Law, only to add, "but don't make liberty an excuse for carnality." [14] Similarly, he warns against the cold works of the Law in order to urge us on unceasingly to works of love.

There may have been some who, out of sincere enthusiasm, were in favor of calling the orders and the leaders of the Church to better things. But I am not quite sure whether they are the ones who, under this pretext, long for the wealth of the churchmen; I consider nothing more abominable and subversive of public peace than this. If they think it is right to lay hands on the property of the priests because some priests sinfully use their property for worldly magnificence or things in other respects less than honorable, not many—either citizens or important personages—will have very secure possession of their own goods. A pretty state of affairs indeed if priests are wickedly robbed in order for the soldiery to use the plunder in an even worse fashion. Such fellows throw away their own property, and sometimes that of others, in such a way that it is of no use to anybody.

I don't even agree with those men, my dear Jonas, who say that Luther could not maintain a Christian moderation because he had been provoked by the unbearable effrontery of his opponents. Regardless of how others behave, anyone who is taking such a role upon himself ought to be consistent with himself and indifferent to all other matters. Furthermore, he should have looked for a way out before he let himself down into this hole, lest the same thing happen to him as to the goat in the fable. Even in religious matters it is stupid to begin something you cannot finish, especially if a not very felicitous attempt only causes the most drastic problems instead of the hoped-for advantages. We now see affairs brought to that state where, realistically, I see no way out unless Christ by His own art converts the recklessness of these men into a general good.

Some make excuses for Luther because, impelled by the pressures of others, he first wrote too sharply and then did not entrust himself to the judgment of most merciful Leo and the Emperor Charles, by far the best and gentlest prince of the faith. But why was he more willing to listen to people like that than to other friends, neither unlearned nor inexperienced in such matters, who were urging him to pursue a different course? And just how, I ask, did a great many of the sort who supported him try to protect him? With silly little books and empty threats! As if, indeed, foolishness of this sort would either frighten their adversaries or please the good men to whose judgment the whole movement should have been submitted if they had really wanted their story to have a happy resolution.

Now what a host of ills this rashness has created: to no slight degree hostility confronts the study of good letters, as well as the good men who at the outset were not particularly unfriendly to Luther, either because they hoped he would handle the matter differently or because of the enemies they had in common. For it happened that in the beginning, for whatever reason you wish, those who were directing the opposition to Luther were also the foes of learning, and for this reason the disciples of letters were less unfriendly to Luther in order to avoid strengthening the hand of their own enemies by joining the ranks of his adversaries. Even if, whatever the case may be, the concerns of religion ought to have priority over those of studies.

And here, my dear Jonas, I have been constrained at times to hope for some indication of the Gospel spirit when I saw Luther— but especially his backers—working with a kind of guileful cleverness to the end of involving others in a detestable and perilous undertaking. What purpose was served in loading Reuchlin, already burdened enough, with a more crushing ill will? Why was it necessary to mention—often invidiously—my name when the situation did not demand it at all? I had admonished Luther, in a private, sealed letter; it was soon published in Leipzig.[15] I had advised the Cardinal of Mainz, in a sealed letter, not to rashly turn over Luther —whose cause, so far, was acceptable to most good men—to the capricious passions of certain men. It was printed, in substance, before it was delivered. Pirckheimer complains in his letter to me that some missives, which no one had even delivered to him, had been printed and were being circulated. In these letters they urge him to keep on the course which he had begun—by which it is obvious that they would make him, willy-nilly, a member of their faction.

From books of mine which I wrote before I even dreamed of the rise of Luther they have plucked out certain distasteful passages which seemed to have kinships with some of Luther's teachings and published them in a German translation.[16] And those who do this wish to seem to be friends of mine, although no deadly enemy could do anything more damaging. Those who would like to do me the most harm have less talent for doing it. They have furnished my enemies with a weapon, so that now these foes are proclaiming in public sermons the points on which I am at one with Luther. As if a lie, indeed, may not have a resemblance to truth on each side, once you overstep the line.

Somewhere, perhaps, I advise against the heedless taking of vows; and I do not approve of the type of people who, leaving at home a wife and children whose lives and moral well-being ought to be their main concern, dash off to St. James or Jerusalem, where they had no business. I advise young men not to be lured into the bonds of the religious life before they know themselves and what the religious life is. Luther, so they say, utterly condemns all such vows. Somewhere I complain that the burden of confession has been made heavier by the traps set by certain men. Luther, they say, teaches that all confession should be rejected as pernicious. Somewhere I have taught that the best authors should be read first, adding that the books of Dionysius [17] may not be as profitable as their titles seem to promise. Luther calls the man silly, I gather, and unfit to be read at all.

A fine similarity, I must say, when another man, going beyond my meaning, twists the sense of what I was saying accurately, in the appropriate context, and with moderation! The laws will be treating me most unfairly, though, if I am to be compelled to guarantee that not even in the future will anyone misuse what I have written. If we may believe his colleague Peter, this felicity did not even befall the Apostle Paul.[18] Still, to speak frankly, if I had foreseen that a time like this would come to pass, either I would not have written some things I did write, or I would have handled them in a different manner. My desire is to benefit everyone in such a way, if possible, as not to injure anyone. Pamphlets of conspirators in which Erasmus is also depicted are being distributed, but as far as I am concerned, there is no name more abhorrent than that of conspiracy or schism or faction.

This whole business, whatever the story is, has been started against my advice and, of course, with my steady disapproval of the tactics. My letters have never been at the service of any partisan group except that of Christ, who is the common possession of us all. I don't know what I accomplish by these letters or by this mode of thinking; certainly I have tried and wish to do good not only to Germans, but to French, Britons, Bohemians, Russians, and even to Turks and Saracens, if I can. That is how far I am from ever wishing to be connected with a faction so dangerous as this.

In the meantime I also hope for common sense in these men who believe anyone can be inveigled into their camp by tricks of this sort. If they want to alienate any sensible man, what better way of doing it? They protest enough that this is *sykinen epikounian*,[19] as the saying goes, although they rely upon such supports in such a hazardous affair. Moreover, I am woefully afraid that this business is going to bring great dishonor to our Germany among the other nations, since the common run of men ordinarily impute the folly of a few to the whole nation.

So, just what has been accomplished, pray tell, by so many venomous little books, by so much foolish talk, so many fierce threats and so much windy rhetoric, except that what was once debated in the universities as a probable opinion may henceforth become an article of faith, and that it may then be hardly safe to teach the Gospel, while there will be nothing that will not be pounced on for the sake of false accusations, every problem having been exacerbated. Luther could—with great benefit for the Christian flock—have devoted himself to the evangelical philosophy. He could have enriched the world by bringing out books if he had refrained from these works which could not but result in dissension.

He has also deprived my works of a good part of the benefit they possessed. Not even the disputations in the universities, which used to enjoy the utmost leeway, are now free. If it is right to hate anyone because of personal injuries, the Lutherans have hurt no one more than me. Nevertheless, I would wish even so that this far worse discord be resolved, and resolved by those methods that will not cause it to erupt later on in a worse fashion, as a badly treated ulcer is likely to do.

NOTES

1. Mysterious and secret.
2. Acts 2:40.
3. Acts 2:13-15.
4. Joel 2:28-32.
5. Acts 3:14.
6. Acts 2:29.
7. 1 Cor. 9:22.
8. Acts 17:22-31.
9. A Greek didactic poet of the third century B.C. The verse quoted by Paul was from an invocation to Zeus opening one of his poems.
10. Recanted.
11. Acts 23:2-5.
12. See, for example, Eph. 6:5, Col. 3:22; Titus 2:9-10.
13. Cf. *Adagia* (*LB*, II, 51C). Cited by Allen, p. 489n.
14. Gal. 5:13.
15. Written in May, 1519. The letter is translated in J. Huizinga's *Erasmus of Rotterdam*, pp. 229-231.
16. Perhaps a reference to Spalatin's German translation of the letter to Volz included in this selection (Allen, p. 491n).
17. The so-called "Pseudo-Areopagite," highly regarded in the Middle Ages, who attached the name of the original, named in Acts 17:34, to certain of his own writings, including "On Divine Names" and "On Mystical Theology." He is thought to have lived sometime during the fourth or fifth centuries.
18. 2 Pet. 3:15, 16.
19. Frail support. Allen (p. 492n) cites *Adagia* 685, in *LB*, II, 245F-255C.

*From a letter to Duke George of Saxony,
from Basel, 1526 (EE, VI, 1743).*

I HAVE READ REPEATEDLY the letters in which you answer
the contentious Luther, wonderfully good-humored, candid, and
clever; and, as is appropriate to a Christian prince, they possess
sufficient sternness but much more of mildness. Would that the
Lord would prevail upon the mind of that man to defer to the most
wholesome advice with which you close your letter. I can never
marvel enough at the spirit and character of the man. If he is
moved by an evil and perverse genius, what has ever arisen more
deadly to the Catholic Church? If by a good one, I miss in many
respects—not to say in every one—the fruits of the spirit of the
Gospel. If he is drawn by a composite of good and bad traits, who
can have had such enormous vitality of two types within the same
heart?

Many views no longer to be countenanced have crept into the
life of Christians; some have become so absorbed with traditions
that these are identified with virtues. A great many things disquiet
the devout, things they would like to see changed if they could
accomplish this short of world-wide chaos. Of this mind, I know,
is the emperor. But to Luther everything is wrong. That party of
his, though—even if no one were to attack what he has written,
even if the pope and the emperor were to approve it—will eventually disintegrate, so great is the disagreement among the members
themselves, not to mention the character of this populace whom
this evangelism has produced among us, which is scarcely evangelic! It remains for wisdom, strengthened by the authority of the
rulers, to so restrain the seditious license of the Lutherans that a
more perilous conflagration does not spring up in another quarter.
I am talking about the bad monks and a good many theologians of
the same stripe; what sort they are among you I don't know, but
among the Spaniards and Hungarians and Poles and Netherlanders
—but especially among the French—these fellows have without
exception kicked up an extraordinary row in opposition to good

174

letters and me, by whom they suppose these studies have been either invented or encouraged. By their uproar and slanderous books —for they rely upon such tactics as these—they would have prevailed had not the power of the princes and patrons checked their impotent and two-faced agitations. This is what the most Christian King of France did a few days ago; if Your Highness should wish to learn about any aspect of this story, he can do so from the letter we have sent to Jerome Emser, a recipient of your favor. I have not presumed to belabor Your Most Illustrious Highness, so busy with affairs of state, with gossipy trifles.

How I am equipped to oppose Luther, or what we may have started in our treatises, I do not know; for what has my *Diatribe* [1] accomplished except that he has asserted his own dogma even more intransigently? Certainly, as far as my powers, however insignificant, carry me, I will not desert Catholic unity, to which I owe my life. One part of *Hyperaspitae* came out long ago, but the plotting of certain people whom I have just now been talking about having sprung up throughout every quarter of the world, this compelled me to meet a current evil with books and letters and to abandon the work in hand. This summer, for instance, Paris has sent me five volumes full of rabid accusations against me.[2] They have been producing the same stuff in other places also. Even so, I would have made out satisfactorily in both matters except that in June such an illness seized this good-for-nothing body of mine, frail even at best, that the physicians provided no relief or dared to extend any hope. So I am alive only by the grace of God, surviving as long as He sees fit. I will take up now what I began, and—if the Lord gives me strength—will finish it shortly.

I have sent a copy of Luther's letters to Your Highness, and your replies to him, to the English court. . . .

NOTES

1. His *De libero arbitrio*, which Luther had answered with his *De servo arbitrio*. The vituperative tone of Luther's treatise led Erasmus to reply in kind with his *Hyperaspitae*.

2. A reference to, among others, the *Annotationes* of Natalis Beda, part of which were directed at Erasmus, and the attacks of a Petrus Sutor (Le Couturier), a Carthusian theologian, who had condemned all new translations of the Bible, including Erasmus' Greek New Testament. (Allen, pp. 132n and 286-7n).

From a letter to Simon Pistorius, con-
temporary with the letter to Duke George
(EE, VI, 1744).

T HE FACT THAT you plead my case with the Prince [1] to say
that I have never sincerely departed from the principles of the
Church is a remark, my dear Pistorius, which is not very clear to
me; I have never departed from what is acceptable to the Church
either sincerely or insincerely. But it is necessary to make distinctions between the regulations of the Church. Some are those of
general councils, some are from rescriptions, some are the work of
bishops, some that of the Roman Pope but equivalent to ordinances
of the people, such as those of the Camerlingo. Again, certain ones
of those made by synods are permanent, while others are made
for the time being. Similarly, certain ones are hallowed and to be
considered as resting upon Holy Writ; others are of the sort that
can vary in accordance with the current situation.

Now, however often I stress the necessity of changing regulations, I am thinking only of these which can be changed without
throwing overboard anything essential to piety. Nor do I ever argue
that even this should be done without the backing of eminent authority. To be quite frank about it, when this disastrous upheaval
worsened I was openly of the opinion that if a few of these rules
were modified, that tempest might be stilled to some kind of tranquillity. In the meantime, I will not talk about the vices which,
under the guise of religious worship, have invaded the Church and
become so oppressive that they have virtually extinguished the last
spark of evangelic vitality.

Why this is, not everyone understands. Secular rulers are right
in guarding against any loosening of the bonds of public order; but
this is a matter of moral awareness. When I now see neither side
willing to give an inch to the other, I pray only that God will grant
a lucky solution. I don't know who else can achieve it. Many think
that his evil can be put down by laws and penalties—and maybe
it will be quieted—but only for a time. And even if it can be quelled

176

permanently, the surreptitious mutterings and problems of conscience will not stop. The authority of the Church does not crumble just because some things have been altered, for cogent reasons, by leaders of the Church, something that has already been done not infrequently by our predecessors.

THE FACT that I have written that neither side seems reasonable does not mean that I am attacking the Church, but there are those who would force more upon us than it is necessary to believe. I was talking about certain theologians and monks, not the Church. For example, those on the other side of the Alps would like us to believe that one pope of Rome is more mighty than the universal Church and all of Christendom. Those on this side[2] also have certain convictions, some of which I am unwilling to defend; nevertheless, if I don't do so, they raise a hullabaloo. So, I have not said that I belonged to neither party, only that I was blindly committed to neither. Anyone who is slavishly obedient in every respect is so committed. It is not so important to conform in opinions so much as in character and moral tone, which I have found to be most corrupt in a good many people who most noisily parade their Ecclesiastical orthodoxy.

In regard to there being no immediate necessity of burning Luther's books, this seemed, considering the times, more politic in terms of the public situation. If the Church were to allow the use of the sacrament in both kinds, I don't see the least bit of harm from it; She once did allow this to the Bohemians. I don't approve, however, of anyone's stirring up a hubbub among Christian people by this dispensation. I do not condone marriage for priests, nor would I soften the vows for monastic life unless this comes about by the authority of pontiffs, with the intention of strengthening the Church, not destroying it. I consider it barbarous to force boys and girls into it, and an act of piety to free those imprisoned in it by fraud. In the early Church priests and monastics had to *prefer* celibacy and an ascetic life. Now, since practices have become so corrupt, perhaps we should choose the lesser evil. If this view doesn't please the dignitaries of the Church, let it be dismissed as nonsense.

As to what you write about the ungodly licence of some, I have encouraged no one in such excesses; I have to some degree restrained many. You are fearful of paganism. I see Judaism preempting almost everything. If, religious and secular, high and low, we were to turn with sincere hearts to Christ, the Head of our faith, and if each of us, acknowledging his own sins, were to pray for His mercy with unanimous devotion, we would shortly see a happy end to these tumults. Now, as long as most people are intent upon serving their own personal interests, not even the public interest is properly taken care of.

NOTES

1. Duke George.
2. The orthodox party in Germany (Allen, p. 402).

To Willibald Pirckheimer, a wealthy patron of learning and art as well as an author and translator, from Basel. 1527. (EE, VII, 1893)

PEACE IS PERISHING, and love and faith and learning and morality and civilized behavior. What is left? . . . I have said, certainly without dissimulation, and from the heart, that I have never swerved from the truth of the Eucharist. Just how much weight the authority of the Church has with others I do not know: for me, certainly, it has so much that I could agree with the Arians and the Pelagians if the Church had approved what they taught. It is not that Christ's words do not suffice for me, but it should not seem strange if I follow the Church as an exegete by whose authority I was persuaded to believe in the canonical scriptures. Perhaps others have either more talent or more industry; I acquiesce in nothing more securely than in the positive judgments of the Church. There is no end to opinions and argumentation . . . .

From a letter written in 1527 to Martin Bucer, a Dominican monk who later became prominent in the Reform movement. (EE, VII, 1901) Reprinted in full in J. Huizinga, Erasmus and the Age of Reformation *(New York, 1957), pp. 243-246.*

Y OU GATHER TOGETHER many conjectures as to why I have not aligned myself with your church. You should know, however, that the first and most cogent of all reasons for my not joining that group was my conscience; if it could have been convinced that what was being done proceeded from God, I would long since have been campaigning in your camp. A second reason is the fact that I see in that herd of yours many who are alien to any evangelical commitment. I dismiss rumors and suspicions; I am talking about what I have experienced—I may even say, to my hurt—and not just at the hands of the mob, but even those who seem to be *somebodies,* not to say leaders. It is not my business to censure what I know nothing about; it is a big world. But I have known some who before they joined your faith were very fine men; what kind of men they are now I do not know. At any rate, I have discovered that several of them have been made worse, none of them better, so far as human judgment can ascertain.

A third reason which has discouraged me is the bitter dissension between leaders of the movement. To say nothing about the Prophets and the Anabaptists, with what corrosive pamphlets Zwingli, Luther, and Osiander quarrel among themselves. I have never approved of the tyranny of the rulers, but the behavior of some of these people provokes this ferocity when, if you really had what you claim, they ought to have been advancing the cause of the Gospel by the holiness and forbearance of their character. To pass over other things, what purpose was served by the kind of abusive treatment Luther offered the King of England when, with the world's approval, he had undertaken so difficult a task? [1] Did he not give a thought to the part he was playing? Did he not con-

sider that the eyes of the whole world were fastened on him alone?
And here we have the principal figure of this movement, whom I
am not annoyed with just because he has treated me so derisively.
What disturbs me deeply is the fact that he has abandoned the
cause of the Gospel, the fact that he has stirred up princes, prelates,
pseudo-monks, and pseudo-theologians against the principles of
good men, the fact that he has doubled a slavery which was already
intolerable. And I seem to see ahead a cruel and bloody time if
the offended faction gets its breath again, something which it is
plainly doing now. You will say that there is no crowd which does
not have some bad men in it. Obviously the leaders should have
exercised especial care as to their conduct, nor should they have
deigned to encourage liars, perjurers, drunkards, and whoremongers.
Now I hear—and virtually see—that things have turned out far
otherwise. If the husband had found his wife easier to get along
with, the teacher his pupil more respectful, the magistrate the citizen more responsible, the contractor his workman more reliable,
the customer the merchant less tricky—that would have been the
great recommendation for their evangelicalism. Now the conduct of
some of them has made people grow cool toward this movement
who at first, out of a love of piety and dislike for Pharisaism, favored
it. And the princes—while they see an *atakton* populace springing
up, made up of vagrants, fugitives, bankrupts, the down-and-out and
wretched, a great many even evil-doers—are cursing, even those
who in the beginning had entertained high hopes.

I mention these things, not without grave concern, not only because I foresee that an affair badly handled will become worse,
but also because I myself will have to smart for it. Certain carping
critics impute to my writings the fact that scholastic theologians
and monks are in several places made less of than they would like,
the fact that ceremonies are neglected, and the authority of the
Roman Pontiff is disregarded, although it is no mystery what the
origin of this evil is. Those people were stretching the rope too
tight, and now it is parting. They very nearly set the authority of
the pope before that of Christ, they measured all religious devotion
by ceremonies, they stiffened confession beyond reason, monks
were in control without check, already thinking of out-and-out open
tyranny. So, finally, it came about that, as the proverb has it, *to
kalodon teinomenon,* the string snapped. It could not have turned
out any other way. Again, considering the way the other side began

the action of their drama, it could not have ended in any other way than we see. Pray God we not see even more barbarous events!

If the leaders of this movement had Christ as their object, however, they should not only have refrained from vices but even from any appearance of evil; they ought not to have given even a slight impediment to the Gospel, carefully avoiding those actions which, even if they are permissible, are still of no help. First of all, they should have shunned all seditious acts. If they had carried on with moderation and sincerity, they would have enlisted the support of princes and prelates, for they have not all been given up for lost. Nor should they have heedlessly uprooted anything without having something better ready to take the place of the worse. Nowadays those who have given up doing the canonical Hours, pray not at all. Many who have taken off the Pharisaical robes are worse in other respects than they were before. Those who scorn the regulations of bishops do not even obey the precepts of God. Those who neglect the selection of foods pamper their palates and their bellies. It is a protracted tragedy, part of which we ourselves hear every day, part of which we learn about from others. I never liked the abolition of the Mass, even though I have always disliked this sordid and greedy breed of mass-performers. And other things could have been changed without such chaos. As it is, some people like nothing at all that has been an established practice, as if they could create a new world all at once. There will always be some things which good men must endure. For that reason, if anyone thinks that the Mass should be abolished because many people misuse it, then the sermon should also be abolished, though this is virtually the only custom you accept. I feel the same way about the invocation of saints and about images.

NOTE

1. A reference to Henry VIII's *Assertio Septem Sacramentorum* which Luther had replied to in his *Contra Henricum regem Angliae*. The abusiveness seems to have been shared by both tracts (see Rainer Pineas, *Thomas More and Tudor Polemics* [Bloomington, Indiana, 1968], pp. 8-14).

From a letter to John Longlond, Bishop of Lincoln, in 1528, defending the Colloquies, *under attack in England and recently condemned in Paris.*
(EE, VII, 2037)

THE *COLLOQUIES* APPROVE of confession; those people who are commercializing their own interests under the seal of the Gospels are the ones who growl. Thus, a soldier on his way to confession is laughed at, just as the crowd is accustomed to laugh. There is nothing to offend the critics except that I say somewhere that the confession made to God is best, and a young man remarks that he had never followed this practice invented by men. But I am talking about this kind of confession now practiced, which nowhere do I censure. No one has yet been able to show me that it was instituted by Christ, nor is it of that semblance. If anyone should show me, he would win my applause. In the meantime, however, I maintain that it ought to be kept as if Christ had instituted it.

In my little book on the manner of confession[1] I do not argue that we should not practice it but that we should confess in a beneficial way. I could not accomplish this purpose without making some disagreeable points which I do not ascribe to confession itself but to faults in both those who make it and those who receive it. Now, when the whole world is full of tales about shameful carryings on and wickedness indulged in under the cover of confession, they are angry with me because I have touched upon certain things in the most temperate fashion. Nor do they take into account how many things of this sort I have kept silent about out of a sense of Christian propriety, or so that even a hint could not taint the mind of the reader. Many monks, however, are zealous for this business of confession not out of love of righteousness, but because they reap a rich harvest from it as long as they dominate the homes of rich men whose secrets they have learned, as long as they attend people at the point of death, as long as they get a bite out of the wills. Let my critics take a close look at the Lerna of evils which have thus far been born of confessions and cease to be aghast at what I have suggested about confessing in the right way. Let them likewise consider how much superstitition there has been in connection with the worship of saints, what a plague has descended from man-made ceremonialism, and they will see that our warning was vitally necessary.

The most pleasing worship of saints is to imitate their lives, though no one need look for a more exemplary model for life than that of Christ himself. I promote this true worship. For such people as these, however, the superstition was more profitable; hence their loud outcries. In no place do I condemn ecclesiastical ceremony, but I point out how ceremonies should be used and I make an appeal for things more beneficial. If Christ teaches this very same thing, if Saint Paul does, if it is righteous and holy, why are they shouting against me? But some exclaim, "Who does not know that the ultimate goal of righteousness should not be defined by ritual?" In reality, though, who does not know that nowadays all religon has been reduced to ritualism and because of that, evangelical vitality has been virtually dispensed with? This condition was rather convenient in terms of prestige and profit for certain men. Christ, however, yearns for another kind of profit; His prestige is consonant only with the highest understanding. Let them congratulate themselves upon their true piety; if this is lacking what is the ostentation of ceremony but hypocrisy?

I have made a full reply to Natalis Beda[2] concerning the choosing of foods, if the man had any sense of propriety. No one is really so devout, if he looks carefully at the matter, that he would not prefer that duty be changed into exhortation. Assuredly these are times not so much for laying snares as for observing fasts in the heart, especially if the lives of priests offered a shining example of moderation and Christian temperance. In France, it is reported, two men are being tried for no other reason than the fact that, afflicted by illness, they ate meat on two days of Lent. You see what ceremonialism does. Obviously it causes us to stultify the teaching of God on account of the regulations of men; we regard parricide more tolerantly than slighting the arrangements of popes, even though no pope has forbidden that a sick man should eat what his health requires.

I censure the extravagant proliferation of feast days, particularly now that no days are more given over to sinning than these holy days. I thoroughly approve of moderate feast days, but I would like them devoted to the sacred observances for which they were intended, not to carousing and debauchery. As for miracles, today the Christian religion does not hinge upon them; without question, a great number of tales of such things are being foisted upon the world by men shrewdly promoting their own interests with the aid of fake miracles. Let us believe all the more steadfastly in what sacred scripture contains, even if we do not swallow every trifling fabrication of men.

I F ANY IMPROVEMENT is to be made, let there be practiced that moderation which befits Christians, as we see it was practiced by the early Fathers, whose learned piety successfully dealt with so many troops of heretics. What do they think is accomplished by these stupid uproars, this malicious syncretism, vicious disparagement, abusive impudence, worse-than-belligerent censure, and out-and-out lies? The Church, the Dove of Christ, is not accustomed to overcome malice with malice, folly with folly, wickedness with wickedness, but has learned to conquer evil with good. No one can question my intentions. I could have been a leader in the Lutheran church but preferred to arouse the hatred of all Germany against myself rather than withdraw from the fellowship of the Church. I could be the founder of a new faction; I have cultivated no disciple of my own, but everybody I could I have entrusted to Christ, preferring to have fellow Christians rather than followers. I seek no fortune, although I have long been solicited by the most eminent princes, and no small number of them. If I seem to speak arrogantly in this respect, let it only be understood that I speak with absolute truth. I persevere in indigence, nor do my continuous and arduous labors provide a staff for poor health and advancing age to lean upon.

These things show how much I detest heresy. If certain aspects of my writings give offense, those who are offended disregard how much more deeply people for whom the admonition was intended have offended and are in need of healing. I am not sorry for the fact that I have tried to recall the theology of the schoolmen to the founts of Scripture and the interpretations of the early Fathers, especially when I think of the frivolous nit-picking it has succumbed to. If they would like to restore theology to her pristine dignity, let them do it, not by ranting at others but by revealing a sensible theology worthy of Christ, such as is now being done in several schools. Devoutness itself and a moral sense led me to make some suggestions concerning monks, although often enough here too I have often made concessions to Christian modesty and the name of religion. These people will more successfully restore the authority they once had if they show that they are really monks in their holy and righteous behavior rather than by vilifying somebody else's reputation with stupid lies. And if they really want to promote the dignity of their orders, let them restrain such brawling pettifoggers, who particularly disgrace them by their words and actions, and have recourse to that integrity of life which at one time won them such great good will from the world.

In brief, a sincere effort should be made to bring about the triumph of Christ in these turbulent affairs and the obtaining of victory for Him alone, not for the sake of human passions which are seen in every faction strenuously claiming victory for itself. Let pope and cardinals win if the center of their regard is Christ; let the monks win if you please if they are performing the work of Christ. But if they are concerned for their own reputation, their own bellies, their own profit and power, they are warring not in the name of Christ but of the world. The evil is not removed but disregarded; the sickness is not cured but changed, perhaps for the worse. What Luther has sanely taught and advocated let us follow, not because he taught it but because it was sound and in accord with holy Scripture. I see a danger now that we will not be set straight in agreement but, as it usually happens, will be pushed apart into diversity. For example, although formerly there was quite enough superstition in the culthoods of saints, now they will intensify the practice just to be that much more unlike Lutheran teaching. But this is a place for temperance, not extremism. People should be taught that images are nothing but tokens provided for the understanding of the laity. Saints should indeed be venerated, but not worshipped, as they say. It is finer to lift up the heart to Christ without the aid of corporeal images than with them; it is better to ask Christ for whatever we wish to obtain. It is more salutary to display Christ imitated in ourselves than any saint whatever; saints are venerated most devoutly by following the example of their good deeds. The indiscriminate collecting of images is not appropriate to the Church; in this matter there should be a regard for measure and propriety. But to put it briefly, if in everything else the emphasis were upon not extreme measures but restraint, it would be possible to hope for a happy resolution of this furor.

This will never happen, however, unless princes and leaders of the Church eliminate private passions from their policy and have regard for nothing but the glory of Christ and the general welfare of the Christian religion. Let God be thus present in our actions and He will convert tumult into tranquillity. It is clear enough that this tempestuous situation has been visited upon the world not without the will of God, just as He once inflicted various plagues upon the Egyptians to bring them to their senses. It would therefore be the wisest position for all of us to take refuge in God's mercy and for each of us to recognize his own culpability. As it is, some attribute all the sin to others; no one acknowledges his own. We are seeking, not a cure for evils, but revenge.

NOTES

1. *Exomologesis.*
2. Beda, a conservative theologian at the University of Paris, had been critical of Erasmus' *De esu carnium.*

From a letter in 1529 to Justus Decius, author and patron of arts and letters in Poland. He gave Erasmus an annual pension of 20 florins in 1532. (EE, VIII, 2175)

THE THINGS LUTHER is upbraiding us with are truer than I should like. Free will, good works, merit, and like matters are subjects which could be debated by the learned to the benefit of right living, if the obstinacy hostile to truth and the animosity that blinds all judgment were absent. And those things which Luther advocates, if pursued with moderation, would in my opinion approach more closely the meaning of the Gospels. That which has been hatefully objected to in the matter of images did very little for piety but a great deal for dissension. Nor do I see why the Mass should be totally abolished, even if Oecolampadius were teaching the truth, for neither the body nor the soul of Christ referred to in the observance is what is adored. His divine nature, however, which is adored, is never absent.

But here, they say, the general run of men fall into error. Nothing is easier than teaching the people that nothing made by man ought to be adored at all in the service. In another respect, no one is sure that the host has been truly consecrated except the celebrant. But it is the silent and constant assent of the worshiper that frees him from the peril of idolatry. If it were not for the fact that I am influenced by the very substantial agreement of the Church, I should be able to adopt the view of Oecolampadius; [1] now I abide in that which the Church, as an expounder of Scripture, has handed down to me. Otherwise, I find no passage in the Holy Scriptures where it can be firmly established that the Apostles consecrated bread and wine in the flesh and blood of the Lord.

NOTE

1. Oecolampadius upheld the metaphorical against the literal interpretation of the word "body" in the Eucharist.

188

*From a letter written to John Botzheim in
1529. Botzheim, like Erasmus, was at first
favorably inclined toward the Reformation
but afterwards revolted by its excesses.
(EE, VIII, 2205)*

SOME PEOPLE HAVE provided no small occasion for these
disorders by stretching the rope too tight, preferring to break
it rather than save it by easing the tension. The Roman Pontiff, for
instance, being the ruler of the whole Church, ought to be granted
the very great honor in keeping with his very great authority; but
those who have endlessly proclaimed his might, if they have not
broken the rope, have certainly frayed it. Pontifical indulgences,
as long as they stayed within reason, the people reverently accepted. On the other hand, where pardoners and monks with an
eye on their own profit bring them in with unbelievable ostentation, where they advertise them to the skies, and peddle them
greedily, while endlessly every church is filled with the cross and
the scarlet chest, while on every post is fixed the papal insignia with
the triple crown, while some men are even encouraged to reword
them—something they say has virtually been done in Spain—then
they have very nearly snapped the rope.[1]

Furthermore, when people distort the invocation and reverence
of saints into superstition, or even exalt it beyond measure, here
the rope is nearly snapped. The practice of supplying images and
statues was a fine one, either for showing honor or as a reminder
of those whose example could move us to piety of life; but when
churches everywhere are crowded with unseemly paintings, when
we are slipping into virtual idolatry in these superstitious practices,
we have provided a chance for breaking this rope.

It is also an established custom, as well as a pious act, to praise
God in hymns and spiritual songs; but when one hears music in
church better suited to weddings and dinner parties than to divine
worship, when the sacred text is drowned out by the strenuous
bellowing of the voices, when even trifling popular tunes of the
people are sometimes sung in place of sacred ones; finally, when

189

nothing but this droning is heard in churches, this rope begins to be in peril. What can be more sacred than the Mass? But when dirty, ignorant mass-priests learn perhaps three masses without any understanding of them, and go through them like a cobbler making a pair of shoes; when those who have just approached the Lord's table are living in open sin, when this sacred rite is not performed with that reverence which is fitting, when they turn so holy an observance into a public fair, then they have all but broken this rope.

What is more salutary than private confession? But when they make this too stringent and too much a cause of uneasiness, when under the pretext of confession they are after the money of simple people, when they are laying an ambush for the chastity of maidens and committing other unmentionable crimes, when this practice devised to be therapy for the soul they turn to their own power, have they not provided great help to the breaking of the rope?

Thus it is that when no rationality or limit is applied to human arrangements, when many men either set up certain practices or pervert them to their own profit and power, this rope is put in jeopardy. So, perhaps, when priests are not eager to lead a life worthy of respect but nevertheless demand excessive respect, in the eyes of many they become contemptible. In the same way, when monks do not seek to gain the good will of men with their uprightness of life and character, but depending upon riches, numbers, intrigue, and other evil practices, are zealous to crush by force those they cannot deceive by guile, when they attribute so much to their robes as the power of warding off sickness, bringing good luck to the home, and guarding against evil spirits, what else have they accomplished except that whereas they were once regarded as gods, now they are scarcely considered even good men.

I do not mention these things, my dear Botzheim, to support those who, because of the culpability of evil practitioners, assail things good in themselves, and prefer to overthrow just institutions rather than improve them: rather, I bring them up partly so that we may on this account react with more restraint toward those to whom we ourselves have given provocation, and partly so that I may indicate means by which this turbulent situation may be restored to tranquillity. As we now see human zealotry, I am afraid that whichever way the die falls, those who with sincere heart aspire to the glory of Christ and the honor of His house are going to be no better off. Those who ingratiate themselves under the label of Evangelicals behave altogether in such a way that they seem to be eager for vileness, or money, or anarchy and unrestricted liberty to do whatever they please. Certainly no one becomes better; most become worse. As for the other faction which insists on being regarded as Catholic, there are those who will so little suffer anything whatever to be taken from long-standing practices that they even add to them a great deal of superstition and Pharisaism. There are those who, though on the face of it they execrate Luther verbally, nevertheless in many things practice his teachings, if indeed he ever did teach this. They neglect the Hours, nor do they pray at all; they disregard the fasts prescribed by regulations of the Church, dining even more lavishly on these days than on others. They boldly disdain the edicts of the Roman Pontiffs concerning clerical immunity, shunning of simony, attacking the clergy, and many more things, so that I can hardly decide whether any people are more damaging to papal ordinances than those who set themselves up as their very special defenders.

NOTE

1. Cf. Philip Hughes, *A History of the Church*, III: 500-502.

Appendix to a letter to Archbishop of Cologne, Hermann Von Weid in 1528. (EE, VII, 1976)

AFFAIRS OF *bonae literae* were going along famously, except that the violent factiousness of certain people, trying to give us a new world all at once, has virtually ripped apart the fabric of the state with discordant views and contentious dogmas, and has shattered the harmony of the whole Church. And here, indeed, has vanished my fruit and recompense for so many sleepless nights, so much toil, so many years spent.

Personal loss, however, would matter little if it were compensated for with public good, especially, of course, the glory of Christ, who ought to be the only goal of all our actions. There can be nothing felicitous and prosperous in human affairs except what Christ performs in us so that, with our human passions subdued, our will may serve His will.

We already had a plethora of these ills without adding to them the unyielding rages of monarchs. Although these rages have brought so much calamity upon the world, nevertheless they are more and more exacerbated every day, threatening utmost chaos in everything unless some deus ex machina appearing suddenly brings an unlooked-for solution to this turbulent tragedy. Meanwhile, with hope almost abandoned in such a tempest, since virtually nothing remains but prayers, we cling to the fragments of the vessel just in case Christ should reveal a port somewhere to those who have been tossed about so long and so violently. . . . But even though widespread warfare brings with it a host of evils, these things make men more wretched than wicked. More critical is the crisis in the matter of belief, which, being the most costly of all, takes away from us good understanding. Here there is almost more obstinacy of contention than in warring monarchs. I don't know how it happens that no one inflicts more damage upon this cause or that one than those who seem to themselves to be cherishing it most stoutly. Thus some men pull in opposite directions on the little rope of contention until, having stretched it too tight, as the saying goes, it snaps and they all sprawl upon their backsides.

There is no point in prying into everything, much less in making pronouncements about them. It is enough to deal with those matters which are particularly relevant to gospel teaching. The world has certain claims of its own and schools have their own disciplines; but nothing should be disseminated among the people except that which is not open to question, is essential to matters of faith and conducive to righteous living. Some, just as an example, curtail confession too much; on the other hand, some accept the whole of it, when there is some middle ground between the two. Similarly, certain people exalt the Mass to such an extent that it is a good livelihood for ignorant and venal priests or celebrants, as well as the assurance that men will go on living sinfully. Again, others reject the Mass entirely. And here is occasion for moderation which would let us be of the opinion that the Mass should be made more pure and consecrated without wiping it out of existence. By the same token, some people in their credulously extravagant veneration of saints virtually do away with the worship of Christ, while others damn as impious any reverence for them. Some try to abolish completely every order of monasticism; others too much respect these human arrangements, rituals, titles, and kinds of robes. In these matters, and in others, a modest good sense would make it possible for us to possess more definite and more sound articles of faith, for there to be a more heartfelt and less perturbed kind of confession, a more devout and more reverent kind of mass, to have, if fewer, certainly better priests and monks.

Although I am deeply distressed by this tempest of the world I still have some hope that Divine Providence will change these tumults ultimately for the good. Prudent moderation on the part of leaders will be most conducive toward this end, a moderation which shuns factious impiety in such a way as to always have an understanding of true righteousness, plucking up weeds, that is, in such way as not to damage the wheat. This would be done more readily if, purging ourselves of private interests, we all fixed our sights on one target, the glory of Christ. At present most people are pursuing their own advantage and thus it happens that neither privately nor publicly is it well with us. Some of us place the blame on others when this disaster of the world is really the hand of God summoning all men to the improvement of their lives. If we would all take refuge in Him, He would easily turn this storm in human affairs into peaceful calm.

From one of the Epistolae Floridae, *addressed to Cuthbert Tunstall, 1530. Tunstall was Bishop of London and Durham, and one of the English humanists sympathetic with Rome.* (EE, VIII, 2263)

THE OLD FRIEND preserves his old practice through it all, heaping kindness upon kindness and with the most affectionate, loyal advice and counsel looking after the welfare and good name of his friend!

To the extent that one can divine the future from the prologue of this affair, after the prolonged wrangling by voice and pamphlet this business will very shortly be conducted by cannon and battle-axe. Were it not that the welfare of my soul takes precedence over that of my body and material condition, I would rather be in the camp of those from whom I have fled. But far be it from me that I should forsake the unity of the Church for the mere pittance of life remaining to one who is not only advanced in years but also nursing the stone—that is to say, certain death—in his bladder. What some petty priests of that Church draw from my lucubrations they themselves will understand. If men like Augustine now dominated the Church, I could readily come to agreement with them, but I am afraid that if Augustine were to write now what he once wrote he would not be attuned to what this age demands much better than is Erasmus. What you write is pious; that fire is not to be extinguished by fire; but it is an impiety to endure the calumnies of ungodliness. What did Augustine do? I could assemble countless passages from him which now would be labeled heresy, and almost as many from Saint Paul. They will consider me, of course, to be a ninny; but meanwhile mere ninnies can lament the fact that some people have emasculated the life out of the Gospel with their man-made subtilizing. What this life is many do not understand, and many abuse with this verbalizing. If the scholastic theologians and monks think they are going to restore peace to the Church by this method, they are patently deluded. We must take refuge in Christ. Here, here alone is the Truth, the fire not to be extinguished by fire. *This* conflagration has sprung from the authoritarianism of Rome and bad monks, and to extinguish the flame those people are adding oil to it. We see these things and are grieved by them, but we leave the turning point of the drama to Christ, the Choragus. Here I know that I am holding on between the devil and the deep blue sea,[1] nor do I see how I may safely rescue myself. The only thing left is to commend ourselves to the Lord.

I am not unreservedly happy for Thomas More, even if I do not grieve on his account. I earnestly congratulate your Britain, which means something to me also.[2]

I had translated three homilies of Chrysostom on Acts; his works displease me because I see nothing of Chrysostom there. Nevertheless at your urging I took the codex in hand, but I have never read anything more unskillful. I have written better things when I was in my cups and snoring. It is full of inane and clumsy little observations which it is impossible to handle satisfactorily.

THE FRAGMENT of Origen[3] I have rendered faithfully; even if it had contained some error, it was not dangerous, since no one reads him today as an expounder of dogma, the errors of the man having long since been exposed.

The early Fathers reverently discussed the Eucharist some time before this had become a subject for debate. Not even now, perhaps, has the Church clearly explained in what way the Body is present, as the effect of the accidents or of the very bread. It is certain, too, that in the time of the Apostles there was a gathering together which the laity carried on among themselves and which was devoted to prayer and blessing. This bread, it is likely, they called the Body of the Lord, so that frequently, even in Holy Scriptures, the same term is applied both to the symbol and the thing symbolized. It can be supposed that Origen is talking about this communion in that passage. One can find no place in canonical writings where the Apostles clearly consecrated the Body of the Lord as it is now consecrated on the altar, with the exception of one passage in 1 Corinthians, chapter 11. Nevertheless, in chapter 10, on which these remarks of Paul are based, he does not seem to be dealing with priestly consecration. Now it is not a foolish remark for us to believe that Origen was speaking here of a true consecration. What is material there, that is to say, the bread or the accidents, disappear, nor is there any benefit in the partaking of it if faith is lacking. It is not irreligious for the Real Body there to be called a type or a symbol, since the invisible Body lies concealed within the tokens and this itself, the Real Body that is partaken of, is a symbol of the unity of the Body with the Head and of the members with one another.

As to the fact that you advise me to clarify my own position over and above this, why should I do that rather than anyone else, since I have never thought, spoken, or written otherwise than what Catholic truth maintains? However, what you suggest has been taken care of both in the letter sent off two years ago to the Council at Baden and shortly afterwards in the treatise published this year.[4] This pamphlet has even been translated into German. But what shall I do for those who don't read me? I know that you are too busy.

I have answered the Bishop of Lincoln[5] concerning the *Colloquies*. Those who say that I am making fun of Christian fasts, devotional offerings, ecclesiastical ceremonies, the abstinence from foods directed by the Church, the invoking of saints, and pilgrimages undertaken on account of religion are—to put it baldly and succinctly—judging *atechnos*.[6] I laugh at the superstition of certain people in such matters as these, something that very properly deserves laughter. If you had time to read what I have replied to the Spaniards and to Beda, you would see that those people are manufacturing slander out of nothing. It is something else that goads them on. In Brabant the monks are in control, especially the Observantines. These fellows have prodded a certain young man of their group, brazen, of boundless loquacity and unbridled impudence, a type created for spitting on Erasmus, balking at nothing if only he gets notoriety. By the educated he is laughed at, but he nevertheless is well pleased with himself. Now, I don't wonder at a youth crazy with the thirst for glory; I do wonder at such fathers as those, by whose encouragement he dares to do these things. If they do not see how much hostility and disgrace the boy's callow effrontery is going to attach to the order, I hope they acquire better judgment; if, as I think, they are applauding and supplying the cold water, I hope they acquire a more temperate attitude.

We have developed a thick skin in regard to these things. If I could get rid of the stone I have had in my bladder for two years now, I could easily disregard the other matters. It is a continual discomfort, but thus far endurable. I am not afraid of death, but I should prefer a milder form of it. Many urge an operation but I will bring in the surgeon when I am finally tired of living. Here there is a strong hope that the Emperor's influence may repress the boldness of the sectarians, which is now unendurable to anyone. Would that this might be done, though, without great bloodshed and that the victory might not go to the power of monks and pontiff but to piety and to Christ! We all work for vengeance but no one strives for a more faultless life.

NOTES

1. For *"inter sacrum et saxum."*
2. A reference to More's appointment to the chancellorship.
3. According to Allen (VII, 101), a reference to a fragment of Origen's commentaries on the Gospel according to Matthew.
4. The *Detectio Praestigiarum.*
5. John Longlond. Cf. Epistle 2037.
6. Naively or simple-mindedly.

From a letter of 1530 to Balthasar Mercklin,
an influential churchman in the service of
the Emperor Charles. (EE, VIII, 2284)

INNUMERABLE QUESTIONS EXIST concerning this sacrament; how does transubstantiation come about; how do the accidents remain without the subject; how do they retain the color, smell, taste, and even the effect of filling, of quenching thirst, of nourishing, which the bread and wine had before consecration took place; at what point does it begin to be the body and blood of the Lord; when does it cease to be the substance of body and blood, and another substance follow in the species that have been consumed; how can the same body be in countless places; how can the real body of a man be contained in such a tiny piece of bread, and a great many other questions which it is proper for those who have trained intellects to discuss reasonably among themselves.

For the mass of men it suffices to believe that the real body and blood of the Lord is there after consecration, that it cannot be divided or damaged, that it is not exposed to any indignity, whatever happens to the species. If the body of the Lord were defiled by being discharged into filth of the latrine, or when it descends into the stomach of a man, it would be no more so than when it is partaken of by a man polluted by sins. Of course the sacramental species of the Christian religion are to be treated with all reverence; nevertheless, just as God, who in consequence of His nature is in sewers no less than in the heavens, cannot be harmed or defiled, so the body of the Lord is not enhanced. To put it briefly, over against all the questions raised by human rationalism we should place, first of all, the immense power of God, to whom nothing is impossible, for whom everything is easy; next, how inconceivable are the qualities of the glorified body, especially that of the Lord Jesus. It remains then for us to observe worthily that which we have been persuaded of, and to show in the observance itself that we do believe. For how much purity, how much reverence and awe this mystery to be adored over and over again requires! Who can adequately express it in words?

But who would believe in the sincerity of belief of those people who, during the performance of this sacrament, stroll around the church and gossip or, as is the custom everywhere, stand in the square in front of the church doors killing time with idle stories? At one time that was a place for penitents and catechumens. Some people, just as soon as the mysteries have been shown, rush out to a tavern, leaving the church empty. What kind of practice is this? When some trivial play is being performed, you stay until you hear the "*Valete et plaudite*," but you can't wait for the termination of a sacred sacrament? The most worshipful angelic spirits surround that table; there is the Presence on whom the whole host of heaven rejoices to look. And you belch and yawn, or chatter or tipple, just as if they were putting on some inane show.

Nowadays I see a practice accepted by most, one which perhaps I ought not to call irreligious since it seems to be a product of a certain permissibly human piety of emotion, but even so has been introduced over and above the traditional practice of the Church and is hardly consonant with it. While the sacrament of Consecration is being performed, a choir carols a pretty tune accompanied by a long-winded prayer to the Virgin Mother. Is it appropriate to call upon the Mother, with the Son Himself present? If we wish to preserve the practice of the early Church, this was a time when no voice was heard in the whole church; rather, the people, prostrate on the earth, gave thanks with silent emotion to God the Father, who had given over His Son to death for the salvation of mankind. To this end, surely, the priest is exhorting us when, addressing the people, he says, "Lift up your hearts! Let us give thanks to the Lord our God." Nothing is more appropriate to ineffable mysteries than silence, nor can the amazing love of the Lord Jesus for us be more fittingly praised in any other way than with that most eloquent silence, while, with the din of human voices stilled and with body humbled, the uplifted heart speaks to God.

However, in order for the people to venerate this sacrament as it should be, the way of life of the priesthood is of no little importance. There was a time, when the Church was in its prime, when there was only one sacrament, which only the bishop performed. The religious service first began to attract a crowd of mass-performers and then led even to money-making. Now at last a situation has come about in which many learn to say a mass for the same reason that a common workman learns a trade—this one shoe-making, another brick-laying, still another tailoring. To these people the Mass means nothing but a living. It is right, of course, that he who has served the altar should live from the altar,[1] but it is hardly appropriate for this mystery to be run like an inn; the ministers of this ceremony of worship ought to reflect the dignity of their office, not so much in their gestures or robes or words as in the conduct of their lives. How very appropriate to them are sobriety, modesty, purity, contempt for crass pleasures, and a love for sacred letters!

How incongruous it is for the priest, immediately after such a sacrament, to spend the rest of the day in drinking-bouts, indecent chatter, cards or dicing, in hunting or idle strolling about, and to give very little time, if any at all, to the reading of sacred books or to meditation on things heavenly. Let priests recognize the sublimity of their own profession. When they stand at the altar, they have angels as ministers; when they depart from it, some of them don't hesitate to become the boon companions of the lowest dregs of humanity, to put it rather mildly. The character of those who fill an office of angelic dignity should not, I insist, offer more provocation to heretics to conceive irreverent opinions about so indescribable a mystery; let them honor their own ministry, so that God may in turn honor them, not only among men, but also before his heavenly Father.

NOTE

1. Cf. I Cor. 9:13.

From a letter to Jacopo Sadoleto in 1531.
Sadoleto was later to become a cardinal
in 1536. (EE, IX, 2443)

I SEEM TO INFER from your letters that there are two matters in which you wish I would either be more circumspect or more restrained: first, in mocking these matters which, even if they are not perfect piety, are nevertheless not at odds with true religion, such as the invoking of saints and the use of images. Second, in refuting the charges of anyone, I ought either to wholly disregard those things of which you are the author, or answer them in such a way as not to seem annoyed. Indeed I will not deny that I have been at fault in both respects, and I would much like to undo what I have done in many cases. Certainly—the only thing which I can do now—I correct or moderate many things in the lucubrations which have been brought out, acting as a no less severe critic of my own writings than Saint Augustine, whose example my friends frequently invite me to follow, was of his. But would that you, or someone like you, had been present as a timely advisor for me, for I now realize of what little use to me are the plaudits and speech of those who cry "Good man! Well done!"

Nevertheless certain malicious charges are of the sort that it would be wicked to keep quiet about, as when in repeated sermons or publications I am presented as the originator of impious dogma, the subverter of papal dignity, an *akineton*[1] falsifier of the Scriptures, the founder of schism. A man who would endure these things in silence doesn't seem righteous at all to me. Now that there is no consideration whatever for my good name, what could be less conducive to peace in the church than that a great many people should become convinced of what they, with conniving malice, invented. I have had no bitter disagreement with anyone who either censured only my talents or felt that something was wanting in my behavior. I very readily yield the palm for erudition to anybody you please, and in my behavior I confess that I am only human. But to be speechless before an open accusation of impiety, what is that

201

but to acknowledge the crime, since to reply even mildly and with constraint does not free one from the double suspicion that either he was intellectually too naive or that he is craftily comspiring with traitors to the Church. The peril is not as Cicero imagined it in regard to himself: "Unless you had the thought in mind, Erasmus, you would not act in this way."

Not even here, however, have I had tongue or pen for everybody. Some people, because they deserved such treatment, I have ridiculed, to put it fairly accurately, rather than debated with, never more temperately than those who were exasperating me, as my reputation attests. It is both possible and characteristic for emotion to affect my discretion, and I am, I confess, one who can heat up with anger but who does not nurse his wrath, and is as easily forgetful of injuries as anyone else. But when the thing is done in widely read books I customarily exercise the least forbearance in my anger. This remark you might not totally disapprove, perhaps, if you were free to read their accusations and my defenses. But the saints forbid that you should take so many precious hours from your most devout labors to spend them upon such dismal ditties. That I have no natural talent, furthermore, for such brawls, worse than gladiatorial, as these is made evident by the fact that I have written many defenses, true, but so far nothing but defenses—not even a single attack. But Cato is considered a good man because he was more often leveling charges at others than being brought to the bar himself.

The situation is even more disagreeable because while I am in the arena wielding the net and the hook against the people whose annihilation as the chief foes of religion these fellows are praying for, fighting for them at great risk to fortune and life, one after another they spring on me from the rear. . . .

So much for that part of your letter in which you advise me either to treat the yapping of pettifoggers with silent scorn or to confute them in such a way as to seem very little stirred by anger. I should not want you to think that I say these things, my dear friend, as if I were absoluely blameless and you were admonishing me either uselessly or beyond what I deserve, but in order that you may be more fair to me and pardon more readily my faults thus far.

I come now to the other part of your letter, where you wisely advise me not to oppose popular enthusiasms too acrimoniously when, granting that they are not of unadulterated piety, they are nevertheless not associated with ungodliness—for example, the veneration of saints and the proliferation of paintings. I don't know what has been reported to you, but don't think that in my books I have ever condemned reverence for saints or the use of images. I censure anywhere the superstitious and perverted worship of saints; I consider it a superstition when a soldier about to start upon a looting expedition promises himself a safe return if he kneels respectfully before a statue of Barbara and recites some little prayers, very closely akin to magical incantations, in her honor. I consider it a perversion when saints are worshiped in wax and paint while the whole life of the worshiper is incompatible with their character; the most acceptable way to worship the saints is to imitate their holiness. Pictures and tokens, since they are excellent adornments of life, I have never believed in abolishing, although I should like to see nothing in churches except what is appropriate to such a place.

Over this matter of the invoking of saints and adoration of images there is fierce contention. First of all, there is no passage in Scripture which allows us to invoke saints—unless, perhaps, it pleases us to distort the fact that in the Gospel parable Dives cries out for the help of Abraham. Nevertheless, although in such an important matter to alter anything contrary to the authority of Scripture can be justly reckoned a dangerous procedure, I nowhere censure the invocation of saints, nor do I think it ought to be censured, provided only that superstition—which I frequently find—be absent from it.

Nor is this without reason, for I consider it superstition when saints are petitioned for everything, as if Christ were dead, or when we pray for the aid of saints with the attitude that they are more easily influenced by prayer than God is, or when we beg for particular things from particular saints, as if Catherine might be able to get this for us while Barbara couldn't; or when we appeal to them not as intercessors but as the creators of those blessings which God bestows on us.[2] I don't think it seems blasphemous—or even superfluous, I am sure—to suggest these things, if you have detected the outlandish superstition of our people in this matter.

Now along the same lines the worship of images for which Scripture indeed gives us no support is a graver peril, so that it should seriously worry us. If the fine-spun sophistry of Scotus is accepted, that images ought to be worshiped with the same reverence that is accorded to what the images stand for, those early

Fathers were extraordinarily thick-witted when they objected so strenuously to any images' being placed in the churches of Christians. In our day if the same kinds of adoration, what for the images of God and images of saints, do not exist side by side—since the people bare their heads in the very same way before the images of saints, prostrate themselves on the ground in the same way, crawl up on their knees, fondle them with their hands, caress their cinctures—how can you distinguish one kind of worship from the other? And what should I say now about those persons who gossip with images just as they would if they were alive, and are not stirred in the same way with respect to all images of Christ and saints, but hope to get from this one what they dare not ask from that one?[2]

Although these things are only too true, still I will not try to get out of a punishment if someone can point out anywhere in my writings that I have condemned wholesale either the invoking of saints or the veneration of images. If you will deign in this matter to take my word for it before that of others, I promise not to trick or deceive you. But if someone has convinced you otherwise, if you have little faith in me, I ask you to order these people who are accusing me to point out the passages to you. As soon as you have examined them you will see that their fearsome insinuations are nothing but unadulterated smoke and vapor.

Even if they are, in themselves, totally inconsequential and you refer to them so mildly and considerately, nevertheless, in the guise of friendship you deprecate my boldness and temerity with an excessive modesty sharply at variance with the practices of some persons who, although they themselves stray completely from the path, still make a to-do, with every third word about schisms and heresies. I will suffer patiently being admonished by similar remarks, or even slaps, from you, dear Sadoleto; I am far from taking offense at such mild counsels, unless the very fact that you don't counsel me more freely should offend me.

NOTE

1. Persistent or stubborn.
2. Cf. The *Enchiridion of Erasmus* (tr. Himelick, p. 99 and *n* 10) and the colloquy "Military Affairs" (Craig, pp. 14-15).

*From a letter written in 1532 by Erasmus
to Martin Bucer, emphazing the differences between his views and those of the
Reformers. This letter (EE, IX, 2615) is an
answer, it would seem, to one written by
Bucer, in which the latter had apparently
reviewed the whole history of Erasmus'
relationship with the Evangelicals.*

I HAVE READ WITH utter astonishment that I am in agreement
with you upon all matters of religion. If this is the case, I have
been totally unaware of it so far. What creature could be more
vile and despicable than I if I used my pen against those with
whom I am in happy agreement upon all matters of religion? You
bring up my writings as evidence, but where do my writings reduce the number of sacraments? Where do they revile the Mass?
Where do they dispense with Purgatory? Where do they deny that
the body of the Lord is in the Eucharist, or teach that it is not
permitted to invoke saints, or argue that man has no freedom of
will? I pass over the rest. I have made it plain that I disliked the
fact that the Reformers were disseminating a great many *para-
doxoteros*, the fact that some of them so violently attacked bishops,
secular rulers, and others who differed with them, the fact that
against the will of their rulers they have altered public rites and
ceremonies. Such things, I say, have displeased me; but such things
are not all that you prudently cover up. Thus I have said that I
was unhappy with the way the business was being carried out, that
even if it was a movement righteous in conception it should have
been handled by other methods, in the same way that time and
again a play good in itself is hissed from the stage because of an
actor's ineptness. You know I am speaking figuratively, not literally.
As for the rest, what would be more perverse, more vacillating in
me than, in books I have brought out, to assail beliefs with which
I agree? In regard to this movement, you acknowledge that some
things have been maliciously conceived, that rulers have been unjustly assailed in insolent pamphlets. But in a matter of this sort

which you consider so very pertinent to the health of the whole
Church it is no trivial fault to render a good cause odious by the
way it is handled. Again I am speaking of it as a general thing.

You plead the necessity of making changes in ceremonies. But
how does it promote the success of the Gospel to smash statues
and deface paintings, no matter how pious they are? I say nothing
about the other things. I see a pit I am unwilling to get further
into. Many aspects could have been gradually corrected, and some
had been best ignored. If the power of the pope were obstructing
the Gospel, his despotism should have first of all been restrained,
something that was not at all difficult except that some men, as
the oft-repeated saying goes, preferred the whole to the half. And
remember that this is said as a generality, lest you think what I am
talking about here is a reference to your own state, which I have
never complained about nor have I heard anyone else. But about
the Swiss and the people of Basel many complain every day, although there is no time to recount these charges, which are innumerable, nor is it safe, since it has to do with civil authorities.
Let us turn to doctrines.

You say: "We propound no dogmas concerning the sacraments
any different from what you teach, for we would have the Supper
to be nothing but bread. This principle of Christ's presence, which
is the only thing we deny, you long ago wrote ought to be insisted
upon by no one, since you do not acknowledge it to have been
established by the Church, however unwilling you are to align
yourself with those who oppose it."

Here, my dear Bucer, I plead for that honesty of yours which
you so frequently tell us about and even swear to. Why do you
not cite the place where I have written anything of that sort? In
the *Epistolae Floridae* I have found one passage in which I say
something to the effect that the laity ought not to demand to know
how the body of the Lord might be in the Eucharist, but I add,
"whether as a part of the substance of bread itself, or as part of
the accidents, or whether in what some call the species." The place
you refer to is among the *Epistolae Floridae* in a letter to Cuthbert
Tunstall.[1] My words are as follows: "The early Fathers have spoken
reverently concerning the Eucharist; not even now, perhaps, has
the Church clearly explained how the body might be there, whether
by way of the accidents or in the bread itself."

Here I appeal to your conscience, Bucer: does this passage show that I have the same views of the Eucharist as you teach? I have some question about the Church's explanation, but this question has as its basis whether the real body of the Lord is there in terms of the substance. Having followed the authority of the Church and Scripture, I accept this, nor have I ever written or believed anything to the contrary. Who does not know that the Church has explained that the real body of the Lord is in the consecrated bread, His real blood in the wine? My reply to the treatise of Oecolampadius shows that I have not abandoned the position. And here you thank me, forsooth, for distinguished services to the Church. But is this one of those distinguished services? If the Church did not define the limits, then the matter could be deliberated upon. Now it is not objectively open to do that. Show me any such assertion, which I have never considered; if the dogma ought not to be made hard and fast, why do you make so much uproar in insisting upon another part of it? If you had left it undecided, the tumults of the world would have been of a milder sort and you would have had more followers, for there are a great many who, while they either approve of or tolerate the other things, still shrink back from your bread and cup. But let us grant—something that is really not true at all—that we are in agreement about the Lord's body, does it follow forthwith that you are preaching nothing but the things I teach?

WHAT RULER, moreover, wants a situation in his state of the sort that seems to have arisen in some—where one is not able to reject the religion embraced by majority there, where a sacred rite is denied, the Eucharist denied and those who are convicted of having received it elsewhere are manhandled, where a Catholic meeting is prohibited and ecclesiastical confession forbidden and even the church is closed, where people in their own country live not much more agreeably than Jews among Christians; nay, what is worse, they are forced by threats to a communion they dislike (you will pardon me; I report what I have heard, but I have heard much from many quarters, and this at first hand), where, on the other hand, those who follow the new dogmas, or pretend that they do, can do what they please; they are not subject to laws or bound by contracts, public or private; (here is one example out of many: in the treaty of alliance established by the inhabitants of Basel with the Swiss they had stipulated that if any trouble came up between the Swiss cantons, Basel would restore peace but would function only as a mediator; now it is obvious from how fiercely they have rushed into war under Zwingli's leadership that they are going to take sides); where priests are so mistreated that they go into exile voluntarily, where monks are either banished or closely spied upon, as they say of the Carthusians at Basel; where a confidence is not kept in either pamphlets or in sealed correspondence; where a citizen who, because of either his religious faith or his fear, has gone away, cannot be a guest in a neighbor's house but is compelled to go to a public inn; where monasteries are turned into barns, churches abandoned; where a liberal education in good letters is utterly given up. I see learned men inveigled into the sect, but I see no one in the sect who has learned any letters or who wants to learn any. The principles of the movement are presented, but where are the pupils? Recently I sent a servant to Basel. He heard a sermon in church. I asked how many heard it. "Three men," he said, "and ten women." Nor among these people themselves was any real spirit of piety in evidence. Nearly everyone drawn to that sect immediately conceives a fierce hatred of those who differ with them, very scanty proof of the Evangelical spirit.

Let me repeat what I have already said: I have known no one who has himself become better through this Evangelicalism, that is, who has become less given to whoring, to gluttony, to dicing, more forgiving of injuries, more indifferent to getting even, less intent upon serving his own interests. I have known many, though, who have been made worse. I am not basing my judgments on what I know nothing about. All we hear is "The Gospel, the Gospel! Faith, faith!" Now I should like nothing better than that such a state of affairs may chance to have a happy ending, but insofar as I can conjecture and infer the rest of the book from its preface, the situation suggests the complete disaster of Christian authority, and this not only in outward affairs but even in the goods of the spirit. What will this life be without learning and education? And when even now piety is lightly regarded, what can we look forward to but paganism? If already in individual states the management of worship depends upon the church structure and no one controls many states, one has to fear that eventually we have as many sects as states. What could be a more unhappy state of affairs than this? Hence it is that princes are afraid that the same thing will happen to them that in several places has happened to bishops and abbots.

Nor do those people who, either wicked or stupid, lurk in the obscurity of the Evangelical label, win for you any insignificant share of opprobrium. Because church officials do not dare to scold them sharply, they encourage them with flattery or pretend to ignore them. So it comes about that not even the clergy are free as long as they are afraid of being deserted by the people. But as to the most likely outcome, what else can be born of all this but schism? Unless you think that perhaps the whole world will come around to your opinion. I do not see on what grounds you hope for this, since you differ among yourselves.

NOTE

1. Cf. the letter to Cuthbert Tunstall, Epistle 2263 above.

This fragment of a letter to an unknown recipient lacks both beginning and end. Written in 1533, while the Liber de sarcienda Ecclesiae concordia *was still fresh in Erasmus' mind, it appears to be little more than a brief summary of the concluding pages of that book.* (EE, X, 2853)

THUS BOTH SIDES have pulled the rope tight, so that it is parting to the detriment of both, and hence this general uproar in the world. They do away with all images, very helpful and beautiful adjuncts. Superstition in worshiping should be abolished; images inappropriate and too ornate should be removed from churches, and this should be done gradually, without furor. They want to throw out the priests; let them take pains that priests are learned and devout, that no one is carelessly admitted to this dignity when he does not deserve approval. There will be fewer of them, but what of that? Better to have three good ones than three hundred worthless.[1]

They don't like the Church's form of worship. Many unsuitable things are sung and performed in church; let the faults be amended, but gradually. Let the worship service remain. They revile masses, detesting that disgraceful breed of priests who have learned nothing but how to recite the words, in other respects more profane than the laity. Those hireling performers should be removed and, as was the custom with the early Christians, one religious service celebrated in the church, or two on feast days—a private one early in the morning for the household and guests, another around the tenth hour.

Indulgences, by which the world has been exploited—with the help of monks and conniving theologians—for several centuries, are now jeered at. Those who think that masses and prayers for the dead do no good for the departed should spend on the living poor what the common run of men order at death. Those who are convinced that the good offices of the living are beneficial to those

210

dead who have been careful to do them themselves when they were alive, should not be harassed. People who are persuaded that the saints are of no use in interceding with Christ should faithfully call upon the Father, Son, and Holy Spirit. Let them honor and venerate the saints by imitating them, but without raising a din against those who in pious devotion do worship and invoke them. Superstition is to be censured; but sincere feeling, even if mistaken, should be accepted. So the saints do not listen to prayers? Even so, Christ listens, and He grants what we seek in their stead.

Some are sure that confession is not a part of the sacrament, that it was not instituted by Christ; until the Church decides otherwise, nevertheless, let them keep it as a salutary practice introduced by the Fathers and accepted by the consensus of many centuries. Let there be genuine candor in confessing, but no superstition. The person who chooses a suitable priest, who confesses only those sins clearly mortal, and who has been careful not to commit a capital crime will not be much inconvenienced by confession. As to Purgatory, let every man enjoy his own opinion; Christian charity should not be torn apart on account of these things. Let theologians debate freedom of the will in the Sorbonne; let laymen proceed in simple trust. Whether or not good works justify is a meaningless question; let it only be agreed that faith without good works is not enough for salvation.

Let baptism be preserved because the Church has preserved it for so many centuries. Every parent, however, should be left to decide whether he prefers to have an infant baptized at once, or to postpone the rite until adolescence; only let the child in the meanwhile be instructed in orthodox doctrine and religious character. The Anabaptists should not be tolerated at all. The Apostles order us to obey our magistrates, but those people chafe at obedience to Christian leaders. Let the sharing of goods come as a result of love, but let ownership and the right to distribute them remain in the hands of the possessor.

If they argue about the Eucharist among themselves, so that every day they give birth to some new and absurd notions, how much sounder a practice it was to remain in the traditional opinion until either a general synod or divine revelation discloses a truth less debatable. Scruples about the matter of adoration are easily disposed of; no one adores the Eucharist unless the whole Christ is there. Neither is anyone so mad as to adore the human nature of

Christ in place of the divine. The divine nature, however, is never absent. Abuses of this sacrament could be corrected.[2] At one time it was not displayed but kept shut up in a select spot. It was not carried around in spectacles or through the countryside by a mounted priest. It was offered only to those wishing to receive it. Now in England there is no house, no tavern—I almost said no brothel—where the sacrament is not offered. Street walkers are peddling these things.

In other respects too, if moderation were applied by both sides, perhaps these disorders would gradually subside into some condition of tranquillity. This policy has been followed by the duke of Juliers, and he acknowledges that it has worked out well. I don't doubt that your city would do the same if the clergy would allow it, but I am afraid that those fellows don't attend to their own business, in order to be in a secure. . . .

NOTES

1.   One is reminded of More's Utopia, which had "priests of exceeding holiness and therefore very few. . . ." (Everyman ed. [London, 1946], II:124.)

2.   In *Ecclesiastes* (*LB*, 840A-D) Erasmus describes some of these abuses existing in England and on the Continent.

ECCLESIASTES

Ecclesiastes, a shortening of the full title, could be said to do for neophytes among the clergy what such works as his De copia verborum ac rerum *and* De ratione studii *had done in a more secular way. It is one of the longest of Erasmus' treatises, consisting of four books (LB, V, 769-1100C) covering an enormously wide range of topics pertinent to the art of preaching. Here one may find doctrinal exegesis, explanation and discussion of the manifold senses of scriptural reading, suggestions as to pulpit techniques, the structuring of sermons, the ways and means of amplifying and supplying copia, discussion of rhetorical "places" and organization, his views—inevitably—on ritual, ceremonies, mass, and concluding with a section on "concordia," suggesting as always the singular importance Erasmus attached to the role of peace and unity in the Christian faith. From* Ecclesiastae Sive De Ratione Concionandi *(LB, V, 1070C-1072A)*

RESTRAINT OUGHT TO be exercised in the exegesis of dogma, lest we seem like inept doctors who in treating the liver ruin the stomach. When the uneducated laity hear over and over that the whole Law has been set aside by Christ, who redeems us from the curse of the Law, they take it to mean that everyone is free

213

to do whatever he wants to, since now, the Law having been repealed, he is less a sinner. But the Law has been set aside for those who in faith and charity surpass what the Law enjoins and yet are not smug about their own good works but ascribe them to the grace of Christ. If anything has been neglected or left undone because of human frailty, they apply to the bounty of Christ and there replenish what was insufficient in themselves.

By the same token, when these people hear that a man is justified by faith alone, that there is no justification through our own good works no matter what those works are, they should understand only that our justification is in Christ. The vulgar jump to the conclusion from this that good works are unnecessary, although the Apostles stressed hardly anything more strongly than that those who have died with Christ in baptism will rise with Him into a newness of life. Even if all our works are evil, as some teach, there is a vast difference between bestowing one's goods on the poor and stealing somebody else's, between abstinence and drunkenness, between prayer and spouting obscenities.

It is pious to denigrate reliance upon human works, especially those not originating in faith and love, which everywhere possible puts itself in the service of his neighbor, but instead are concerned only with ceremonialisms like eating or dressing in such and such a way or trotting off on pilgrimages to Compostella or Jerusalem. Similarly, whenever the common run of people hear that Christ has accepted the punishment for our sins and absolved us of the debt, they interpret this as having a licence to sin with impunity and be secure in their wrong-doing. This error is more perilous than the belief that making amends is the third part of sacramental penitence. It is unnatural that anyone believing in God as the punisher of evil-doers would not fear Him as a judge, or that anyone reflecting upon His ineffable benevolence should not glow with love for Him, that he should displease Him by his unworthiness and not expect punishment for offending a Being so great and of such a nature with his sins. One might also mention in passing that those who persist in their sinning do not ordinarily have a faith that justifies. Faith is a vital force; wherever it really exists it cannot be inactive.

Let them see to it, then, that they are not comforting themselves with words while they either are devoid of the gift of faith or have only a lifeless one, a kind they share with evil spirits. Is it conceivable that anyone who has been squeezing the poor will not—if he really has been reborn—try to compensate for his injury by benevolence? Some reject the word *repayment* [1] but accept *recompense.* [2] Words can be changed; the thing itself stays the same. There is no need, though, to speak specifically in those offices of the conventionally accepted remission of sin, but rather of divine mercy through faith in Jesus the Redeemer. I have, by way of example, touched upon a few things out of many. In all such matters the preacher should exercise the same circumspection lest, while he is diligently promoting some virtue he dig a pit into which certain listeners will tumble, lest he bump the heads of the fallen when he is trying to raise them up.

IF ANYONE is eager to promote harmony [3] let him first define what true harmony is, the union of good men in a good cause. The banding together of evil men in evil things is not concord but conspiracy. Men are said to be in accord because they are of one heart, just as they are said to be *unanimous* because the many are of a single *anima,* or mind, something which is not possible among those whose hearts are deceitful, who utter one thing by mouth and hide another intent in their breasts.

The creator of this concord is that heavenly spirit which unites and binds all things together. For just as the spirit of man, as long as it lives in him, preserves the individual physical body, which after that spirit has left him, falls into dissolution, so, after the Spirit of Christ had descended upon His disciples they all were of one heart and one mind, as Saint Luke testifies. To be sure, they felt and spoke alike in exalting God, not in their opinions as men. But just as God is the first and foremost author of concord, so Satan first sowed discord between God and man. The highest, archetypal example of concord is the identical nature, will, and power of the three Persons of the Trinity. Next is Christ, in whom His Church has been incorporated in such a way that God, man, and the whole fellowship of the devout form one entity, and through this union we become co-heirs of God and the Holy Spirit. The body is one with the Head. The Head is one with the Father and the Holy Spirit.

A third example is the community of members of the mystical body with one another, an example which Saint Paul repeatedly reminds us of. The various members have been designed for different functions, but they form one body insofar as an injury to any member whatsoever affects the whole body, and the glory of individual members is shared by all the others. The symbol of each concord is in *Sinai,* that is, in the communion of the Lord's body and blood.

A fourth example is the wedlock of man and woman. Out of two persons one flesh is made to the extent that they are so tenaciously joined together by love that man can more readily be separated from his mother and father than from his wife.

A fifth example is the linking of body and soul, which are themselves coupled in a kind of marriage. The soul corresponds to the husband, the body to the wife. Soul gives the orders, but lovingly; the body obeys. Moreover, their separation indicates how inextricably they are united, for nothing is more grievous than death. How much body owes to soul the lifeless corpse exemplifies. Where then is the beauty, the sight, the hearing, the voice, the movement? Soul in turn can not rest when divorced from body until it is recalled to its former partnership.

A sixth example is that of celestial bodies, which, by the ordination of their Creator, although they move in diverse ways nevertheless observe a harmony for so many thousands of years in perpetual agreement.

A seventh is in the elements, which, differing in their respective qualities, nevertheless work together with one another in a marvelous commingling. Static earth holds everything it encompasses in equilibrium, water refreshes it, air warms it, fire activates it.

An eighth example is that of animate creatures of diverse kinds. Bees and ants work together for the common good, at peace with one another in an admirable social organization. When cattle see a wolf, they join ranks as if in a battle line. Doves flock together at the sight of a hawk. Indeed, primitive men also sought the federation of a political state in order to live more safely and happily. And a state is nothing more than the concord of many, harmoniously obedient to the same laws and protecting themselves by giving aid to one another.

Illustrations of harmony can even be found in inanimate objects. Arrows can be broken easily one by one; bound together they are very strong. Thus it is that many things survive when united, are destroyed when separated. Wine, for instance, grows flat in a cup but keeps its body in a large jar. In the same way, water goes stale

in a jug, stays fresh in a well. Since a vine cannot stay alive by
itself it supports itself by the embrace of stronger ones. A gourd
does the same thing.

One might also point out that no battle line is more invulnerable
than when, in a dense phalanx, it mutually fortifies its members
with its shields, nor can soldiers easily be beaten in battle unless
they break rank and isolate themselves from comrades or unless
there is disunity among their officers. Unity is such an effectual
condition that even brigands and pirates know that what they do
will not succeed without a friendship of sorts to hold them together.
This is why nature herself entices and impels us to friendship by
so many means. She has instilled innate affection between parents
and children, between brothers and sisters, between relations by
blood and marriage, between men of the same state and nation—
to put it summarily, between all like men: for instance, between
boys, between old men, between learned men. Thus it is that jackdaws like the company of jackdaws and cranes fly away all at the
same time. Endowments of body, talent, and even fortune nature
so distributes among men that no one is self-sufficient; everybody
needs the reciprocal help of other men.

From these examples the reader easily sees how many examples
of concord can be brought together from every aspect of life. Just
as Satan enforces his tyranny with discord, so Christ strengthens
His rule with concord. This is what we ask for every day in the
Lord's prayer: "May Your kingdom come, Your will be done, on
earth as it is in heaven." The Church seeks a universally peaceful
kingdom, free from all strife. Christ was the cornerstone joining
together both walls, that of the Jews and that of the Gentiles; he
broke down the barrier separating God and men, canceled the
indictment of guilt under which Satan held us bound, and fastened
to the Cross a new inscription of peace and grace for us, signed
in His own blood, through which we have been made sons of God
instead of enemies. He himself is mediator and intercessor between
God and man, and reigning today with the Father is our advocate,
saying those things which make for our peace.

How peaceful His nature was in evinced by the fact that He
showed gratitude to Pilate and Herod: "When I shall have been
exalted above the earth," He said, "I will draw all to me." How
many were the gods in the world which were worshiped as devils,
in place of the divine will! How many nations, differing in lan-

guage, rites, customs, were all drawn to the worship of the one God, called to the same grace and welded into one state or, rather, into one body.

Hence we must distinguish between various kinds of concord. First there is the oneness of man with God, which comes by faith and innocence. A second is that of man with man, which Christian charity makes possible. A third is that of each man with himself, which is present when a mind is sensitively aware of itself and the carnal part is obedient to the spiritual. These are all so closely inter-related that either they are all present or all lacking. No one has inward peace with God who has strife with his neighbor. After these kinds, examples of unity will be found in the Scripture, in Genesis 13 for instance. Abraham, in giving up his own rights to a subordinate Lot, avoided strife and encouraged amity. In a like manner Jacob gave way to the rage of Esau, besides soothing him with mild words and gifts on his return. With equal courtesy he took care to avoid discord between himself and his father-in-law, Laban. In the first chapter of Judges, Judah and Simeon join forces to conquer Canaan, in accordance with the old saying "In the man, let the brother be present."

By gentleness peace is fostered; by harshness dissension is be-gotten: this is the lesson of 3 Kings,[4] chapter 12, on Raboa, who by pursuing an immature policy estranged himself from the ten tribes. An impressive number of like examples could be culled from sacred writings, no fewer from secular works. Passages abound which commend unity to us—immediately, for example, in Gene-sis: "It is not good for man to be alone; let us make him a helpmate similar to himself." Likeness is the mother of love; friendship is a help in adversity and a delight in prosperity. In the fourth chapter of Ecclesiastes we read, "Woe to the man who is alone, for if he falls he has no one to help him up," and so on. In chapter 18 of Proverbs we see, "A brother helped by a brother is like a strong state." In the twenty-fifth chapter of Ecclesiasticus, among those things approved by both God and man, these are recorded: the con-cord of brothers, love of neighbor, and harmonious agreement of husband and wife. What is the function of those innumerable pre-cepts in the New Testament about charity, about loving even one's enemies, all the exhortations of Saint Paul to oneness of heart, to love one another as brothers except to call us to unity? "Keeping peace with all men," he says, "insofar as is in you, dearest brethren,

and not defending yourselves." And among the pagans such senti-
ments have been forcefully expressed, as in "In concord small things
prosper, in discord great things come to naught."

I will not pursue the point further; what I have pointed out
already should suffice. Your partitioning of the topic will supply
both the order and enrichment of arguments. Nothing is more in
accordance with the nature of man than friendship: "lo, how good
and how pleasant," and so on. Nothing is more pleasing to God
than the harmony of good men; nothing is more conducive to both
physical and spiritual well-being.

NOTES

1. For *satisfactio*.

2. For *pensatio*.

3. Beginning at this point, cols. 1097D *et seq.*, in the fourth book.

4. In the Vulgate. In English versions the reference would be to 1
Chronicles.

SELECTED BIBLIOGRAPHY

Latin Editions

Erasmi Opera Omnia. Edited by Jean LeClerc. Leiden, 1703-06.

Opus Epistolarum Des. Erasmi Roterodami. Edited by P. S. Allen and H. M. Allen, Oxford, 1906-41.

Erasmi opuscula. Edited by W. K. Ferguson. The Hague, 1933.

Desiderius Erasmus Roterodamus: Ausgewählte Werke. Edited by Hajo Holborn. Munich, 1933.

(A modern critical edition of the complete works, edited by J. H. Waszink and others, is in progress at Amsterdam. Texts are in Latin, introductions and notes in English.)

Modern Translations into English

Letters:

Epistles of Erasmus. Edited by F. M. Nichols. London, 1901-18 (to 1517 only).

Froude, J. A. *Life and Letters of Erasmus.* London, 1894.

Huizinga, J. *Erasmus and the Age of the Reformation* (appendix). New York, 1957.

Olin, John C. *Christian Humanism and the Reformation: Desiderius Erasmus.* New York, 1965.

The Praise of Folly:

The Praise of Folly. Translated by Leonard Dean. Chicago, 1946.

The Praise of Folly. Translated by Hoyt Hudson. Princeton, 1941.

Colloquies:

The Colloquies. Translated by Nathan Bailey. London, 1900.

The Colloquies of Erasmus. Translated by Craig Thompson. Chicago, 1963.

Ten Colloquies of Erasmus. Translated by Craig Thompson. New York, 1957.

The Enchiridion:

The Enchiridion. Translated by F. L. Battles. Abridged version in Spinka, W., ed. *Advocates of Christian Reform.* London, 1953.

Erasmus, Handbook of the Militant Christian. Translated by J. P. Dolan. Notre Dame, Indiana, 1962. (Abridged)

The Enchiridion of Erasmus. Translated by Raymond Himelick. Bloomington, Indiana, 1963.

The Adages:

The Adages of Erasmus. Translated by Margaret Mann Phillips. Cambridge, England, 1964. (*Erasmus on His Times* is a shortened paperback version, published in 1967.)

Other Treatises:

The Education of a Christian Prince. Translated by L. K. Born, New York, 1936.

On Copia of Words and Ideas. Translated by D. B. King and H. D. Rix. Milwaukee, 1963.

Julius Exclusus. Translated by Paul Pascal, notes by J. K. Sowards. Bloomington, Indiana, 1968.

Ciceronianus. Translated by Izora Scott. New York, 1908.

Discourse on Free Will. Translated by E. F. Winter. New York, 1961.

Desiderius Erasmus concerning the Aim and Method of Education. Translated by W. H. Woodward. Cambridge, Mass., 1904.

(A complete translation of *The Collected Works of Erasmus* is in preparation at the University of Toronto Press.)

Biographical and Critical

Allen, P. S. *The Age of Erasmus.* Oxford, 1914.

———. *Erasmus: Lectures and Wayfaring Sketches.* Oxford, 1934.

Bainton, Roland H. *Erasmus of Christendom.* New York, 1969.

Born, L. K. "Some Notes on the Political Theories of Erasmus." *Journal of Modern History* 2 (1930):226-236.

Caspari, Fritz. "Erasmus on the Social Functions of Christian Humanism." *Journal of the History of Ideas* 8 (1947):78-106.

Ferguson, W. K. "The Attitude of Erasmus Toward Toleration." in *Persecution and Liberty.* New York, 1931.

———. "Renaissance Tendencies in the Religious Thought of Erasmus." *Journal of the History of Ideas* 15 (1954):499-508.

Huizinga, J. *Erasmus of Rotterdam.* New York, 1952.

Hyma, Albert. *The Youth of Erasmus.* Ann Arbor, Mich., 1930.

Kaiser, Walter. *Praisers of Folly: Erasmus, Rabelais, Shakespeare.* Cambridge, Mass., 1963.

Renaudet, A. *Erasme: Sa Pensée religieuse, d'après sa correspondance 1518-1521.* Paris, 1926.

———. *Études érasmiennes (1521-1529)*. Paris, 1939.

Rice, Eugene. "Erasmus and the Religious Tradition." *Journal of the History of Ideas* 11 (1950):387-411.

Schenk, Wilhelm. "The Erasmian Idea." *Hibbert Journal* 48 (1950): 257-265.

Smith, Preserved. *Erasmus*. New York, 1923.

Spitz, Lewis W. *The Religious Renaissance of the German Humanists*. Cambridge, Mass., 1963.

Taylor, H. O. *Erasmus and Luther*. New York, 1920.

Williams, Kathleen, ed. *Twentieth Century Interpretations of the "Praise of Folly."* Englewood Cliffs, N.J., 1969.

Erasmus and the Seamless Coat of Jesus was printed by the letterpress method on 70-pound white vellum finish Panta offset paper, and casebound in Interlaken Natural Finish Buckram by the Pantagraph Press of Bloomington, Illinois. Caledonia typefaces were chosen for the text, with Caslon used for chapter headings and decorative initials. Warren's Lusterkote was selected for the dust jackets, which were printed by offset lithography by Pantagraph. Moroni J. St. John, Purdue University designer, handled the artwork, and Diane Dubiel, assistant university editor, was editorial and production supervisor.